Transitions from Authoritarian Rule: Prospects for Democracy,
edited by Guillermo O'Donnell, Philippe C. Schmitter, and
Laurence Whitehead, is available in separate paperback editions:

Transitions from Authoritarian Rule: Southern Europe,
edited by Guillermo O'Donnell, Philippe C. Schmitter, and
Laurence Whitehead

Transitions from Authoritarian Rule: Latin America,
edited by Guillermo O'Donnell, Philippe C. Schmitter, and
Laurence Whitehead

Transitions from Authoritarian Rule: Comparative Perspectives,
edited by Guillermo O'Donnell, Philippe C. Schmitter, and
Laurence Whitehead

Transitions from Authoritarian Rule:
Tentative Conclusions about Uncertain Democracies,
by Guillermo O'Donnell and Philippe C. Schmitter

List of Contributors

Fernando H. Cardoso *Centro Brasileiro de Aviálise e Planejamento, São Paulo*

Robert R. Kaufman *Rutgers University*

Abraham F. Lowenthal *University of Southern California*

Adam Przeworski *University of Chicago*

Alain Rouqié *Centre d'Etudes et de Recherches Internationales, Paris*

John Sheahan *Williams College, Williamstown, Massachusetts*

Alfred Stepan *Columbia University*

Laurence Whitehead *Nuffield College, Oxford*

Transitions from Authoritarian Rule

Comparative Perspectives

edited by
Guillermo O'Donnell,
Philippe C. Schmitter, and
Laurence Whitehead

The Johns Hopkins University Press
Baltimore and London

Third printing, 1991

The Johns Hopkins University Press,
701 West 40th Street, Baltimore, Maryland 21211
The Johns Hopkins Press Ltd., London

The paper used in this publication meets the minimum requirements
of American National Standard for Information Sciences—
Permanence of Paper for Printed Library Materials, ANSI Z39.48-1984.

Library of Congress Cataloging-in-Publication Data

Transitions from authoritarian rule. Comparative perspectives.

Papers originally commissioned for a conference sponsored by the
Latin American Program of the Woodrow Wilson International Center
for Scholars between 1979 and 1980.
Bibliography: p.
Includes index.
Contents: International aspects of democratization/Laurence
Whitehead—Some problems in the study of the transition to
democracy/Adam Przeworski—Paths toward redemocratization/
Alfred Stepan—[etc.]
1. Representative government and representation—Latin
America—Case studies. 2. Authoritarianism—Latin America—Case
studies. 3. Democracy—Case studies. I. O'Donnell, Guillermo A.
II. Schmitter, Philippe C. III. Whitehead, Laurence. IV. Woodrow
Wilson International Center for Scholars. Latin American Program.
JL966.T73 1986 321.09′ 098 86-2710
ISBN 0-8018-3192-X (pbk. : alk. paper)

John Roberts

Contents

Foreword

Abraham F. Lowenthal

The three coeditors of *Transitions from Authoritarian Rule* have kindly invited me to introduce this effort because it resulted from the Woodrow Wilson Center's project on "Transitions from Authoritarian Rule: Prospects for Democracy in Latin America and Southern Europe."

The "Transitions" project was the most significant undertaking of the Wilson Center's Latin American Program during the seven years I had the privilege of directing its activities. The resulting four-volume book contributes substantially on a topic of vital scholarly and political importance. I want to highlight both these points, to underline some of its strengths, and finally to say a bit about what is still left to be done.

The Woodrow Wilson International Center for Scholars was created by an act of the United States Congress in 1968 as a "living memorial" to the twentieth president of the United States, a man remembered for his idealism and for his commitment to democracy, for his scholarship, for his political leadership, and for his international vision, but also for his interventionist attitudes and actions toward Latin America and the Caribbean. The Center supports advanced research and systematic discussion on national and international issues by scholars and practitioners from all over the world. It aims to bring together the realms of academic and public affairs, as Wilson himself did.

The Latin American Program was established early in 1977, within the Center's overall framework, to focus attention on the Western Hemisphere. The Program has tried, from the start, to serve as a bridge between Latin Americans and North Americans of diverse backgrounds, to facilitate comparative research that draws on the Center's special capacity to bring people together, to emphasize the highest standards of scholarship, to stress privileged topics that merit intense cooperative efforts, and to help assure that opinion leaders in the United States and Latin America focus more attentively and more sensitively on Latin America and the Caribbean and on their relation with the United States.

In all its undertakings, the Program has been striving to assure that diverse viewpoints—from men and women with varying national, professional, disciplinary, methodological, and political perspectives—are presented, and that complex issues are illuminated through the confrontation of different analyses. But the Program's orientation has never been value-free; it has stood for vigorous exchange among persons who disagree about many things but who fundamentally respect the academic enterprise and who share a commitment to the core values all the nations of the Americas profess. The Program has sought diversity of many kinds, but not artificial balance. It awarded fellowships in the same semester to writers exiled because of their convictions from Argentina and from Cuba, for example, but it has never invited their censors on an equal basis. It has sponsored research on human rights from many different standpoints, but never from the perspective of the torturers. And it sponsored the project on "Transitions from Authoritarian Rule" with a frank bias for democracy, for the restoration in Latin America of the fundamental rights of political participation.

The "Transitions" project was begun in 1979 on the initiative of two charter members of the Latin American Program's nine-person Academic Council: Guillermo O'Donnell (then of CEDES in Buenos Aires) and Philippe Schmitter (then of the University of Chicago), with the active encouragement and support of the Council's chairman, Albert O. Hirschman, and of Council member Fernando Henrique Cardoso of Brazil. During the project's first phase, I served as its coordinator. As the project grew in scope and complexity, it became clear that another Center-based person was needed to focus more fully on it; we were fortunate to recruit Laurence Whitehead of Oxford University, a former Wilson Center fellow, who then worked closely with O'Donnell and Schmitter and became coeditor of the project volume.

The "Transitions" project illustrates the Wilson Center's aspirations in several respects:

Its leaders are recognized as among the world's foremost academic authorities in Latin America, the United States, and Europe.

It attracted the participation of other top-flight scholars from all three continents and encouraged them to work closely together in a structured and linked series of workshops and conferences.

It emphasized comparative analysis, and sharpened the focus on Latin American cases by putting them into a broader perspective.

In its various workshops, the project drew on the perspective not only of scholars but of several persons—from Latin America and from among former U.S. government officials—experienced in politics and public affairs.

Its findings have been made available to opinion leaders from different sectors through specially organized discussion sessions in Washington.

It maintained a creative tension between its normative bias, its theoretical ambitions, and its empirical and case-oriented approach. The project's animus, as I had occasion to say at its first meeting, was never wishful thinking but rather "thoughtful wishing," that is, it was guided by a normative orientation that was rigorous and deliberate in its method.

Finally, the project illustrated a point the Wilson Center's director, Dr. James H. Billington, has often emphasized: to seek tentative answers to fundamental questions rather than definitive responses to trivial ones. All the project's participants know that the complex issues involved in transitions to democracy have not been dealt with conclusively in this volume, but they can take great satisfaction in what they have contributed.

Transitions from Authoritarian Rule

Ultimate evaluations of this book's import, obviously, will have to come from analysts less involved in the project's inception and management than I. I would like, however, to suggest some of the reasons why I think *Transitions from Authoritarian Rule* is important.

It is the first book in any language that systematically and comparatively focuses on the process of transition from authoritarian regimes, making this the central question of scholarship as it is today in Latin American politics.

Its analytic and normative focus on the prospects of building democratic or polyarchic politics in the wake of an authoritarian transition provides a vantage point that organizes the materials in ways useful not only to scholars and observers but to political actors as well.

Its comparisons of cases in Latin America and in Southern Europe and of cases of transition from bureaucratic authoritarianism, military populism, and sultanistic despotism allow for considering several different variables.

Transitions from Authoritarian Rule is rich in nuanced, contextually sensitive analysis, and each of the case studies is written by a leading authority. Although the methods, perspectives, and styles of the various authors understandably differ, their agreement on shared assumptions makes this a coherent volume. The book is filled with subtleties, complexity, and a keen sense of paradox.

Throughout, disaggregation is emphasized. All authoritarian regimes are not equated with each other. No authoritarian regime is regarded as monolithic, nor are the forces pushing for democratization so regarded. Distinctions are drawn between "democracy" and "polyarchy"; between "democratization" and "liberalization"; between "transition" and "consolidation"; between "hard-liners" and "soft-liners" or accommodationists within the authoritarian coalition; and among "maximalists," "moderates," and "opportunists" in the coalition supporting *abertura* (liberalization).

From the various cases, several points emerge that deserve special mention here. These cases show that, although international factors, direct and indirect, may condition and affect the course of transition, the major participants and the dominant influences in every case have been national. They demonstrate the importance of institutions, of mediating procedures and forums that help make the rules of political discourse legitimate and credible in a period of change. They illustrate the vital significance of political leadership and judgment, of the role of single individuals in complex historical processes. They point out, again and again, the importance of timing, the complexity of interactive processes carried out over extensive periods, the various ways in which transitions produce surprises, and some of the ironies and paradoxes that result.

Above all, the cases analyze the ways in which transitions from authoritarian rule are conditioned and shaped by historical circumstances, unique in each country but patterned in predictable ways, by the way in which a previous democratic regime broke down, by the nature and duration of the authoritarian period, by the means the authoritarian regime uses to obtain legitimacy and to handle threats to its grip on power, by the initiative and the timing of experimental moves toward *abertura*, by the degree of security and self-confidence of the regime's elites and by the confidence and competence of those pushing for opening the political process, by the presence or absence of financial resources, by the counseling of outsiders, and by the prevailing international *fashions* that provide legitimacy to certain forms of transition.

The Tasks Ahead

I do not wish to detain the reader longer before he or she enters the reading of *Transitions from Authoritarian Rule*. It remains only to concede, as all the authors would, that this book is incomplete, and that much remains to be done. The cases of transition are still few in number, and each one merits a much more detailed and sustained analysis. The processes of consolidation, so important if these transitions are to be meaningful, are barely considered in this volume, and require separate treatment. The sensitivity that the authors in their chapters show to the dilemmas and choices faced by opposition groups pressing for *abertura* needs to be matched by equally empathetic and well-informed assessments of the choices made by those within authoritarian regimes who permit *abertura* to occur and push for its extension. Some of the categories of analysis—of hard-liners (*duros*) and soft-liners (*blandos*), for example—need to be further specified and refined.

All this and more needs to be done. No doubt the editors and authors of *Transitions from Authoritarian Rule* will be among the leaders in carrying out this research. Some of them will be leaders, as well, in the very processes of building democracies. They, and many others, will go much further than this volume can, but they will build upon a solid foundation.

Preface

Between 1979 and 1981 the Latin American Program of the Woodrow Wilson International Center for Scholars, in Washington, D.C., sponsored a series of meetings and conferences entitled "Transitions from Authoritarian Rule: Prospects for Democracy in Latin America and Southern Europe." As this project grew in scope and complexity, Abraham Lowenthal, program secretary from 1977 to 1983, provided indispensable encouragement that enabled us to turn it into the present four-volume study. We wish to acknowledge our special debt of gratitude to him, and also to thank the Woodrow Wilson Center, the Aspen Institute for Humanistic Study, the Inter-American Foundation, the Helen Kellogg Institute of the University of Notre Dame, the European University Institute in Florence, and Nuffield College, Oxford, for their financial and logistical support. Louis Goodman, acting secretary of the Latin American Program in 1983–84, also gave us much-needed assistance. Needless to add, only those named in the table of contents are responsible for the views expressed here.

All of the papers published in these four volumes were originally commissioned for a Woodrow Wilson Center conference or were circulated, discussed, and revised in the course of the "Transitions" project. They have, therefore, some commonality of approach and outlook, but it was never our intention to impose a uniformity of interpretation and terminology. On the contrary, we deliberately set out to widen the range of serious discussion about regime transitions in general, and to promote informed debate comparing specific cases. In Volume 4, O'Donnell and Schmitter present the lessons they have drawn from this experience of collaboration among scholars working on Latin America and Southern Europe. Volume 3 contains a series of discussion papers analyzing common themes from different perspectives. Volume 1 (on Southern Europe) and Volume 2 (on Latin America) contain country studies, some of which were written during or immediately after the launching of a democratic transition, and some even before it had begun. Two cases (Uruguay and Turkey) were added to our sample at a later stage in the project as developments in these countries called for their inclusion, whereas the chapter on Italy refers to a transition completed more than thirty years earlier. Because of these differences in timing, and the delay in publication, readers should be warned that not all chapters carry the analysis right up to date (end of 1984).

Although the three editors are listed alphabetically in volumes 1, 2, and 3, they, of course, established some division of labor among themselves. Primary responsibility for Volume 1 rests with Philippe C. Schmitter, Laurence Whitehead took the lead in editing Volume 2; and Guillermo O'Donnell had first responsibility for Volume 3. This has been very much a collective endeavor, however, and all three of us share credit or blame for the overall result.

Transitions from Authoritarian Rule

Comparative Perspectives

1 ·

International Aspects of Democratization

Laurence Whitehead

Introduction

How important are the international factors influencing attempts at redemocratization? What motivates some major governments to proclaim the "promotion of democracy" as an important goal of foreign policy, and how realistic are such claims? Is this either a feasible or a desirable element in the foreign policy-making of powerful states? Are there substantial differences between leading democratic nations in the emphasis given to this objective, and if so how can such variations be explained? How important are nongovernmental organizations (churches, political parties, human rights lobbies, aid agencies) in the promotion of democratic transitions? What instruments are available to those in or outside government that might influence the reestablishment of democracy in countries subjected to authoritarian rule, and what results can be achieved by the use of such instruments? How far may the contending political forces engaged in a process of redemocratization manipulate international support for sectional advantage, rather than for "democracy" *tout court*? What type of "democracy" is most likely to be favored by strong international encouragement, and what other variants of redemocratization may be hindered? These are a few of the many questions concerning international aspects of transitions from authoritarianism. This chapter formulates some provisional answers derived from recent experiences in Latin America and Southern Europe. It compares the record of the U.S.A. with that of the European Community.

There can be no universal, timeless answers to such questions. Apart from the transition in Italy, all the transitions or potential transitions studied in the Wilson Center's project took place after 1945 and in conditions of peace. This circumstance excludes one very important variant of "democratization," namely, the case of imposition by conquest.[1] Historically, Washington's most memorable experiences of promoting democracy overseas took place at the end of successful wars (1898, 1918, 1945) when, of course, international forces were in a position to overwhelm domestic political tendencies. The U.S. invasion of Grenada, in October 1983, was a reenactment in miniature of this type of experience. However, since 1945 Washington has generally possessed only much more indirect means of leverage over the internal political affairs of the independent states of Latin America, the Caribbean, and the Mediterranean. As for the European powers, apart from a short-lived French attempt to rid Spain of Franco by closing the frontier (1946–48), it has been in the context of retreat and withdrawal, rather than of expansion of power, that the promotion of democracy has been attempted (mainly by the British, in the course of decolonization). With exceptions, the governments of Europe, when designing postcolonial institutions, have invariably found themselves without the means to impose political arrangements of their choice on other countries. The postwar governments of Western Europe have become accustomed to coexisting with a variety of undemocratic regimes whose internal political arrangements were tacitly accepted, not only in Latin America, but even on the immediate periphery of the European Community.

The cases chosen for study in the Wilson Center's project on "Transitions from Authoritarian Rule" shared a variety of defining characteristics. Not only were they postwar peacetime attempts at transition, they all concerned transition from an authoritarianism of the "right"; and they nearly all concerned countries whose political traditions included a substantial amount of liberalism and constitutionalism. The differences separating these cases were of course large, but they remained within certain quite limiting bounds. Thus none of the countries under consideration has experienced a fully established Communist government; and, with the possible exception of Turkey, none is subject to such anti-Western ideologies as Islamic fundamentalism. Politically these countries are all "children of the French Revolution"; in socioeconomic terms they are all developing or newly industrializing countries in which a dominant social aspiration is to approach the levels of material well-being and the forms of political organization associated with the leading liberal capitalist powers; and geopolitically they all find themselves within the Western system of postwar alliances, either as full members or in a strategic reserve.

These shared characteristics may seem unremarkable if viewed separately, but if taken in conjunction they become fairly restrictive. The generalizations proposed in this chapter may only apply within these restrictions. Thus, for example, in all the peacetime cases considered here internal forces were of primary importance in determining the course and outcome of the transition attempt, and international factors played only a secondary role. But this generalization only holds for a particular geographical area and in a specific historical period. Within postwar Czechoslovakia the internal forces may well have been as favorable for a democratic transition as within most of the countries considered here, but the geopolitical location was adverse. Similarly in interwar Europe various attempts at democratization foundered, not necessarily because of an unfavorable social or political context in the country in question, but because of the rise of Fascism and Nazism in other parts of the continent. By excluding such cases, the "Transitions" project narrowed its frame of reference to those recent experiences of attempted redemocratization in which local political forces operated with an untypically high degree of autonomy. The international setting provided a mildly supportive (or destructive) background which was often taken for granted and which seldom intruded too conspicuously on an essentially domestic drama. Even so, in a country where from an internal viewpoint prospects for democracy seemed finely balanced (e.g., Portugal in 1975, or the Dominican Republic in 1978) quite a modest impetus from outside might tip the outcome one way or another.

In the official discourse of Washington, London, Paris, and Brussels the promotion of democracy has long provided a recurrent theme. It would be tedious to recite the full catalog of historic declarations and even binding treaty commitments that embody this idea. Nevertheless it must be recalled that President Wilson led America into World War I on the argument that "the world must be made safe for democracy." In December 1940, President Roosevelt proposed to convert the U.S.A. into a "great arsenal for democracy." In August 1941 he prevailed upon a reluctant Churchill to accept point three of the Atlantic Charter, advocating "the right of all peoples to choose the form of government under which they will live" (a death knell for the old European empires). In March 1947 the "Truman Doctrine" explicitly listed a series of characteristics that would qualify Greece as a "democracy" entitled to U.S. aid against a Communist insurgency (the will of the majority, free institutions, representative government, free elections, guarantees of individual liberty, freedom of speech and religion, and freedom from political repression). In 1948 the Organization of American States (OAS) was established, and all the member states endorsed a "Final Act of Bogotá" on "the Preservation and Defense of Democracy in America," pledging themselves to defend "the free and sovereign rights of their peoples to govern themselves in accordance with their democratic aspirations." In May 1949, ten West European democracies created a Council of Europe which not only committed all its members to the rule of law, human rights, and fundamental freedoms, but which provided for the suspension of member governments who violated these precepts. The preamble to the NATO Treaty of 1949 commits all signatory states to "safeguard the freedom, common heritage, and civilization of their peoples, founded on the principles of democracy, individual liberty, and the rule of law." Although the 1957 Treaty of Rome specified no explicit political conditions for membership of the European Economic Community, in 1962 the Birkelbach Report was adopted, establishing that "only states which guarantee on their territories truly democratic practices and respect for fundamental rights and freedoms can become members of our Community." In March 1961, President Kennedy launched the "Alliance for Progress" to demonstrate that "economic progress and sound justice can best be achieved by free men working within a framework of democratic institutions." In 1977, President Carter declared that the defense of "human rights" would be one of the guidelines of his foreign policy, and by extension gave support to various movements in favor of redemocratization. In June 1982, President Reagan addressed the British Parliament proposing a bipartisan and international effort "to foster the infrastructure of democracy the system of a free press, political parties, universities—which allows people . . . to reconcile their own differences through peaceful means"; and the following year the U.S. government created a "National Endowment for Democracy" intended to coordinate the efforts of American political parties, trade unions, and business organizations to promote democracy overseas. In January 1984, the Kissinger Commission proposed an ambitious and long-term package of measures intended to uphold U.S. interests, and allegedly also to promote democracy, in Central America. Most recently, at the London Summit of June 1984, seven Western heads of state and the president of the European Commission issued a "Declaration on Democratic Values" which once again restated a commitment to "genuine choice in elections freely held, free expression of opinion," and so on.

It would be misleading to recite this litany of statements without some comment on its relationship to observable behavior. On his inauguration in 1913 President Wilson had declared his administration not only the friend, but the "champion" of constitutional government in the Americas. In fact he established long-term U.S. military governments in Nicaragua, Haiti, and the Dominican Republic, all countries subsequently notorious for their lack of democracy. During the 1930s the European democracies acquiesced in the destruction of constitutional governments in Spain and elsewhere. When they finally determined to resist Fascism it was in defense of authoritarian Poland rather than of democratic Czechoslovakia. After Pearl Harbor, when President Roosevelt led the U.S.A. into World War II, it was as one of twenty-five nations who collectively (as the "United Nations") declared war against Axis aggression, nine of whom were U.S. client states in Central America and the Caribbean. His cosignatories therefore included a remarkable collection of tyrants—Somoza, Batista, Ubico, and Trujillo among others.

Postwar the same pattern has persisted. Thus the Greek beneficiaries of the Truman Doctrine were a heterogeneous assortment, but they certainly included many state officials and security personnel inherited from the preceding period of dictatorship and occupation, who used U.S. support in the Civil War to avoid being purged, and eventually to collaborate with a new military dictatorship. Among the signatories of the resonant-sounding "Final Act of Bogotá" was a Somoza who had just emerged unscathed from an exceptionally flagrant act of contempt for electoral and constitutional niceties. Portugal was a founder member of NATO notwithstanding the language of the treaty. Moreover the dictator Salazar made no secret of his disconformity with the preamble, which he described as "manifestly unfortunate" and containing "worn-out and disturbing formulas." He signed on the basis that Portugal would "feel bound by the obligations of the Treaty and by its general aims— not (in any way) by doctrinal affirmation pointing to the unity of political regimes."[2] Indeed the most inquisitorial of his repressive laws (e.g., the October 1949 decree empowering the secret police to detain anyone for 180 days without charge) was adopted immediately after entry into NATO.

In more recent times, the rhetoric of democracy has frequently masked support for less appealing practices. Despite the high expectations announced by the Alliance for Progress, constitutional governments were overthrown in a succession of Latin American countries in the early 1960s, and the Kennedy administration soon abandoned any illusions it may have had about blocking such developments. It is sometimes believed that it was not until after the assassination of President Kennedy that U.S. policy shifted toward favoring military governments, but with regard to the collapse of democracy in Brazil (much the most important episode in the series) Kennedy had already decided that "he would not be averse" to the overthrow of the elected Brazilian government by forces more friendly to the United States.[3] In his last year in office President Carter authorized large-scale support for a military-dominated "reformist" junta in El Salvador which was as heterogeneous in its composition and as ambiguous in its commitment to democratic values as the Greek government of 1947. President Reagan followed his June 1982 speech in London with a visit to the Philippines where he spoke to President Marcos of the struggle for democracy in Asia during World War II, "a struggle in which you, Mr. President, participated." "The Philippines have been molded in the image of American democracy," he added. There was no criticism of the eight years since 1972 during which Marcos had ruled by martial law, nor any urging of the need to conciliate the democratic opposition (a need that became all the more manifest when, in August 1983, senior officials in the Philippine army assassinated opposition leader Aquino on his return from enforced exile).

There should be no great surprise that official declarations in favor of democracy in the abstract correlated poorly with observable behavior affecting specific real interests and international relationships. Nevertheless, it should not be concluded that the former is always and entirely unrelated to the latter. On the contrary, *some* of the official statements summarized above have considerable practical force (the Birkelbach Report, for example). Most are of indeterminate significance until a practical test arises, but certainly cannot safely be disregarded. Often they express a commitment that is more qualified than it appears, perhaps because other unstatable considerations are also known to be in operation (e.g., the U.S. base in the Azores antedated Portugal's accession to NATO, and was known to occupy an important role in Washington's global military planning); or perhaps because of a tacit understanding that some key term in the general declaration would be given a highly specialized meaning ("free elections," for example, can embrace a multitude of practices according to the favor or disfavor with which a given regime may be viewed).[4] In any given situation it is a matter of negotiation how loosely or strictly some general statement of principle is to be applied—negotiation *within* the foreign policy-making establishment of each dominant power, negotiation *between* leading democratic states, and negotiation with the peripheral regime which needs international approval for its efforts to democratize, to liberalize, or indeed to preserve the status quo. Clearly certain types of transition from authoritarianism (those that pose no risks to the existing system of external alliances, those that preserve or strengthen existing political and economic ties with the dominant powers) are more likely to succeed in these processes of negotiation. Other types of transition (those that seem to threaten too many established interests, or that create too much insecurity and uncertainty), are less likely to receive effective international support, even if on the face of it the same declaration of principles would seem to apply.

Later in this chapter I examine more closely these multiple processes of negotiation, paying particular attention to the motives of the various parties, the instruments available to those governmental and nongovernmental agencies that seek to influence the outcome of a transition, and the not-always-intended results that ensue. Some significant contrasts emerge between North American and West European experiences, and an attempt is made to account for these. Before disaggregating the cases in this way, however, I should make three general points that apply across the board.

First, all the above declaratory statements either assert or assume a particular model of "democracy" which emphasizes electoral competition among freely constituted political parties, and which enshrines the classical liberal guarantees of individual freedom. In some statements Communism is explicitly identified as the enemy against which democracy must be protected (e.g., the Final Act of Bogotá). In others, such as the 1984 "Declaration of Democratic Values," the rights of private ownership are more or less explicitly incorporated into the description of democracy (governments should set conditions "in which enterprise can flourish . . . and in which there can be confidence in the soundness of the currency"). Not all of the political forces promoting redemocratization in Latin America and Southern Europe are thinking in quite these terms about the kind of democracy they favor. Many would argue for a greater stress on social rights and on economic equality, and less emphasis on "abstract" individual freedoms; on this view of "democracy," Communism may be less clearly the major enemy. The point here is not to debate the relative merits of these rival viewpoints, but to emphasize that, when the leading liberal capitalist governments attempt to promote democracy internationally, it is the first variant (private ownership and anti-Communism) that meets with their strongest approval, and that is seen to pose the least threat to their real interests. Although the second variant (social rights and economic equality) may also secure some international support, it will be more contested, there will be more scope for misunderstanding and backsliding, and the assistance provided will be weaker and more erratic.

Second, as O'Donnell and Schmitter emphasize in their presentation of the internal aspects of the transition process, a clear distinction should be made between the "liberalization" of an authoritarian regime and full democratization. In the international conditions prevailing since 1945, powerful minorities that wish to defend and preserve their privileges have often found it advantageous to adopt at least an appearance of sympathy for democracy. Alternative ideological positions were partially discredited by the outcome of World War II (except insofar as they could be revived under the guise of anti-

Communism). For political interests of this kind, one obvious response to international pressures for democratization was to offer a limited liberalization, arguing that to go further would be too destabilizing. This is only one example of the way in which international support for democracy is likely to be manipulated by the contending forces engaged in a transition process. It is argued elsewhere in these volumes that transitions from authoritarianism are characterized by unpredictability, and by uncertainty about the underlying strength and the true intentions of the various domestic forces in play. For most of these competing political organizations the eventual democratic outcome (if it materializes at all) is likely to be a "second best" solution from many points of view; quite often, indeed, formerly substantial political groupings fail to survive the transition at all. Given such circumstances, the enlistment of international support will be a high priority for many of the parties engaged in the transition process, even if only insubstantial and symbolic forms of endorsement are available from outside. Rival political groupings may go to considerable lengths to win international acceptance of their "democratic" credentials, including disguising and misrepresenting their antecedents and even their intentions. Agencies like the World Christian Democratic Union and the Socialist International have become deeply involved in this aspect of the transition process. It is not that such agencies are easily misled but rather that a subtle game of mutual adjustments is involved, as we shall illustrate later in this chapter. The more general point is that we should not think in terms of a homogeneous front of aspiring democrats who approach the international community for united support of an agreed project. A more typical situation would be an uneasy and rivalrous alliance of not always entirely democratic forces who find themselves launched on an uncertain transition, and turn to competing sources of external support in their attempts to push the transition process in directions that will be advantageous for their own separate interests. Neither the international nor the domestic actors engaged in such maneuvers can afford to be too purist about the bargains they make.

The third and final general point is that there is a center-periphery aspect of all the international relationships under consideration here. The countries claiming to promote democracy beyond their frontiers are all relatively stable, rich, dominant liberal capitalist societies. The countries attempting transitions to democracy are all less rich, less stable, and may all be classed as "peripheral" or even perhaps "dependent" capitalist societies. Schematically, then, one can suggest the following typical pattern of international influences. The peripheral society aspires to "catch up" with or "fully belong to" the more prosperous and stable communities at the center of the system. To catch up in material terms would require national unity, social discipline, and the sacrifice of present welfare for the sake of future growth. These requirements favor the introduction of authoritarian forms of government, and create deep dissatisfaction with weak democratic regimes that seem characterized by indiscipline, disunity, and shortsightedness. "Full membership" of the developed capitalist world is desired not only for the material prosperity it offers but also for the political freedom, personal security, and social justice that are an equally important part of its promise. To catch up in political and social terms requires the establishment of political democracy, even if the associated reforms impede the process of economic growth. Within the terms of this highly simplified schema the countries of this capitalist core transmit two somewhat contradictory impulses to the societies on their periphery. International support for efforts at redemocratization is only the most visible part of one of these dual impulses. The full story of the relationship is more complex, and more ambiguous. This sketchy interpretation may help to account for one crucial characteristic that many of the peripheral countries seem to share, namely, the tendency to alternate between authoritarian and democratic forms of government without becoming irreversibly committed to one or the other.

This chapter will now review some recent history, considering the motives, the methods, and the results of American and West European efforts to promote democracy in Southern Europe and Latin America.

Motives

The simplest and most fundamental motive for the promotion of democracy is to extend to foreigners the benefits of a system that is valued at home. Citizens of the established liberal democracies readily believe in the superiority—both moral and practical—of their form of government, and most would find it hard to doubt that the world as a whole would be a safer and happier place if it were generalized. (Though I shall not attempt to refute this proposition, many Soviet citizens probably take the same view of *their* system, likewise many Iranian fundamentalists. In general, expansionary powers have almost invariably promoted some such view of the merits of their domestic system of government.) Given that political democracy is now well established in all the leading countries of Western Europe and North America, verbal expressions of support for redemocratization efforts in peripheral countries are virtually *de rigueur*, and should be interpreted first and foremost as affirmations of internal legitimacy. However, it is not official rhetoric that requires analysis here, but the manner in which these declaratory statements are translated into effective action in a given set of circumstances. To explain this, a rather more complex and nuanced set of motives must be considered, and distinctions must be made between the various agencies providing international support for democracy.

The basic distinction is between the U.S. government and the governments of Western Europe. Their contrasting histories, their distinctive geopolitical roles, and their present differences of political structure, all give rise to marked variations of conduct and motive. First of all, the U.S.A. views itself as a great nation whose success is founded on a long tradition of internal democracy (in important aspects traceable back to the origins of the Republic), and whose international supremacy is connected with the implementation of democracy by force of arms, not just in one instance but repeatedly. Given such a view of the sources of America's past and present strength, policies involving the "export of democracy" are likely to be conducted in an assertive and self-confident manner, with limited concern for the complex calculations of the contending forces within the country in question. More important will be whether domestic U.S. support can be enlisted for the foreign policy in question. For this purpose no precise criteria of what counts as a "democracy" are needed; but foreign governments that are not reliable allies of the U.S.A. as a global power, and political movements overseas that do not share the official American world view, will find it hard to secure recognition in Washington as truly democratic, however liberal their electoral practices or their political philosophies.

By contrast, the history of democracy in Western Europe is far more checkered. European greatness was traditionally associated with colonial empires rather than personal freedoms. The postwar consolidation of liberal democracy throughout Western Europe came in the wake of two great wars both originating in European imperial and territorial disputes. That consolidation required external assistance, and the painful renegotiation of political relationships within Western Europe. It was achieved not through conquest, but through defeat; not as part of an expansion of Europe's power in the world, but in the aftermath of its contraction. It had to be constructed piecemeal, country by country, and always with a view to placating the geopolitically dominant powers (mainly the U.S.A., but also to some extent the U.S.S.R., notably with regard to Austrian and Finnish democracy). This contrasting history naturally gave rise to substantial differences of approach compared with the U.S.A. over the "export of democracy." For one thing, the West Europeans had to concentrate their efforts on their own region and on their former colonies, that is, where an extension of democracy must signify a loss of privileges to some previously dominant European interests. Quite soon after 1945 it became apparent to the newly liberated peoples of Western Europe that they lacked the means effectively to promote democracy either in Eastern Europe or in the Iberian Peninsula (let alone in Latin America). Postwar West European efforts to promote democracy were therefore far more tentative and introspective than their American counterparts. Lacking the power to impose any kind of democracy on their enemies, West Europeans had to proceed with tact and patience if representative government was to take root among their neighbors and in their ex-possessions. Therefore they had to deal cautiously with political movements that vigorously repudiated the official European world view, and with governments that were unreliable or even downright antagonistic. Nevertheless, the West Europeans had an interest in strengthening whatever democratic or semidemocratic potential they could discern in such situations. At the same time, if the recently restored democracies within Western Europe were themselves to be preserved from the temptations of pseudo-democracy, it would be necessary to agree on clear and inflexible criteria for distinguishing between fraudulent imitations and the real thing. (As we shall see below, the Birkelbach Report of 1962 was critical in this respect.)

Clearly the U.S.A. and Western Europe have different regional spheres of influence ("backyards"). Moreover they have also adopted a division of responsibilities concerning their global alliance. The prime responsibility for military security rests with the U.S.A.; political and economic strategy in Europe and in the Lomé states (ex-European colonies) is largely a matter for the European Community. This role specialization has contributed to the differences of approach that have arisen concerning specific instances of democratic transition. For example, West German analyst Christian Deubner has contrasted the American and German responses to the collapse of the Iberian dictatorships in the mid-1970s:

> All the Western European bourgeois governments [were concerned about] the political stability of the Southern flank of capitalist Europe [but the West German position was] crucial, not only because of its government's accepted ability to influence the granting or withholding of substantial economic or financial inducements, or to serve as an intermediary with privileged access to the U.S. administration, but also because of the enormous influence which West German political and social organisations, such as political parties and trade unions, exercise at the level of subgovernmental transnational political processes in Western Europe, because of their organisational and financial strength. . . . Western Europe is up to now essentially a "civilian superpower" (to use a term of Johan Galtung) which, if only for lack of military might in the Mediterranean, cannot rely on this form of power coupled with threats for control of Mediterranean affairs as the U.S. appeared to do, but has to use the potent means of transnational processes and of inducements. Even the enlargement policy of the EC is, in the end, a clear political outflow of the fact that military force is not an available or acceptable means for inter-European stabilisation or coercion today.[5]

Even on its immediate perimeter, then, the European Community lacks the *military* means to project its power, and relies instead on political and economic inducements to stabilize its southern flank and to draw its neighbors into its system of commitments. By contrast, the U.S.A. has more plentiful military resources which are available to reinforce the security of its alliance system, not only in the immediate vicinity of North America, but also in many more distant places, where U.S. economic and political influence may be relatively weak. This contrast becomes especially clear when America's worldwide network of military agreements is taken into account. Thus, for example, the armed forces of Greece, Portugal, Spain, and Turkey all view their missions within the context of an American-led alliance. In general, civilian political groupings and social organizations look first to Western Europe as a source of external guidance, but the men in uniform look first to Washington, and this division helps to account for the differing roles played by the Americans and the Europeans when redemocratization came on to the Southern European agenda.

As noted above, both the NATO Treaty of 1949 and the treaty creating the

Council of Europe, in the same year, contain explicit language requiring a commitment to constitutional democracy. (Such language was adopted partly with an eye to excluding countries with Communist governments from participation in "European affairs," and similar considerations influenced the language used at the creation of the Organization of American States in 1948.) But NATO and the OAS were treaty systems dominated by strategic considerations that would apply whether or not political freedoms were being upheld by member states. Thus NATO included Salazarist Portugal, the Greece of the colonels, and military-ruled Turkey, whereas the Council of Europe excluded the first of these and suspended the other two because of their lack of democracy. (Spain was also excluded from the Council and did not gain admittance to NATO until 1982, but the United States entered into a military alliance with Franco in 1953.)

William Minter explains the strategic considerations that motivated the inclusion of Portugal as a founder member of NATO:

> The nature of Portugal's domestic policy was blurred . . . by the grant of the use of the Azores for the final stages of the war. Salazar seemed to slip quite easily from the close ties to Germany in the thirties, through neutrality, into the congenial context of postwar anti-communism. [The United States continued to use the Azores base on an ad hoc basis when peace came.] With military considerations soon uppermost in the minds of postwar American policy-makers, and with the Azores cast for an important role in this global military planning, the inclusion of a dictatorship in an alliance for the defence of "democracy" did not seem strange.[6]

Exhausted by three years of civil war, Spain remained technically neutral in World War II, but the Franco regime had more to lose than Salazar from an Allied victory. It was only after the United States and Britain halted shipments of oil and gasoline to Spain, in 1943, that the Madrid government promised to cease providing strategic commodities to Germany, and sheltering Nazi espionage activity. Even after this promise was made (in May 1944) and oil supplies were resumed, the Franco government continued secretly aiding the Axis powers. Consequently, in July 1945 the Allies declared at Potsdam that the Franco regime lacked "the necessary qualifications" to become a member of the United Nations, and Spain was excluded from the founding conference at San Francisco. However, it was one thing to declare Franco a pariah, and quite another to incur casualties in an attempt to overthrow him, or to foment another civil war. So in March 1946 the French, British, and Americans (not the Russians) issued a joint note urging a "peaceful transformation" of Francoism, an unlikely prospect considering the background. The French provisional government, itself so recently the product of an armed struggle to restore democracy, took the commitment more seriously than the rest, and for two years the Franco-Spanish frontier was closed. In December 1946 the United Nations voted by thirty-four to six in favor of a withdrawal of ambassadors and the application of economic sanctions. Because of this resolution, Spain was excluded from the Marshall Plan when it was launched in 1948. Although these sanctions were ineffective in political terms (indeed, they created some patriotic support for the Madrid authorities) they were extremely harmful in economic terms. However, President Perón of Argentina provided sufficient credit and food imports to enable Spain to withstand the blockade until the cold war came to Franco's rescue.

Many leading figures in West European political life had fought for the Spanish Republic, and much electoral opinion saw in the Southern European dictatorships not reliable allies, but barbarous relics and even possible sources of danger to European freedoms. More specifically, the parties of the European Left and West European labor movements have well-established fraternal ties with the counterpart organizations of Southern Europe that stand to gain most from democratization, and that are most at risk in the event of an authoritarian resurgence. These parties share some elements of a common history, a common "anti-Fascist" orientation, common ideological orientations, and similarities of social base. The conservative parties of Western Europe also have an anti-Fascist component derived from the legacy of World War II, and since they are in electoral competition with the parties of the Left, they too have sought to promote and protect democratizing counterparts in the Southern European dictatorships. These connections provide relatively strong and broadly based European support for democratizing alliances in Southern Europe (although the internal frictions and rivalries they engender should not be underestimated).

To understand the West European policy, and how it differs from that of Washington, it is necessary to consider the underlying political forces and distributions of opinion to which these respective centers of power must respond. One particular political organization—the Socialist International (SI)—is of particular interest here, because so many of the leading political figures of Western Europe have been associated with its campaigns in favor of democracy, and because no important political forces within the U.S.A. have been associated with it. Thus, a consideration of the role of the SI may help to explain differences in behavior on the two sides of the Atlantic on the question of promoting democracy in Southern Europe.

One theme running strongly through the entire postwar history of the SI was its hostility to the Franco regime. It was, of course, in response to a Socialist election victory that Franco had risen and launched the Civil War, in 1936. In prewar days, as idealistic youths, many of Europe's established social democratic politicians fought with the International Brigades in Spain, or knew those who had. In the early 1940s, all the Socialist parties of mainland Europe were reduced to refugee status in London and Stockholm, and the tradition of international solidarity with oppressed parties was greatly reinforced. In the immediate postwar period, when European Socialist parties began once more to enjoy the fruits of public office, they felt a special duty of solidarity toward their Spanish coreligionaries who still suffered the full force of a dictatorial repression. In July 1951 (at the height of the Korean War), a conference was held in Frankfurt to reconstitute the Second International, at this time renamed the Socialist International. The declaration of principle asserted: "Socialism can be achieved only through democracy. Democracy can be fully realized only through socialism." It adopted a seven-point definition of democracy that requires considerably more than the mere existence of free and competitive elections. (It is in marked contrast to the narrowly procedural view of "democracy" often invoked by Western governments.) In addition, the declaration argued that "every dictatorship, wherever it may be, is a danger to the freedom of all nations" and that "democracy can only be defended with the active help of the workers, whose fate depends on its survival." Although directed as much against the Communist regimes of Eastern Europe as against the "Fascists" of the Iberian Peninsula, the declaration involved a far stronger political commitment to the redemocratization of Spain than Washington policy-makers were ever likely to contemplate.

In recent years the major political parties of Western Europe have also taken an increasing interest in the fortunes of sister political parties struggling to establish democracy in Latin America. Here too there has been a contrast between the outlook of Europe-based organizations and their American counterparts, although the newly established National Endowment for Democracy apparently represents an attempt to bring U.S. practice closer to the European pattern. By 1984 nineteen parties or political movements in the Western hemisphere were full members of the Christian Democratic Organization of America (ODCA; originally founded by the Chilean Eduardo Frei, and others, in 1947), an affiliate of the World Christian Democratic Union, which derives most of its backing from Western Europe.[7] In the same year fourteen of the forty-nine full member parties of the Socialist International came from the Americas, together with six of the seventeen consultative parties. In Rio de Janeiro, in October 1984, the president of the SI, Willy Brandt, chaired the largest meeting of Socialist parties ever held, which was also the largest gathering of Latin American and Caribbean political parties.[8] Similarly the Liberal International also has a network of Latin American sister parties, and there are analogous links between European and Latin American labor movements.

Throughout the thirty-nine long years of Francoism, the Spanish Socialist party benefited from the encouragement and support of the other European parties, until it was finally once more legalized after Franco's death, and swept back to electoral victory in 1982.[9] Following legalization, the party's secretary general (now prime minister of Spain) became joint president of the SI, with special concern for the Spanish American parties. Both the current Socialist prime minister of Portugal and the present prime minister of Greece received the support of the Socialist International when their countries were subjected to authoritarian rule, and both now play an active role in promoting the Latin American objectives of the SI (although the Greek party does not actually belong to the organization).

Just as the Spanish Civil War served to catalyze the opposition of European parties to the Iberian dictatorships, so the 1973 overthrow of President Allende by the Chilean military spurred equivalent European efforts in Latin America.

In particular, the Nixon administration's efforts to destabilize Allende's government in Chile, and the tragic destruction of Chilean democracy, produced a strong impact among West European Socialists. Although many of the established party leaders regarded Allende's policies as far more radical than they themselves would endorse, they were bound to express solidarity both with his general aims and with his apparent reliance on democratic methods. His fate revived memories of Europe's struggles against Fascism, and reignited distrust of American foreign policy priorities. It was particularly disturbing to those parties for whom electoral interest might lead to a popular front tactic of alliance with the Communist party. The French, Italian, and Spanish parties were the most affected by this consideration. (Mitterrand, for example, needed to attract nearly all of France's large Communist vote if he was to win a presidential election.) For both ideological and practical reasons, therefore, Mitterrand's forceful remarks (during a visit to Mexico in 1977) concerning the military regimes of the Southern Cone were not entirely out of line with general SI opinion in Western Europe: "The only answer to personal dictatorship or to the bourgeois class in Latin America is socialism. Twenty years ago, traditional democracy as developed by the liberal bourgeoisie, could have been another answer. But this possibility disappeared from the moment that the liberal bourgeoisie, faced by the demands of the masses, had to turn to dictatorship."[10]

Washington policy-makers have operated under a different set of domestic political constraints, and so have tended to view the Latin American Left with far more fear and distrust than is common among the Europeans. On the other hand, the right-wing and dictatorial forces of Latin America generally encounter relatively little support in postwar Europe (where the associations with Fascism evoke an emotional rejection), but they often have rather strong links with some important business, military, and ideological groupings within the United States. In general, the Europeans have rather little to lose in the way of economic or strategic investments from the downfall of authoritarian regimes in Latin America, whereas powerful American interests may feel far more directly threatened.

Certainly, during the presidencies of Truman, Kennedy, and Carter and perhaps more generally, there were active forces within the Washington bureaucracy who sought to combat the antidemocratic forces of the Latin American Right, but almost always their efforts were overshadowed by the greater need to oppose Communism and therefore to unify anti-Communist forces.[11] A State Department background paper prepared by the Policy Planning Staff for the Bogotá conference of April 1948 (which gave rise to the Organization of American States) put the issue as follows: "Two new forces threatening democracy have, during and since the war, made their appearance in Latin America: a brand of Fascism deriving in part from Nazi ideology, and, second, Communism." Once the U.S.A. had made its peace with Peronist Argentina (by mid-1947), the defense of democracy became conflated with anti-Communism.[12] As the State Department report continued, "Ample precedent for common measures to combat Communism in the Americas existed in the programs and activities carried out during the last World War." Exchanges of information, and police cooperation, were particularly mentioned. *But* the report went on:

> There are strong and extreme reactionary forces and governments in Latin America which, through selfishness and lack of any sense of social responsibility, impose a minority will through military or other dictatorial governments and so alienate large segments of their populations which otherwise probably would be anti-Communist. These reactionary forces often adopt a strong anti-Communist line but frequently apply repressive measures to all political opponents, alleging that the latter are Communists whether or not that is the fact. . . . Consequently, co-operation of the United States with these reactionary elements, even in anti-Communist measures, should be very carefully considered in the light of our long-range national interests.

The report hinted at ethical as well as pragmatic reasons for caution: "The Catholic Church, the armed forces, and the large landowners naturally provide strong opposition to Communism. These three elements frequently work together and dominate governments. Unfortunately, they sometimes come close to the extreme of reaction which is very similar to Communism as concerns totalitarian police state methods." So, although recommending a series of measures to combat Communism, the paper argued that the U.S.A. should try to resist Latin American pressure for the adoption of anti-Communist measures "so drastic in nature that they would . . . increase international tension, give dictatorial governments in other countries a means of attacking all opposition and might even infringe constitutional liberties in the United States."[13]

Within the U.S. political spectrum, this was a rather progressive position and not one that could be sustained consistently. It was particularly likely to be overruled at moments of crisis in the cold war, such as those occasioned by Korea, Vietnam, and the Cuban and Nicaraguan revolutions. Within the political spectrum of postwar Western Europe, by contrast, this would rank as a moderately conservative position. Even during heightened phases of the cold war, major political forces in Europe were wary of alliance with the authoritarian Right, remembering only too clearly what such an alliance had led to in interwar Europe.

In summary, then, European and American attitudes on the promotion of democracy differ, in part because of the legacy of European Fascism. European definitions of "democracy" seem to give more stress to social and economic participation, whereas the Americans give almost exclusive emphasis to the electoral aspect. The political spectrum in most West European countries is reasonably congruent with that likely to emerge in Southern Europe and Latin American nations as they redemocratize. Thus major political currents on both Left and Right are likely to find counterparts in Western Europe, whereas the U.S. spectrum may only correspond to that ranging from the Center to the far Right, leaving emergent left-wing currents with no *interlocuteurs* in the American political process. In any case, European parties are organized differently from U.S. parties, with a programmatic basis that facilitates identification with similar currents in other countries, and a structure that enables them to pursue more or less sustained foreign policy goals, even when out of office. American parties, by contrast, have less structure and continuity, and less commitment to explicit doctrinal positions. They therefore have less solid relationships with "fraternal" parties in other countries. In order to mobilize U.S. domestic opinion around any foreign policy goals, U.S. leaders often need to deploy a moral, patriotic, or anti-Communist rhetoric that expresses American exceptionalism and that some external opinion may perceive as expressing an American wish for hegemony. If the rhetoric is effective enough to arouse domestic enthusiasm, it is also likely to impede the process of international confidence-building required for the promotion of autonomous redemocratizations abroad. The hopes and fears that U.S. promises of support generate among the contending political forces engaged in a democratic transition reflect more than just the rhetorical aspects of the process. Washington has strong economic and strategic interests to defend in many parts of the world, whereas the Europeans have partially withdrawn from some of their most far-flung positions, and elsewhere they can to some extent shelter behind Washington's alliance system. Of course they have large interests in adjacent Southern Europe, but these interests are not entirely congruent with those of Washington, and in any case, they have found that political and economic inducements, rather than reliance on military ties, may best serve to consolidate their positions there. The apparent success of these methods in Spain, Portugal, and Greece has subsequently strengthened the European inclination to apply them further afield, notably in South America and most recently even in Central America, a region where Europe's direct interests are minimal. It may be partly in response to this increased European activity in what has been traditionally regarded as a U.S. sphere of influence that Washington has also stepped up its support for prodemocratic currents in Latin America.

There is, of course, a large area of overlap between European and American approaches to the promotion of democracy, and a considerable degree of cooperation exists between them. The differences of emphasis indicated above should not be overestimated, but equally they should not be overlooked. These nuances can be of great practical significance for particular political organizations engaged in negotiations over a specific redemocratization project. The underlying source of all these differences of emphasis arises from the fact that in the postwar period the fundamental concern of the European Community has been to consolidate democratic institutions in their own region. After the recent experiences of Fascism and Communism, these institutions were known to be insecure. For them, therefore, the promotion of democracy *outside* the European Community was intimately related with its internal consolidation.[14] By contrast the U.S.A.'s democratic constitution has not been under any serious internal threat, and in consequence Americans have given more attention to protecting and extending the international supremacy of their nation. The security of their *external* alliance system has naturally been the top priority of their foreign policy, and if that meant condoning some undemocratic regimes within the "Free World," many Americans could reasonably judge that such a posture would pose no real threat to their domestic freedoms.

Methods

Governmental

It should now be apparent that a wide variety of methods are available to assist the promotion of democracy in Latin America and Southern Europe. It should also be apparent that many of these methods are of uncertain effect, some may be mutually inconsistent, and all are difficult to apply in a sustained manner over the long term. Moreover, since the promotion of democracy is never more than one among a series of competing foreign policy objectives, the methods used to serve this end have to be evaluated with regard to their impact on other goals as well. This section will briefly consider the role of international treaties; the scope for diplomacy in interpreting and modifying the terms of treaty provisions; the part played by economic incentive and "aid packages"; and the activities of nongovernmental organizations such as the SI, the ODCA, and the churches. Once again, the experiences of Western Europe and the U.S.A. will be compared.

All these methods involve encouraging transitions to democracy, but without directly "intervening" in the strictly internal affairs of another sovereign state during a time of peace. In practice, the boundary between exercising legitimate external influence and improper intervention is far more blurred than most governments are willing to admit—a significant part of the political process may consist in trying to persuade one or another set of audiences of the appropriate label to attach in particular circumstances. A method that would be effective if accepted as noninterventionist can become counterproductive if seen as illegitimate interference. As noted above, for example, the victorious democracies brought some pressure to bear on both Spain and Argentina after 1945, although in both cases it was clear that force would not be used. Franco and Perón both survived these pressures, in part by presenting themselves as defenders of a national sovereignty threatened by an external imposition. The Mexicans have enjoyed great success with this approach, ever since President Carranza rejected President Wilson's demand for early elections, just before World War I. It should be noted, however, that even where external pressures fail to bring about a desired redemocratization they may have other profound effects both on the internal politics of the country under seige and on patterns of international alignments. Thus, for example, Perón had to contest at least one relatively fair presidential election, and in the process he became more reliant on his trade union supporters than might otherwise have been the case.

Likewise Spain and Argentina were driven together, and so forth.

The methods used against Franco's Spain, in 1946–48 (exclusion from the United Nations, and from Marshall aid, closure of the frontier, official support for—and even in some cases recognition of—a government-in-exile) represent probably the most drastic attempt to induce redemocratization anywhere in the postwar period, short of outright invasion. Current campaigns against the Sandinista government in Nicaragua may constitute the nearest equivalent. That such methods failed in Spain, and that after four years similar efforts in Nicaragua still fall well short of achieving their ostensible aims, confirms the view that in peacetime external factors can play only a secondary role in redemocratization. Unobtrusive but inflexible inducements and penalties are likely to be more effective than more fleetingly dramatic approaches, but even the most effective methods will only produce results over the long haul, and when the internal processes are favorable.

In November 1950 the United States, seeking anti-Communist unity during the Korean War, persuaded a majority at the United Nations to rescind the anti-Franco resolution of 1946. Spain joined the United Nations shortly thereafter, and in 1953 signed a bilateral treaty with Washington exchanging economic aid for military bases. Membership in the United Nations has not subsequently been used as an incentive to democratize. Similarly, as we have seen in the case of Portugal, membership in NATO despite its preamble has never been made conditional on the maintenance of domestic freedoms. (Indeed repressive governments such as the military in Turkey have felt more at home within NATO than recently democratized Greece, Spain, and Portugal.) Similarly, although the Organization of American States proclaims democracy as one of its major values, only Castro's Cuba has been expelled. Allende's more or less constitutional government in Chile came in for strong posthumous criticism from the OAS, whereas a variety of highly undemocratic right-wing regimes remained untroubled within the organization at least until the mid-1970s, when the organization began campaigning against gross human rights violations by member states.[15] Thus the only two international organizations that have stood clearly and consistently for the maintenance of constitutional democracy among all member states are the Council of Europe and the European Economic Community (EEC).

In May 1949, ten West European democracies joined in creating the Council of Europe, in what was to prove an abortive effort at political unification. According to Article 3 of the statute every member of the Council "must accept the principles of the rule of law and of the enjoyment by all persons within its jurisdiction of human rights and fundamental freedoms." To stiffen this provision, Article 8 added that any member "which has seriously violated Article 3 may be suspended from its right of representation and requested by the Committee of Ministers to withdraw." (This provision was invoked against Greece in 1967, and against Turkey in 1981.)

The Treaty of Rome (1957), creating the European Economic Community (EEC), offered West European democracies a further path toward integration.

Unlike the 1949 Statute, the 1957 Treaty contained no explicit requirement of democracy, in part because of the need to include Western Germany and the expectation, still prevalent at that time, of an eventual reunification of the two German states. The Rome treaty simply states that any other European country may apply for membership in the Community, with the terms of admission being a matter for negotiation between the original signatories and subsequent applicants. The treaty also provided for the creation of a European Assembly to be elected, initially, by national parliaments of member countries. In strictly constitutional terms, this treaty need not have debarred Spain from membership if the other European states had been willing to recognize the representatives of the Francoist Cortes. However, notwithstanding the vague language of the treaty, European democratic politics proved an insuperable bar to the acceptance of authoritarian Spain. This fact became apparent when, in February 1962, Franco's foreign ministers wrote to the Gaullist chairman of the Council of Ministers requesting negotiations. Despite the sympathy shown by Adenauer and de Gaulle, there was sufficient protest from leaders of the Belgian and Italian Socialist parties, and from others who had supported the Spanish Republic against Franco's dictatorship, to obstruct this development. Because of their Europe-wide presence, Socialists have been the largest single bloc in the European Assembly since its creation. From the outset the Socialist group took a close interest in the conditions for membership in the Community, and the terms on which it would grant economic concessions to associated states. This group was determined to oppose the admission of Spain and Portugal until constitutional government was restored in the Iberian Peninsula, together with the granting of full legal recognition to the region's Socialist parties and unions. The Birkelbach Report of 1962 was the work of a German Social Democrat who secured approval for strict conditions of membership. It thus became a firm commitment of the EEC to apply quite liberally the terms of the Birkelbach Report, which laid down the conditions for membership: "Only states which guarantee on their territories truly democratic practices and respect for fundamental rights and freedoms can become members of our Community. It is also inconceivable that a State whose foreign policy is diametrically opposed to our own could become part of our Community."[16]

Although a prime target of this excommunication was Francoist Spain, these terms also served to exclude Salazarist Portugal, and the colonels' Greece. Greece was the first nonmember of the EEC to negotiate a Treaty of Association with the Community. It came into effect in 1962, and contained unusually generous economic provisions. Unlike subsequent treaties of association (e.g., with Israel and Turkey), the Athens treaty stated that the objective was to raise Greek living standards to the point where Greece could subsequently join the EEC as a full member. However, the process of integration soon lost momentum. Writing in 1971, Stanley Henig observed:

> A small group of Socialist critics of the negotiations . . . have been proved right: they warned of certain dubious political practices in Greece well

before the *coup d'état* [of 1967] . . . political developments in Greece made her hardly acceptable as a political partner to a democratic Community. Intervention by the Commission led to a cessation of financial assistance and the virtual freezing of relations . . . in [many] respects the Association must be considered moribund ten years after the treaty was signed.[17]

As soon as democracy was restored in the mid-1970s, each of these three countries (Greece, Portugal, Spain) was quick to apply for membership of the (by then enlarged) EEC. Membership in the Community would, it was thought, provide an external guarantee to help the consolidation of democracy. Although it was not European pressure that brought down the Greek colonels in 1974, European influence certainly encouraged the forces of democracy, and added to the regime's problems.[18] Not surprisingly, therefore, after constitutional government was restored, Athens became less cooperative with NATO, but reasserted its desire for full membership of the EEC. The European Commission responded with the following opinion: "It is clear that the consolidation of Greece's democracy . . . is intimately related to the evolution of Greece's relationship with the community. It is in the light of these considerations that the Commission recommends that a clear affirmative reply be given to the Greek request."

In October 1980, Papandreou's Socialist party achieved electoral victory on a platform that included disengagement from NATO and the expulsion of U.S. bases. On 1 January 1981, Greece became a full member of the EEC, with twenty-four MPs in the European Parliament, and the appointment of a Greek commissioner. In view of full membership and the financial support that Greece is now receiving, the Papandreou government has accepted a degree of integration into democratic Europe, while maintaining a degree of distance from the Western security system.

The prospect of membership of the European Community remained an important incentive for the consolidation of democratic processes in the Iberian Peninsula, although the social and economic climate became extremely adverse. West European governments and SI members' parties still faced a major test of the sincerity of their democratizing commitment. In 1982–83 it seemed as if the Socialist government of France might be the major obstacle; by 1985 it was Socialist Greece that raised most obstacles. In June 1985 it was finally agreed that Spain and Portugal would become full members of the Community in 1986.

The EEC is above all an *economic* community, which is governed by rigid rules and treaty obligations, and which minimizes the exercise of political discretion. In consequence, the Community has set up a stable pattern of rewards and disincentives which policy-makers in Southern Europe could hardly hope to vary. The same provisions for membership have remained in place ever since the Birkelbach Report of 1962, although in practical terms they gained in forcefulness from the late 1960s (notably with the enlargement of the Community and the dissolution of the European Free Trade Association

[EFTA] to which Portugal had belonged). Spain, Portugal, and Greece were all eligible to join the integration movement as soon as they became conventional democracies just like Ireland, Denmark, and so on. In these relatively less developed (though rapidly developing) countries, whose leaders were suffering a sense of exclusion from international arenas because of the pariah status of their internal political arrangements, the Community produced a substantial long-term pressure for democratization.

One perhaps decisively favorable aspect of the incentives for democratization offered by the European Community was the guarantees and reassurances it could provide to those conservatives and upper-class groups in Southern European society that were most likely to feel threatened by popular government. Membership of a democratic Europe was also membership of a prosperous community which offered international guarantees for certain things most highly valued by the wealthy classes—free movement of capital, freedom to travel and seek employment elsewhere, legal protection against arbitrary confiscation of property. With these things assured, democracy lost many of its terrors for the Greek and Iberian upper classes. Indeed, it is possible to regard the European Community as the "functional equivalent" for the 1970s of constitutional monarchy as observed by S.M. Lipset in the 1950s. Lipset, it will be recalled, saw the preservation of monarchy as one of Europe's surest devices for easing the transition toward popular democracy. In most stable democracies, he commented, "the preservation of the monarchy has retained for these nations the loyalty of the aristocratic, traditionalist, and clerical sectors of the population which resented increased democratization and egalitarianism."[19] The Spanish monarchy has recently confirmed the continuing significance of this observation, but in a Europe where the upper classes are now overwhelmingly rationalist and bourgeois, membership of the EEC may provide a more than adequate substitute for continuities sustained in the past through heredity and courtly ritual.

The U.S. government has also, of course, offered economic and political rewards to tempt Latin American countries into a democratic course, but if one sets aside the special case of Puerto Rico, these incentives have not been so stable, predictable, long-term, and impersonal. The more typical pattern of U.S. behavior has been that a certain administration may make the democratization of a particular Latin republic a "showcase" for its policies. In the absence of a permanent treaty guaranteeing a continuous relationship, the White House must negotiate a specific package of incentives through all the legislative minefields. Even if one assumes that the original offer of incentives emerges intact from this process, the offer will consist of *temporary* rewards in return for an assumed *permanent* shift to democracy. American incentives to democratize will almost certainly become identified as the actions of a narrow group in the U.S. executive to promote a client faction in a given Latin republic, and so their effects are unlikely to outlast the immediate political conjuncture. In short, U.S. support for democratization will be viewed by all concerned as a superficial commitment, whereas in Southern Europe (though not of course more generally) the EEC could offer something more closely resembling a binding contract.

One major theme running through the recommendations of the Kissinger Commission on Central America was the need for the United States to establish a stable long-term policy toward the region that would, supposedly, offer powerful inducements for local actors to embrace democratic solutions to their problems. The commission was bipartisan in its composition (i.e., its recommendations were aimed at Democrats as well as Republicans); multilateral in its approach (the key idea was to create a development organization with eight member nations, including the United States, under an American chairman); and its recommendations relatively long term in duration (eight billion dollars was to be contributed by Washington over the five years 1985–90, thereby committing in advance whoever might win the U.S. elections of 1984 and 1988). The report commented unfavorably on previous U.S. practices:

> The present purely bilateral process has its drawbacks. It factors political assessments directly into economic aid decisions. This makes the United States the prosecuting judge and jury. It leads to rancorous debate, sometimes poorly informed. This Commission's proposal is an effort to explore a new process . . . [that] should be more effective, more acceptable to Central America and more compatible with present-day views of how sovereign nations should deal with each other.[20]

The report refers approvingly to President Kennedy's Alliance for Progress as a historic model. The 1961 Alliance, in turn, referred to the 1948 Marshall Plan as a precedent. These, together with President Carter's human rights policy, constitute Washington's most ambitious postwar endeavors to use aid and diplomacy in order (among other objectives) to promote democratization overseas. The results of these official American initiatives will be considered in the next section. As far as methods are concerned, these policies all required executive coordination of a wide variety of otherwise unrelated or even conflicting bureaucratic positions. Successive presidents had to "sell" these policies to skeptics in Congress, and in the process convince potential veto groups that value would be obtained for the taxpayers' money, and that there would be continuing opportunities for legislative oversight. Such policies commanded maximum support when the apparent threat to national security was greatest; they tended to lose momentum as the emphasis shifted from "fighting Communism" to other less urgent or more controversial goals. From the standpoint of the foreign beneficiaries of these policies, Washington's methods of policy formation have always necessitated acceptance of a substantial degree of American involvement in internal matters. Recent American and international controversies about Washington's self-described efforts to "promote democracy" in Central America only manifest in somewhat extreme form the tendencies toward distortion and overinvolvement that seem inherent to the U.S. approach.

In Central America, for example, Washington obviously possesses a large array of policy instruments for influencing local developments, and many of them have been used in an assertive and forceful manner (though not always with much consistency or coordination) over the past few years. Military inducements have ranged from the establishment of facilities to train soldiers in "counter-insurgency with respect for human rights" to the denial of arms supplies. A great array of covert activities have been funded to strengthen the hand of some local political groups (e.g., allegedly to secure Christian Democratic success in the May 1984 Salvadoran elections) and to discredit or destroy others. Economic aid has been offered, denied, made conditional on improvements in human rights, and so forth. Political leaders have been refused entry visas, defectors have been put on public display to highlight the misdeeds of their associates, the FBI has been despatched to investigate murders that could not be handled through local judicial process, sugar quotas have been denied, one-way free-trade deals have been offered, the Neutrality Act has been fiercely enforced against some groups and laxly administered against others. This list could be expanded almost indefinitely. The point is that Washington possesses an enormous array of instruments for influencing Central American politics, but that these are often overused, or inappropriately deployed, if the purpose is to strengthen democratic tendencies on the isthmus.[21]

To produce a consistent effect a diverse range of instruments must be coordinated, requiring the cooperation of a variety of agents with divergent interests and perceptions; these external influences must be brought to bear in a manner that elicits the cooperation of local actors without denying them their autonomy or authenticity. For one requirement of any genuine international support for democratization is that local actors must be given sufficient freedom of maneuver to act on their own behalf, and to establish their credentials as authentic groupings, not "puppets" manipulated by external powers. This involves a self-denying ordinance by those external powers wishing to promote democracy. Such restraint may be particularly hard to achieve in countries where genuine progress toward democracy necessitates some clearcut break with a past pattern of power relations. Indeed the consolidation of democracy may actually require the eclipse of local forces (such as the Nicaraguan National Guard) that have been closely aligned with Washington. At least tacit agreement to tolerate such developments may be required for any genuine democratization to occur.

Nongovernmental

The discussion of treaty arrangements, aid packages, and official diplomacy covers the range of direct methods available to Western governments that wish to support redemocratization. However, there are also other methods available, which can be used by nongovernmental organizations. Here we shall consider only the activities of democratic Western political parties, and in particular the member parties of the Socialist International (SI). The previous section pointed out a contrast between the major political parties of Western Europe, which carry out something resembling international diplomacy on their own account, and which actively support "fraternal" parties in other parts of the world, and the exceptionalism and lack of international presence of the major U.S. parties. There are, of course, organizations within the American political process that carry out many of the same functions as the ODCA and the SI, namely, relaying information between like-minded politicians inside and outside the U.S.A. and coordinating policies.[22] These are, however, largely Washington-focused organizations in contrast to the multinational instruments established by the European parties. There is no general answer to the question which of these systems is more effective in supporting processes of redemocratization. Much depends upon the geopolitical circumstances of the country in question, and on the specific configuration of political forces in Washington, or within particular European countries at the time. Given the range of experiences under consideration here, it is possible to discuss only the activities of one of these nongovernmental organizations. The SI has been selected for examination because it is perhaps the most important instance of party-to-party cooperation for the promotion of democracy, and also because its history is relatively little studied and can easily be misunderstood. Washington's response to the sometimes inconvenient activities of the SI is also of interest.

Up to World War II, the Second International (forerunner to the present SI) had been composed exclusively of European parties. In part, this exclusiveness was a reflection of Europe's political and economic role in the world, but it also reflected the prevalence of Eurocentric social theories and even prejudices. After 1945 this outlook was no longer tenable. In the early postwar years, many West European Socialists looked with hope toward Eastern Europe. Both the Comintern and the Second International were formally dissolved, and efforts were made by the strong democratic Socialist parties of Eastern Europe to cooperate with the Communists in the areas under Soviet military control. However, following the destruction of the independent Czech Social Democrats in 1948, a main preoccupation of international Socialist gatherings became solidarity with the persecuted Social Democrats of Eastern Europe. Nevertheless, the tribulations of the Southern European parties (including the Greeks, caught in the middle of an implacable civil war) were not forgotten. It took an American Socialist, Robert Alexander, to point out to European Socialists in 1947 the importance of adding a Latin American dimension: "The Socialist Parties of Latin America need the aid of the European Socialist Parties, but they feel that the Europeans also need the participation of extra-European elements in SI gatherings, and specifically they need the participation of the Latin American Socialists, who now constitute one of the strongest groups of socialist movements anywhere in the world, and with perhaps more future than many of those in the Old World."[23]

Within a year of its foundation in 1951, the SI was able to report applications to join from parties in thirty-six countries, including Argentina, Jamaica, and Uruguay. In addition, the Secretariat had established contact with thirty-five nonaffiliated organizations, including the Socialist party of Chile (shortly to be affiliated), Acción Democrática of Venezuela, and organizations in Brazil, Colombia, Costa Rica, Cuba, Ecuador, Haiti, Mexico, and Peru, as well as countries in the British Caribbean. The first report paid tribute to "thousands of good comrades in Spain who feel united with us but who are politically oppressed . . . also . . . our friends and brothers in the Fascist or semi-Fascist countries of Latin America" (a reference to the Socialist party of Argentina, facing repression from Perón); in July 1953, the third congress noted "with concern the growth of anti-democratic and dictatorial governments in Latin America" and urged "moral aid and encouragement to all those in Latin America . . . who are fighting . . . for the re-establishment and expansion of democracy." SI publications showed particular concern with Argentina and Venezuela. Peru and Paraguay were also mentioned.

In October 1955 (immediately after the overthrow of Perón in Argentina) the Bureau of the SI decided to set up a Latin American Secretariat in Montevideo, and in May 1956 it convened the first conference of Latin American Socialist parties, which promptly denounced "the present policy of domination which the Republican Party of the U.S.A. exercises through the State Department and which has led to the supremacy of the dictatorships and the economic impoverishment of Latin America." It expressed approval for the idea of convening "a Congress of the democratic parties of Latin America to survey publicly and condemn the despotic regimes of many countries of Latin America and the internal and external forces which support them" (the Dominican Republic, Venezuela, Nicaragua, Paraguay, and Guatemala were specifically mentioned in this context).

Two years later, in May 1958, the third conference of the Latin American Secretariat took place in Santiago, under much improved conditions. Seven parties were represented (including a delegate from Castro's 26th July Movement), and the conference provided a platform for Senator Allende's narrowly unsuccessful bid for the Chilean presidency. It also "paid tribute to the people of Venezuela and to Acción Democrática for the defeat of the Pérez Jiménez dictatorship," and urged democratic governments to break diplomatic relations with the Paraguayan and Cuban dictatorships. Of particular interest is the attitude expressed toward the new civilian government of Colombia, which had recently taken over from a military dictatorship. It was described as "imitation republicanism" in which "public offices were being shared out by the oligarchy." "The conference was disturbed by the new policy of the U.S. State Department which, when it can no longer keep dictatorships in power, uses its influence to replace them by oligarchical governments, paying no heed to popular forces."

In 1958 the SI was on the crest of a wave, but it was not to last. That year there were democratic elections in Argentina, Brazil, Chile, Uruguay, and Venezuela, in all of which SI-associated parties made at least a respectable, and in two cases a strong, showing. The following year another loosely associated organization, Castro's 26th July Movement, came to power not through elections but by armed struggle. The aftershock of that event transformed the panorama throughout the continent. As is well known, the Castro regime initially spoke of elections, constitutional government, and a Socialist humanism entirely consistent with the doctrines of the SI. Within two years, however, the Cuban Revolution had moved rapidly toward Marxist-Leninism, alliance with the Soviet Union, and the promotion of guerrilla movements in other Latin American countries. Worst of all for the SI, not all these guerrilla movements were directed against right-wing dictatorships. Another target was the recently established democracy of Venezuela, governed by the most successful Latin party with which the Socialist International had established fraternal links. The European Socialist parties were bound to dissociate themselves from the Cuban experience, not only for reasons of doctrine, or from a wish to conciliate the U.S.A. In addition, the SI was deeply affected by the fate suffered by compatriate parties in Eastern Europe. Furthermore, its opposition to Franco and Salazar drew strength from the contention that there was a democratic alternative to right-wing dictatorship, a point disputed by supporters of Iberian authoritarianism, who had always portrayed Francoism as the only defense against a worse form of tyranny. Thus, although many individual European Socialists maintained solidarity with Castro in his conflict with the U.S.A., as the polarization intensified the Socialist parties of Western Europe pulled back from Latin America. In Latin America, on the other hand, SI-affiliated parties could not so readily disengage. Their electoral prospects rapidly dimmed as counterinsurgency doctrines spread. Some parties embraced the Alliance for Progress and therefore cut themselves off from the Left (without, as it turned out, securing any effective assistance from the United States against the authoritarian Right). For many others, armed struggle provided a strong temptation, and only in Chile and Uruguay were there significant Socialist organizations able to withstand these twin pressures. Thus, for the decade preceding Allende's election as president of Chile in 1970, the Latin American dimension of the Socialist International's activities was greatly diminished.

The Cuban Revolution was not the only cause of this decline. Other factors were at work in Western Europe. Thus, the French Socialist party was overshadowed by Gaullism throughout the 1960s, while the German and Italian parties were also becoming resigned to indefinite terms in opposition. Admittedly, the British Labour party returned to office in 1964, but it gave fairly uncritical support to the American side in the Vietnam War, and took little interest in Third World affairs outside the Commonwealth. During this period, the SI made some important advances in the Western hemisphere, but not in Latin America. Rather, it was in the newly independent states of the former British West Indies that a series of SI-affiliated or associated parties came to office through electoral processes. During the 1960s the parties of the SI took some steps that were later to bear rich fruit, but, as we have seen, it was toward Southern Europe, rather than Latin America, that the main efforts were initially directed.

After the overthrow of Allende, in 1973, the SI's main European leaders (e.g., Palme, Kreisky, Mitterrand, Schmidt, Shimon Peres, Soares, and González) threw their weight behind an enlargement of the Socialist International and an increase in the scope of its activities outside Europe, and in Latin America in particular. This policy was developed under the presidency of Willy Brandt (and largely on the basis of funds provided by the West German Social Democratic party [SPD]).[24] Thus, at the 1979 congress in Vancouver, over thirty parties were listed as full members, including seven from Latin America and the Caribbean. Decisions were taken by consensus, rather than majority vote. A large number of "observers" were sent by nonaffiliated parties. For example, two Venezuelan parties (AD and MEP) attended as "consultative" members, as did the Paraguayan Febreristas. In addition, eighteen other Latin American parties sent "observers," including the PRI of Mexico, APRA in Peru, both the UCR and the Montoneros from Argentina, the Nicaraguan Sandinistas, and the New Jewel Movement of Grenada. Among the keynote speakers at the Vancouver meeting were Carlos Andrés Pérez (ex-president of Venezuela), José Francisco Peña Gómez (secretary of the governing party of the Dominican Republic), Leonel Brizola (subsequently elected governor of Rio de Janeiro) and Edén Pastora, better known as the Nicaraguan guerrilla leader "Comandante Cero" (who subsequently broke with the Sandinistas). This congress created a permanent committee for Latin America, under the presidency of Peña Gómez, whose party had taken office the previous year as a result of international (especially American) pressure on the Dominican military to respect the verdict of the polls. Clearly, this appointment signaled an intention to act more vigorously in encouraging the trend toward democracy then observable in such countries as Ecuador, Peru, Bolivia, and perhaps even Brazil and Mexico. It also signaled a willingness to cooperate with like-minded elements in Washington.

However, as with the SI's temporary success in the late 1950s, the favorable climate of 1979 was not to last long. This time, the crisis in Central America changed the atmosphere. As in 1959, events presented the SI with a difficult and potentially destructive task of self-definition. What sort of "democracy," and what sort of "socialism," was it seeking to promote in Latin America? In his 1977 speech, Mitterrand had implicitly counterposed Chilean democracy (and Allende's brand of socialism) to Pinochet's capitalist authoritarianism. Similarly, in 1979, the SI could readily support the Sandinistas (a broad front promising, among other things, pluralism and free elections) against the Somoza dynasty. But the SI could exert only a modest degree of influence over Sandinist Nicaragua, where the drive to consolidate an imperiled revolution soon clashed with the commitment to observe democratic conventions. As these dilemmas became sharper, the Spanish Socialist party adopted a typically cautious stance, promising that relations with the Sandinistas would remain cordial "for as long as the original plan for the revolution remains in force." However, the Schmidt government in West Germany provided Nicaragua with some $54 million in aid, under a program that was cut off in November 1982, as soon as the Social Democrats in Bonn were forced out of office. The Mitterrand government has even supplied some military equipment to the Sandinistas, ignoring strong protests from the Reagan administration. At the end of 1984, the SI was still seeking to encourage pluralism and nonalignment in Nicaragua, while trying to counter the Reagan administration's policy of destabilization in that country.

Unlike 1959, the aftermath of the Nicaraguan Revolution has not (yet) led to a complete eclipse of the SI's presence in Latin America and of its capacity to promote an interpretation of democracy at variance with the Washington viewpoint. For example the "Final Resolution on Peace and Democracy in Latin America and the Caribbean," adopted in October 1984 by the Bureau of the SI, meeting in Rio de Janeiro, is still at variance with U.S. policy, especially on Central America. On the other hand, it would be a mistake to overstate the cohesion and commitment of the Socialist International when pressing a view against determined American resistance. Central America in particular is recognized by many leaders of the founding parties to be an area of only peripheral significance to Western Europe, whereas it is of far greater (symbolic or real) importance to the U.S.A. The SI capacity to influence or direct events in this isthmus is obviously quite limited (far more so than in relation to the Iberian autocracies, for example), and the main leaders of the movement know quite well that the regional crisis may not result in anything resembling an open democracy, whatever becomes of the American-backed forces. In an effort to take advantage of these difficulties, the State Department has lobbied Brandt, to curb what it considers the excesses of the SI activists, and according to the Dutch and Swedish parties, the United States has also tried to sow dissension within the Socialist International, in particular exerting pressure on those governing parties whose countries are most dependent on Washington for economic aid (e.g., Costa Rica and the Dominican Republic).

Not surprisingly, then, the leading parties of the SI have been casting around for other less controversial ways of supporting the democratization process in Latin America. Mitterrand, for example, has urged a "flowering of public freedoms" in the French-speaking Republic of Haiti; Carlos Andrés Pérez has taken up the question of restoring civilian rule in Argentina; and the new prime minister of Spain, Félipe González, has launched a campaign to celebrate the five hundredth anniversary of the "discovery" of the continent (1992) "with peace and freedom in every Spanish-speaking country." Clearly, he envisages an appeal that would involve Christian Democratic and other non-Socialist parties, and that would enlist support from both the EEC and the U.S.A., with Spain playing the role of strategic intermediary.

It is interesting to observe Washington's response to these SI activities. Even before the Socialist victory in Spain, President Reagan had begun appropriating this kind of language: "Over the past several decades, West European and other Social Democrats, Christian Democrats and Liberals have offered open assistance to fraternal, political, and social institutions, to bring about peaceful and democratic progress. Appropriately for a vigorous new democracy, the Federal Republic of Germany's political foundations have become a major force in this effort. We, in America, now intend to take additional steps, as many of our allies have already done, toward realizing the same goal."[25]

Results

At the time of writing, the three new democracies of Southern Europe seem surprisingly well established; most of South America is also experiencing a remarkable process of redemocratization. Only Chile and Paraguay remain unaffected in South America, and in Southern Europe only Turkey (not a member of the EEC) has proved disappointing. In Central America and the Caribbean, on the other hand, the picture is much less satisfactory. At this particular cutoff point, then, the European sphere of influence looks better than the U.S. sphere. It would be quite misleading, however, to conclude that these more satisfactory outcomes should be attributed to better European policies in support of democratization. As repeatedly stressed in this chapter and in these volumes, in peacetime it is the process internal to each country that is most important in determining the success of democratic transitions; external support is of secondary importance. Moreover, the United States has exerted a substantial degree of influence on the European redemocratizations; similarly, the Europeans have made some contribution to the Latin American attempts. In any case no firm conclusions should be drawn from the distribution of successes and failures at any particular point. In the mid-1940s and again in the late 1950s, for example, the prospects for democracy in most of Latin America looked considerably better than in Southern Europe. Some of the arguments in the introduction to this chapter, and some of the evidence from the country studies, lead to the conclusion that not all the current redemocratizations are likely to prove irreversible. Accordingly, this section adopts a historical perspective. First, the unhappy results of Western attempts to promote democracy after World War I should briefly be recalled.

President Wilson's difficulties in formulating an effective policy for the promotion of democracy in Russia and Germany after World War I foreshadow themes that would resurface perennially in Latin America and Southern Europe after 1945. It was hardly possible to represent the war against Germany as a war for democracy at a time when it required alliance with czarist Russia. Wilson, therefore, greeted the March 1917 Revolution in Russia (a few weeks before his declaration of war) with great satisfaction. "Russia was known by those who knew it best to have been always in fact democratic at heart. . . . The autocracy that crowned the summit of her political structure, long as it had stood and terrible as was the reality of its power, was not in fact Russian in origin, character or purpose," he claimed.[26] Already, in fact, the stage had been set for Washington to embrace a fledgling democracy as not just an ally but a confirmation of the universal validity of American political prescriptions. Characterized in such terms, the first Russian Revolution could not by its nature fail, it could only be betrayed; and those who betrayed it would necessarily become not just antagonists but outcasts.

After American hopes for some kind of liberal democracy in Moscow had foundered, and the Russian ally had withdrawn from the war and become more or less inaccessible to Allied influence, Wilson's attention turned to the prospects for promoting democracy in postwar Germany. Here the problem would be how to implant a suitably moderate variant of democracy on a defeated nation. In this case, too, Washington experienced difficulties that were to become all too familiar a part of future American foreign policy dilemmas. To save the kind of democracy the United States claimed to favor, it would be necessary to defeat the revolutionary Left, without succumbing to the power of the resurgent undemocratic Right. Gordon Levin describes the predicament:

> On the one hand, the President . . . was concerned lest the [postwar German] Revolution go too far to the Left and was, therefore, insistent that Germany be allowed the necessary food, economic relief, and military force to defend her fragile liberal political and economic institutions against revolutionary-socialism. In effect, then, Wilsonians supported the decision . . . to limit the Revolution to the area of formal constitutional democracy while leaving largely untouched the underlying social supports of German traditionalism in the form of conservative civil servants, army officers, Junker landowners, jurists, and large landowners. Yet, having done all he could to prevent the radical revolutionists from dismantling the German social order root and branch, Wilson could not escape the paradoxical but related problem of the threat to liberal stability posed by the still powerful German right.[27]

The problem faced by Wilson in 1919 Germany is one that has confronted Washington-based democratizers ever since.

The results achieved following World War II were, of course, far more satisfying to the victorious Allies. Nevertheless, some qualifications are in order, especially concerning Southern Europe and Latin America. As the wording of clause three of the Atlantic Charter would lead one to expect, the promotion of Anglo-American style democracy was most spectacularly effective among the Axis powers occupied by the Allied forces—Germany, Italy, and Japan. But the Anglo-American sphere of influence in postwar Europe included a number of undemocratic governments that for one reason or another had not joined the Axis powers in defeat. What priority would the victors assign to the "promotion of democracy" in Spain and Portugal, or for that matter in Greece and Turkey? As the cold war deepened, the answer became clear in all four cases, namely, that provided these governments made themselves reliable allies in the global contest with the Soviet Union, they would not be placed under irresistible pressure to "democratize" in the sense applied to the former Axis countries. However, each of these four cases presented rather different features. Furthermore, the Allies did not straightforwardly abandon their proclaimed aim of promoting democracy; rather, they relegated it to an indeterminate future, and in some cases denatured the original meaning of the term.

Similarly in Latin America, as the Allied victory drew nearer, a considerable momentum built up behind the libertarian ideals for which the United Nations claimed to be fighting. A number of the more undemocratic regimes in the Carribean were liberalized at least in part because of this new climate of opinion, which also contributed to the establishment of formally constitutional governments in Argentina, Brazil, and Venezuela.[28] More generally, the Allied victory of 1945 seemed to promise a major extension of the practices of "democracy" (understood to mean some variant of the Anglo-American competitive electoral system, with separation of powers and under the rule of law), wherever American or British influence could be brought to bear.

As we have seen, the Truman Doctrine of March 1947 marked a crucial stage in the development of the cold war, and was enunciated largely with Greece in view. In practice, the Greek regime of 1947 was (not surprisingly) an imperfect exemplar of the values it proclaimed so explicitly. In contrast to neutral Spain and Portugal, during the war the dictatorial government of Greece ended up a government-in-exile behind British lines, while the people of Greece suffered Axis occupation. When the war ended, therefore, two armed groups emerged to claim the fruits of liberation, one supported by the British and one based on the strongest partisan organization, which favored Moscow. Admittedly, Greece was far more of a democracy than either Spain or Portugal, at least in formal terms. For example, despite the Communist rising of 1944, British pressure ensured that the party was allowed to organize above ground, and to publish its own press, in 1946. In practice, however, Civil War was renewed until the final defeat of the Communists in 1949, and the climate of insecurity was so great that formal rights were largely unenforceable (a condition not unlike that prevailing in El Salvador since 1980).

It could, no doubt, be argued that, with U.S. aid, the Greek government had the potential to become a real democracy, whereas its opponents on the Left offered no such prospect. But in practice, the "democracy" that Truman rescued in Greece was of a hybrid composition.[29] Many "Fascist" elements in the state apparatus, and especially in the security forces and the judiciary, were able to escape the purge, and preserve their positions, by working for a "democratic" victory in the Civil War. So long as this intolerant Right enjoyed a secure electoral position, postwar Greece lived with many of the trappings of formal democracy, but when, in the mid-1960s, the electoral balance began to shift toward the moderate Left (not the outlawed Communist party), the Greek military seized power, ruling in an explicitly antidemocratic manner. In 1967, with the benevolence if not the complicity of the American government, Athens abandoned any pretense of promoting the values for which Truman had claimed to stand in 1947. The democratic forces of Western Europe (including most conservative parties) opposed this rebirth of "Fascism" in their continent, and sheltered Greece's outlawed democratic forces, but Greece remained in NATO, and Washington chose to emphasize questions of military security, without regard for the sacrifice of democratic principle. From the U.S. viewpoint, this proved a shortsighted choice, since the colonels proceeded to provoke a war with their NATO neighbor, Turkey, over Cyprus; when (predictably) the Greeks lost, the dictatorship fell. When forced to choose, the Americans naturally inclined toward a more strategically vital ally, Turkey, so when democracy returned to Greece, public opinion obliged Athens to suspend military cooperation with its NATO allies.

The 1947 statement pledged U.S. aid not only to a threatened democracy in Greece, but also to a Turkish ally that was being subjected to Soviet intimidation. Following the arrival of American assistance, Turkey became a full and strategically located member of the Western alliance, joining both NATO and the Council of Europe, and introducing a competitive electoral system. Here, in contrast to the cases discussed above, it can plausibly be argued that U.S. influence assisted a quite well-defined "transition to democracy." It was in fairly direct response to American requirements that the one-party state was dismantled between 1945 and 1950. The subsequent failure of that democratic experiment culminated in the coup of 1980, which initiated a period of severe military repression against all democratic forces and institutions, and which was greeted with dismay in Western Europe. In 1981 Turkey was suspended from the Council of Europe for banning parties and trade unions, silencing and even torturing political and labor leaders, and in general disregarding its treaty obligations to the European Commission on Human Rights. On the other hand, Secretary of State Alexander Haig "exploded with indignation" at the suggestion that U.S. condemnation of martial law in Poland looked like a double standard in view of Washington's simultaneous approval of a somewhat comparable regime in Turkey. In 1982, the military decreed a restrictive constitution, under which an election was held in 1984 and a civilian administration took office, but U.S.-EEC reactions continued to diverge. Turkey was third among recipients of U.S. aid in 1985 ($880 million), but the EEC still withheld $600 million of European aid that had been frozen after the 1980 coup. Meanwhile NATO continued to tilt away from democratic but neutralist Greece and toward a militarized Turkey. However, at the end of 1985 five European countries withdrew a suit against Turkey from the European Commission on Human Rights. In return Ankara agreed to lift martial law, and to permit European representatives to monitor human rights conditions in Turkey.

In Latin America the early postwar period was a time of fairly widespread liberalization or even democratization of political arrangements, as the effects of the Axis defeat worked their way through. Indeed, for a brief period after 1945 there seemed to exist a more or less genuine "democratic" electoral framework in all but two of the nineteen independent republics of Latin America. The only exceptions were the Dominican Republic and Nicaragua.

Within six months of the founding of the OAS, in 1948, however, a right-wing military dictatorship overthrew the democratically elected government of Peru which, after a momentary flurry of uncertainty, was granted diplomatic recognition by the United States. A new Peruvian ambassador hastened to Washington to explain that his government could not be "more democratic," adding an attack on the outlawed opposition and noting that "his country was not yet ready for either the British or American types of democracy."[30]

Shortly after the Peruvian coup, in November 1948, right-wing military forces also overthrew the civilian government of Venezuela, suppressing all democratic freedoms. In his memoirs, Betancourt traces the links between the military conspirators of Venezuela and the military in Peru and Argentina. He notes: "In the days immediately preceding Venezuela's so called military 'bloodless' revolution, the Washington government recognized the de facto regime of Odría in Peru, the result of a military coup. As the Washington press was later to point out, the Caracas conspirators took this attitude of the U.S. as a 'green light for an uprising.'"[31]

Other military takeovers followed in quick succession (El Salvador, December 1948; Paraguay, January 1949; subsequently followed by Bolivia, Colombia, and Cuba). The State Department recognized all these undemocratic governments, but with some embarrassment. A February 1949 confidential memo on the subject reads, "With respect to the accusation that we are encouraging military coups and deserting democratic ideals, our statements deploring the use of force and urging democratic procedures have served as useful and widely accepted answers."[32] However, a marked asymmetry was evident between the lameness of U.S. reactions toward flagrantly undemocratic behavior by the Right, and the same administration's extreme vigilance when dealing with even relatively democratic governments of the Left.

The documents on Guatemala make this clear. According to the State Department:

> In 1944, one of the most ruthless of all Guatemalan dictators was overthrown by an uprising by all segments of the population. Juan José Arévalo, a seemingly liberal and progressive ex-teacher, returned from long exile in Argentina and was elected President by an overwhelming popular vote. Shortly thereafter, Guatemala embarked on a social, economic and political program which in general terms aimed at achieving freedom and democracy for the people. . . . This program appeared at its outset to be commendable. By and large there was freedom of speech and of the press. The first mid-term Congressional elections were conducted fairly, the opposition won seats and there were few political exiles. . . . Soon, however, the Government's excessively zealous approach resulted in a biased pro-labor attitude . . . aggravated as Communists gained strength. . . . U.S. firms . . . became typified as the arch enemies of Guatemala's "democracy" and the revolution. They were charged with being in conspiracy with the so-called reactionary elements to oppose the democratic privileges which Guatemalans were told they were so bitterly winning. . . . The Government . . . has, as the self-styled model of Latin American liberalism, welcomed within its borders political exiles of leftist inclination, radicals, and avowed Communists . . . [and] tends to deplore and in some cases actively to oppose, openly

or covertly, those governments which it considers to be "imperialistic," "reactionary," or "dictatorial."[33]

Aware of the hostility its policies were arousing in the U.S.A., the Arévalo government initially looked for support to the Truman administration, describing the measures it was introducing as a "New Deal" for Guatemala. At the conference to found the OAS, the Guatemalans advocated the strongest antidictatorial line. For example, they proposed the creation of an Inter-American Court to enforce respect for human rights on member states. But this proposal was rejected, and soon after its creation the OAS reacted to the Peruvian and Venezuelan coups by jettisoning the fine promises made under the "Act of Bogotá." Understandably, therefore, the Guatemalans abandoned interest in the OAS, and turned to other means of pursuing their antidictatorial campaigns. They were particularly concerned to strike against two of Washington's most reliable allies, Somoza and Trujillo, for these nearby dictators were, with reason, viewed as a mortal threat to all forms of political freedom and social progress throughout the Caribbean region. By early 1949, the Truman administration was largely reconciled to the new Peruvian and Venezuelan dictatorships, and instead it had embarked upon a collision course with the, at that time, still relatively democratic Guatemalans.

Thus, in May 1949, the U.S. ambassador to Guatemala reported critically on the hospitality and cooperation that the Arévalo government was extending to political exiles from the Dominican Republic, Nicaragua and elsewhere. The foreign minister was described as "up to his neck" in these activities, and President Arévalo was quoted (disapprovingly) as saying "that his utmost desire is to serve out the remainder of his term and then devote the rest of his life to eliminating the Caribbean dictators."[34] The Guatemalans were faulted for sheltering and encouraging such supposedly dangerous individuals as Juan Bosch (opponent of Trujillo and a future democratically elected president of the Dominican Republic). As a result of this and other grievances, in September 1949 the State Department delivered a lecture to the Guatemalan ambassador in Washington, forthrightly expressing "our feeling that Guatemala currently was not following its traditional policy of cooperation with the U.S. and was indulging in certain undemocratic activities."[35]

Clearly, the Truman administration was far more severe with the constituted government of Guatemala (accused of indulgence toward the Soviet Union) than it was with the antidemocratic but "reliable" governments of the Caribbean. For example, in April 1949, the democratic government of Uruguay attempted to raise at the United Nations the question of human rights in Venezuela. The State Department intervened to prevent this initiative, arguing that public discussion "of the charges against Venezuela would play into the hands of the Soviet bloc and might produce an undignified squabble among the Latin American nations."[36] With Washington taking this line, the authoritarian Right throughout the hemisphere was bound to feel encouraged. Once power had been seized it would obviously prove easy to assuage American scruples. Thus, dictatorships of the Right, however implacable, knew that they had little to fear from the U.S.A.; far less, at any rate, than the reprisals faced by even relatively open governments if they could be accused of tolerating pro-Soviet activity.

Similar calculations have been repeated in different parts of the world throughout the postwar period. Truman's Latin American policy has been given so much attention here not because it was exceptional but because it was such a formative period, and because the official U.S. documents are available. Neither the space nor the evidence is available for a comparable discussion of later periods, but Jerome Slater, for example, has analyzed some closely analogous episodes in the early 1960s. Reviewing the first fifteen years of the OAS, he concluded that it had not only ignored the commitment to representative democracy contained in Article 5d of its charter "but in fact the OAS has often *impeded* the development of democracy in Latin America."[37]

Against this view, Robert A. Packenham has described President Kennedy's Latin American policy as "probably the most sustained explicit attempt since the late forties to foster democracy in the Third World." But even this attempt was not all that sustained or unqualified, as Packenham's account makes clear. "It was a typically 'liberal American' effort, which defined political development as constitutional democracy and excluded radical as well as Communist politics from that definition. It was a learning experience, of considerable importance for President Kennedy, about the limits of America's capacity to promote democracy in the Third World."[38] When the Alliance began there was only one unconstitutional regime in South America (Paraguay). After five years there were four, including the two most influential states (Argentina and Brazil).

Despite all the limitations of its foreign policies, the Carter administration can claim at least one fairly clear success for the promotion of democracy in Latin America. After the 1978 elections in the Dominican Republic, a blatant fraud was attempted to keep the defeated right-wing faction in office. However, firm pressure was exerted from Washington to ensure an orderly transfer of power to the mildly reformist party that had won the vote. To a lesser extent, U.S. influence under Carter may have aided the restoration of civilian democracy in Ecuador and Peru after periods of unsuccessful military rule.

All three administrations discussed above were those of presidents belonging to the Democratic party who had stressed the rhetoric of morality in foreign policy. In all three cases, a pressing issue of national security arose (the Bogotazo in 1948, interpreted as part of a Soviet conspiracy; the threat of Castroism; and the Sandinista rebellion in Nicaragua in 1978–79). The consequent national security fears created almost irresistible demands for Washington to change tack and seek accommodation with "reliable" regimes, no matter how undemocratic. Over the postwar period as a whole, therefore, despite the rhetoric, Washington's real achievements in the promotion of democracy in Latin America have been relatively meager. Only a few administrations made the attempt; in most cases they were easily deflected; and for the period as a whole it is considerably easier to cite instances in which U.S.

influence contributed to the weakening of civilian popularly elected governments than the reverse.

Conclusion

Democratization is never easy, and the process will always contain a significant risk of failure, however unified, skillful, and fortunate its advocates may be. General theories correlating democracy with the level of economic development or "modernization," or indeed associating it with some particular type of "political culture," necessarily abstract from such unpredictability. Consequently the stock of available theories is of little help in explaining the timing, the longevity, or the geographical incidence of recent experiences of democratization. It is, for example, rather striking that in the mid-1970s the last three undemocratic regimes in non-Communist Europe (Portugal, Greece, and Spain) all accomplished transitions to political systems we may call "democracies." By contrast, in the same period, two of Latin America's most well-established democracies (Uruguay and Chile) were swept away, and a major attempt at restoring democracy in the country where various "objective" conditions might seem most favorable to it (Argentina) ended in ignominious failure. A few years later, when the restoration of democracy became once again a significant process in the Latin American region, it was in countries where socioeconomic structures and political traditions seemed relatively unpromising that the transition first occurred (Peru, Ecuador, and in a special sense the Dominican Republic). No solid basis exists by which at the beginning of the 1970s an observer could have predicted with a reasonable degree of accuracy this particular pattern of democratizations in the nine countries in question. Even with the benefit of hindsight, it is not possible to attach high probabilities to the outcomes that we now know to have occurred.

However that may be, recent South European experience with democratization has been a remarkable success, contrasting sharply with the record in Latin America. Since the post-Franco transition in Spain, there are now no undemocratic regimes left on the European landmass, other than the Communist countries. Seldom in its history has Europe been so uniform in its political arrangements across a wide variety of competing states. Indeed the three South European "democratizations" of 1974–76 can be viewed as the long-postponed completion of a project for a wholly democratic Europe that had been thirty years in the making.

The Spanish case, in particular, may be taken to indicate that with enough persistence, and relying essentially on the force of example and economic encouragement, it might be possible to generalize the pluralist constitutional form of political organization, even in the absence of a physical confrontation with the forces of dictatorship and their overt defeat. If so, such a generalization would be a great encouragement to the aspiring democratizers of Latin America and elsewhere, for in most of the Third World, dictatorial or authoritarian forms of government have achieved an ascendancy and have established a tradition of authority that seem to bar the way to any easy or painless displacement. Franco's dictatorship established its ascendancy through a three-year Civil War and a postvictory repression of unusual harshness, and Francoism could appeal to authoritarian and centralizing traditions of exceptional power and durability. If, despite all this, even Francoism could be dismantled with so little effort and danger, then those living under less impressive dictatorships in Latin America and elsewhere were bound to examine their own prospects for democracy in a more hopeful light. After all, Spain still occupies a special place in Latin American cultural and political life. The almost simultaneous (though more troubled) eclipse of the forty-six-year-old dictatorship in Portugal, and of the colonels' regime in Greece, powerfully reinforced this message.

Both in Western Europe and in North America there is some political and electoral advantage to be gained in being seen promoting democracy overseas, an activity that simultaneously reflects genuine aspirations and expresses national self-satisfaction. But what really matters, in practical terms, is how the unobjectionable general aim of promoting democracy is translated into practice in particular cases. Here, we have argued that it is the regionally dominant countries that have the most scope to set the terms of the debate, and to define which forces are worthy of support and which deserve exclusion. In Southern Europe, the EEC has been the major source of power for this purpose. But in Central America and the Caribbean, the initiative still seems to lie mostly with the U.S.A. In South America, it may be that no external power possesses sufficient leverage to play such a role. Clearly, then, the geopolitical dimension must rank high in any account of the international aspects of democratization.

Before 1945, if the pursuit of such a prodemocratic foreign policy gave rise to strategic weakness or material loss, it was America's European rivals who would experience the most direct effects. Since 1945, however, the roles have been reversed. The United States has been the dominant power in the Western world and has taken over prime concern for the stability and security of its alliance system. As American power expanded round the world, Washington acquired direct interests in many areas where any attempt to promote genuine democracy would tend to prove quite destabilizing. Consequently, American policy-makers have learned to exercise great caution and discrimination in pursuing this objective, and have stretched the meaning of the term to embrace an extraordinary variety of friendly but repressive regimes. American political scientists have designed rationales to systematize this evolution (the "emergence of the middle sectors" was followed by "crises of modernization," and most recently, the "authoritarian/totalitarian" dichotomy), but the more traditional moralism still retains its hold over significant sectors of American public opinion.[39] Thus, the "promotion of democracy" remains an element in the arsenal of American foreign-policy rhetoric. But when these arguments are placed in context, it becomes apparent that the term "democracy" has been stretched to cover a great variety of political arrangements. The word lends itself quite readily to selective interpretation, extension, and distortion. The observance of minimal formalities can be represented as evidence of a "move in the right direction" when it serves a great power objective. Conversely, any elements of political freedom preserved by an unfriendly government may be exploited to destabilize it, or to provoke a clampdown that will validate a condemnation of its undemocratic practices. Any analysis of Washington's official discourse on this subject must recognize the problem that the moral categories normally required to justify foreign policy to domestic opinion are seldom congruent with the *Realpolitik* categories generally characteristic of alliance politics. (*Realpolitik* may in principle be justifiable in moral terms, of course, but this approach is too complex to figure permanently in official discourse.) The fervor with which a particular regime is denounced for "undemocratic" conduct is only loosely correlated, in official parlance, with variations in the repressive character of its internal politics. Variations in the intensity of great power rivalries seem generally to provide a better indication of when latent moral sentiments will be invoked. Until the mid-1970s this tendency was reinforced by the fact that those U.S. interests that were best informed about the real political conditions prevailing outside the U.S.A. were for the most part not especially concerned with the promotion of democracy in other countries. Perhaps it would be fairer to say that they generally attached a higher priority to the pursuit of other (economic or security) objectives, which may not be readily compatible with the goal of democratization.

The postwar experience of Western Europe has been quite different. A comparison with Europe should serve to place U.S. policy in a better perspective than can be obtained by evaluating it (as previous authors on American policy have tried to do) simply from within its own assumptions, or on the basis of an assumed American exceptionalism or moral mission. After the war, the Europeans lost their international hegemony, and accepted an auxiliary role in the maintenance of international security. Their energies were redirected toward economic and political reconstruction within the heartland of Western Europe, and their primary commitment was to make that area safe for democracy and free from warlike conflict. The smaller North European nations, like Denmark, Sweden, and Holland, have acquired an enhanced influence over European foreign policy which they have deployed forcefully in favor of international pluralism and against great power hegemony. (In North America, the Canadians may have similar preferences, but they have lacked restraining influence over Washington.) Thus, as the Americans began to relegate the "promotion of democracy" to a lower priority among their foreign policy objectives, it became a matter of increased centrality (at least within the restricted geographical arena of the Community) to the formerly tough-minded Europeans.

In recent years, the dominant motive for stressing "morality" in U.S. foreign policy has probably been the need to restore domestic consensus and international repute after a series of national humiliations that could be attributed to the neglect of moral considerations. Exponents of this approach often add the practical consideration that democracy is so strongly desired by the people of other nations that the United States not only acts rightly, but places itself on a side favored by history, when it presses for democratization around the world.

Against this view, others offer a variety of counterarguments: that the existing system in a particular country is neither so undemocratic, nor so vulnerable, as the moralists suppose; or that the status quo is so vital to American interests that it must not be disturbed; or that the United States lacks effective means to bring about desirable changes; or that the means it possesses are too clumsy for the purpose, and are in fact as likely to pervert or discredit the democratic cause as to promote it; or that American-style democracy is not, in fact, either desired or appropriate in the country in question. Each of these arguments rests upon some fairly specific assertions concerning the political affairs of a given country, so that it may be quite consistent to use all of them at different times and in different cases. In addition, there are other less country-specific arguments that do not require specific knowledge, notably a stand on principle against attempts to influence the internal affairs of other sovereign states; a stand on principle against any measure that might sow dissension in the anti-Soviet camp; or, perhaps most interesting from the philosophical viewpoint, but less common in the practical world, the argument that by its very nature "democracy" cannot be given to others, it is only something they can achieve for themselves.[40]

The contrast between European and American attitudes is not essentially a matter of party politics, although it is significant that of all the American republics and the Western European nations, only the U.S.A. has no significant party that is affiliated with the Socialist International. In practice, there is a current of opinion in both mainstream American parties (mostly, but not exclusively, among Democrats) that corresponds quite closely to what I have characterized as the predominant West European viewpoint. Similarly, European opinion contains a substantial element (mainly, but not exclusively on the Right) that endorses Washington's security-minded approach. Nevertheless, there are some powerful underlying reasons why the one point of view receives strong and sustained embodiment in European policy-making, but finds only a fleeting and insecure expression in Washington's official conduct.

The direct experience of Fascism conditioned a broad spectrum of European opinion to oppose and detest right-wing authoritarian regimes. U.S. experience of Fascism was less direct, and from the late 1940s, right-wing authoritarians were in many cases seen in a favorable light because of their eagerness to cooperate in an American-led world order, and their reliability as opponents of the Soviet Union. In many cases, economic interest has powerfully reinforced American ties with antidemocratic minorities overseas, and has created barriers of misunderstanding and suspicion between Washington and foreign popular movements with democratic potential. Some have viewed this economic dimension as the central (indeed the "structural") explanation of America's foreign policy alignments, but in that case, similar processes should be expected in capitalist Europe. The debate on this remains open, but this chapter has treated Washington's real or imagined security concern as a major explanation in its own right, not just reducible to the play of private economic interests. The greater America's security concern, the stronger was its benevolence toward the authoritarian Right. In Western Europe, by contrast, repudiation of the authoritarian Right (as well as the Soviet model) was a prerequisite for the creation of an economic and political community that guarantees private property and is based on representative government.

So long as the Europeans have concentrated their democratizing energies on the smaller and poorer countries on their immediate geographical perimeter, they have been in a strong position to contain the consequences of their initiatives and to protect their security interests. Any conflict between such initiatives and Europe's other regional objectives has been quite mild. The conflict between any democratizing aspirations in Washington and the security and cohesion of the American system of worldwide alliances is necessarily much greater.

The recent extension of Western Europe's democratizing endeavors into Latin America brings Europe into a region where it has far less capacity for directing and restraining events. However, since the United States was for so long successful at displacing European influence in the Western hemisphere, any security problems or material losses consequent on the struggle for democracy in Latin America are much more of a headache for the Americans than for the Europeans. There are resemblances here between Europe's present limited involvement in the Latin American region, and the prewar posture of the United States when operating within the old European empires and spheres of influence. Now the Europeans can volunteer themselves in Latin America as intermediaries with "clean hands," they can adopt a "moral" stance at relatively little cost to themselves, but there are still fairly clear limits to how far they can encroach on what remains an essentially American preserve. Under mild pressure from the EEC, Washington might perhaps shift a little ground toward an actively promoted European position. But if the Americans concluded that European policies were beginning to damage important U.S. interests, they could always warn the Europeans off: Europe's direct stake in Latin America is low relative to its need for American collaboration on other matters.

During the 1970s the Europeans succeeded in generalizing constitutional democracy throughout their part of the continent. So far, constitutional democracy is far more precarious and patchy in the Americas. Those who have argued most forcefully that the promotion of democracy should be ranked high among foreign policy priorities have often claimed that the survival of even one undemocratic regime is a major threat to all democracies. It was therefore as a matter of national self-interest, rather than mere altruism, that the Betancourt regime in Venezuela, for example, advocated sanctions against neighboring authoritarian regimes. What does the evidence of this chapter suggest here? Is it vital to the interests of the most secure and powerful democracies to promote comparable systems of government whenever their influence permits it? Or may it be, on the contrary, that the interests of a major democracy might be better served by accepting, even welcoming, the establishment of undemocratic regimes in its sphere of influence, provided they are stable and pliable? Several basic analytical issues are raised by this questioning, namely, the nature of the link between internal democracy and external security; whether liberals are right to assume that democracies are necessarily "good neighbors"; what degree of priority the "promotion of democracy" can ever attain among necessarily competitive foreign policy goals; and indeed what kind of "democracy" the policy-makers envisage promoting.

We have seen that for a fragile, recent, or isolated democracy (such as Arévalo's Guatemala, Betancourt's Venezuela, or González's Spain) there may be a clear and direct link between a foreign policy of an aggressively prodemocratic character, and the preservation and consolidation of democratic freedoms at home. For a regional power (such as the European Community) without primary responsibility for the provision of global security, the promotion of democracy in contiguous territories may be an attractive policy because it creates regional solidarity and even helps to protect domestic freedoms. However, for a global power (such as the U.S.A.) the calculus of risk and advantage is significantly different. The preservation of a global system of alliances which extends to regions that are socially and geographically distant becomes the central imperative of security policy. An undemocratic ally in a strategic location may not seem much of a threat to domestic freedoms, and may be viewed as a vital asset from the international security standpoint. Ideally, of course, a global power would wish to create political homogeneity and solidarity throughout its sphere of influence in the same way as a regional power, but in practice the greater power has to contend with a greater diversity of allies and less commonality of outlook apart from that created by a shared perception of external threat.

Thus we have concluded that U.S. security objectives (perhaps correctly chosen, perhaps not) frequently conflict with and may even override liberal democratic goals in determining foreign policy. This observation has been particularly true of U.S. policies in the Third World, which Packenham has somewhat charitably analyzed in terms of "liberal America's confrontation with a largely illiberal world." Specifically with regard to Washington's closest neighbors in Latin America, the record suggests that often the risks of promoting real democracy have been held to outweigh the advantages. Mexico provides a particularly significant litmus test of American priorities. Does it not remain an open question in that country how much democracy of the conventional liberal democratic variety would be tolerable to Washington policy-makers? It is as well to add, however, that the shape of popular government in Ireland has for long posed London policy-makers with even more acute difficulties. In general, then, democracies have often encountered grave impediments to the maintenance of peaceful and prodemocratic relations with their neighbors. Theories that assume otherwise are unwarranted.

The essential point, so easily obscured by abstract theory or by official rhetoric, is that at best the "promotion of democracy" will never be more than one foreign policy objective in competition with others. In order for this goal to obtain any degree of priority, the case must normally be argued as either a test of moral virtue or a vital issue of national security. It requires such impetus to overcome predictable objections against interference in the internal affairs of friendly states, the courting of unnecessary risks, and the offending of established interests. Thus only a stark or exaggerated case will serve to set the machinery of policy formation in motion. Yet, except in postconquest conditions, the effective promotion of democracy in other lands will require subtlety, patience, and long-term commitment, none of which is created by overstatement or the atmosphere of crisis politics. Although, compared with other objectives of foreign policy, the promotion of democracy may almost never be of top priority for a major power, nevertheless for countries within its sphere of influence, where the balance between democratic and undemocratic forms of government is indeterminate, a small push one way or the other from the leading power can easily be of crucial importance. The wish to imitate the political practices of the leading country will in any case contribute to the strength of prodemocratic forces. A modest amount of official encouragement is often sufficient to give them victory. Similarly with the encouragement of antidemocratic forces.

Here we can distinguish between three components of the "promotion of democracy," each of which has different requirements. First, there is pressure on undemocratic governments to democratize themselves. We have reviewed various examples in our discussion of U.S. policy toward Latin America, notably under Kennedy and Carter, and have noted a contrast between the initial drama accompanying the announcement of the policy and the subsequent rather modest and short-lived follow-through. By contrast, the European Community was low key in its political rhetoric but persistent in its stance. Second, there is support for fledgling democracies that are attempting to consolidate. Here, certain dramatic gestures and emergency initiatives may be of great value if skillful and well timed. Potentially, Washington could be more effective at this juncture than Brussels. Here there is the least distance between European and American policy. Third, there is the maintenance of a firm stance against antidemocratic forces that threaten or overthrow established democracies. Here the contrast between Europe and America has been the most marked, mainly because, for security reasons, Washington has been quick to condone (often in a rather visible manner) many forms of right-wing authoritarianism that the Europeans, either through political convenience or firm conviction, have wished to ostracize, albeit without too much drama. Another relevant factor has been the strong presence of the Socialist International in Europe, and the absence of any effective counterpart in the U.S.A. From Washington's viewpoint, therefore, the Europeans tend toward overindulgence with the forces of left-wing authoritarianism. This approach is, of course, the reverse of European observations about the U.S.

This chapter has quoted many examples in which, for the official convenience of one government or another, the term "democracy" has been flagrantly misapplied. However, these differences between Europe and America suggest that even when Western political leaders attempt to use the term with integrity they may give it significantly different shades of meaning. For example, there is a narrowly legalist approach, sometimes associated with the State Department, which equates "democracy" with the formal procedures of electoral consultation apparently without regard to the broader political and social context that gives the process its meaning. A second shade of meaning underlay the thinking of the Socialist International about the promotion of democracy, with more emphasis on the political and organizational freedoms available to the lower classes. A third variant is implicit in much conservative thinking about democracy both in Europe and in the U.S.A. Here, emphasis on the freedom of the (abstractly conceived) "individual" and his/her protection from collectivism can legitimize a restrictive form of "democracy" weighted in favor of the dominant classes, recognizing few social rights and classifying many forms of mass politics as unconstitutional. Various authoritarian governments in Latin America have experimented with highly restrictive forms of constitutional government designed to provide a rule of law and elite cohesion, while excluding challenges from the dispossessed. Clearly, when the "promotion of democracy" is an objective of foreign policy, it makes a considerable difference which of these variants is favored. Consequently, disputes over the appropriate shade of meaning form a staple of Western policy-making in this area.

This discussion illustrates a point that would merit more thorough attention than can be given here. Policies aimed at "promoting democracy" in other countries are liable to constitute an open invitation for manipulation by local political actors who are willing to adopt any rhetoric that seems likely to secure them external recognition and support. Portuguese-speakers of both Europe and South America have the phrase *para ingles ver* ("for the English to look at"), which was used in the nineteenth century to explain why elections were being held. Similar calculations are bound to influence some sectors in contemporary Latin America, particularly if they think they will be left free to define the actual content of "democracy" in a manner that serves their traditional interests.

Finally, then, there is an inescapable undertone of ethnocentricity in all attempts by one nation to promote what it considers to be "democracy" among other peoples. There is a deep dilemma here. Political theory asserts most powerfully that democracy expresses a fundamental human aspiration, not confined to any particular territory or period of time. Moreover, there are good theoretical and practical reasons for arguing that democracy is "indivisible," for example, that its absence in one country (or for one social group) threatens its presence in other lands (or for other social groups). On the other hand, however, experience suggests that an "imported" democracy may well be less solid, and less real, than one constructed from within. It also suggests that real democracies are both less pure, less self-critical, and more diverse, than theory sometimes assumes. Consequently, however good the intentions, principled the methods, and successful the implementation of those seeking to promote democracy in other lands, there is likely to be misunderstanding, or a conflict of perceptions, about the results.

On the eve of Mao Zedong's final victory, Han Suyin met an American missionary who was being forced to flee China. "How could we expect anything else?" he asked her. "We taught you a lot of abstract words which were not in your language—democracy, freedom, equality—without bothering to find out what they meant to you, or *even to ourselves.*"

2 •

Some Problems in the Study of the Transition to Democracy

Adam Przeworski

The purpose of this chapter is to identify and analyze some problems involved in studying processes of liberalization of authoritarian regimes and their replacement by democratic forms of political organization. My concerns are predominantly theoretical and methodological rather than descriptive. What we need to know is whether and under what conditions transformation toward democracy is possible today in those countries which suffer from authoritarian rule. The question orienting this chapter is on what bases—with what information and under what interpretation of this information—can we provide a reasonable understanding of this possibility?

Strategies of Research

The first problem concerns the strategy of research. Studies of regime transformations tend to fall into two types. Some are macro-oriented, focus on objective conditions, and speak in the language of determination. Others tend to concentrate on political actors and their strategies, to emphasize interests and perceptions, and to formulate problems in terms of possibilities and choices. Macro-oriented investigations, of which Barrington Moore's is perhaps the prototype,[1] tend to emphasize objective conditions, mostly economic and social, often at the cost of neglecting the short-term political dynamic. They see political transformations as determined, and seek to discover the patterns of determination by inductive generalizations. These studies demonstrate that democracy is typically a consequence of economic development, transformations of class structure, increased education, and the like. Micro-oriented studies, and I would place here Marx's writings on France between 1848 and 1851[2] as well as Juan Linz's recent analysis of the breakdown of democratic regimes,[3] tend to emphasize the strategic behavior of political actors embedded in concrete historical situations.

In practical terms, the question is whether there are indeed good grounds to expect that regime transformations are strongly determined by some economic, social, or political conditions, whether these consist of the stage of accumulation (exhaustion of import-substitution, product cycles, changes in the major export, etc.), social structure ("balance of classes," patterns of land ownership, family structure), or whatever. If regime transformations are indeed strongly determined by such conditions, that is, if in principle a full specification of such factors would uniquely account for regime transformations, then the proper research strategy would be to conduct comparative statistical studies of patterns of historical covariations, and the only possible political strategy would be to wait for such objective conditions to mature.

Clearly, since the number of such factors can be expected to be rather large and the instances of successful transition to democracy rather infrequent, one would face tactical problems. But I want to make a much stronger claim—namely, that objective factors constitute at most constraints to that which is possible under a concrete historical situation but do not determine the outcome of such situations.

Suppose that one does discover a set of factors that jointly account for the observed historical patterns of regime transformations. The epistemological problem which immediately appears is whether one is willing to derive the conclusions that (1) some transformations were inevitable given these conditions, and (2) the observed transformations were uniquely possible given these conditions. It seems that universal franchise was established in Western Europe when the proportion of the labor force employed outside agriculture passed 50 percent. Are we willing to conclude that once this magic threshold was reached the old system could no longer be maintained and changes alternative to democratization were not possible? Moreover, even if we are satisfied with this kind of an answer, how are we to explain the conflict and indeterminacy experienced by the actors involved in extending the franchise and building democratic institutions? Were all the intentional, self-reflective, strategic actors merely unwitting agents of historical necessity?

Objective conditions do delimit the possibilities inherent in a given historical situation and, therefore, they are crucial. But to inquire about objective possibilities does not translate into the same research strategy as would a study of "determinants." Questions concerning possibility are quintessentially theoretical in the sense that they are not reducible to the description of the actual outcomes. Assertions of possibility necessarily involve propositions about actions that are contrary to fact, that is, statements that "if someone had done something different under the same conditions, the outcome would have been (or might have been) different."

Unfortunately, we are still far from being able to define the logical and empirical conditions under which the validity of counterfactual claims can be assessed. None of the approaches to the study of historical possibilities takes us sufficiently far to make counterfactual claims intersubjectively acceptable.

One approach to the study of possibility is structuralist. It consists of specifying some list of invariant elements of which all systems of a particular kind (grammars, kinships, modes of production) are composed and a list of admissible combinations of these elements. A particular state of the world is thus possible in this perspective if, and only if, it is admissible as a combination of elements. This approach, for all its seductiveness, is of little interest in the context of our problem (as Balibar[4] admitted), since it does not specify how one gets from one state of the world to another possible state. At best, if one is willing to accept this bivariate and a prioristic vision of the world, one can list all the possible states in abstraction from any history.

Another approach is given by modal logic, out of which grows an interesting recent formulation by Jon Elster, according to whom "a state s' (t) is possible relatively to [the actual] state s(t), if in the past history of s(t) there is a state s(t − k), such that there is a permitted trajectory from s(t − k) to s' (t); that is, if there is some branching point from which the process may diverge to either s(t) or s' (t)."[5] To paraphrase, I hope without changing the author's intention, the notion is the following: if from some past state s(t − k), k = 1, 2, . . . , t, it was possible to get to the state s' at the time *t* rather than to the actual state s(t), then s' is possible at time (t + 1). Elster then asserts that the larger the *k* the less likely is the possibility of *s'* relative to *s*; that is, the longer in the past the branching point that would have led to *s'* , the less likely the possibility of *s'* at the current time *t*. This approach is designed to describe the actual practice of historians, and as a description of their procedures it has great merits. Moreover, Elster's conceptualization establishes a link between observations of the actual past and the current possibilities—always a thorny problem in the study of possibility.

Nevertheless, Elster's approach has two flaws, each of which is fatal. First, it implies that opportunities are never irrevocably missed. This implication is too counterintuitive to be acceptable. Indeed, this definition is inconsistent with the author's earlier analysis of "situations," which he defines as the current state of affairs and all possible alternatives, and in which he points out that a situation becomes altered when a possibility is missed, even if the actual state of affairs remains the same. Second, on purely logical grounds Elster's approach suffers from infinite regress: we are told that there is a permitted trajectory from s(t) to s' (t) if and only if there is a permitted trajectory from s(t − k) to s' (t), but how are we to know that there was a permitted trajectory from s(t − k) to s' (t)?

Finally, the third approach to possibility originates from the theory of constrained optimalization. According to Majone's notion of "political feasibility," one would say that a state *s'* is feasible relative to *s* "insofar as it satisfies all the constraints of the problem which it tries to solve; where 'constraints' means any feature of the environment that (a) can affect policy results, and (b) is not under the control of the policy maker."[6] This approach is fine as far as it goes, but in fact it goes one step behind Elster. The problem is to discover what these constraints are, and Majone's own attempt is not very helpful.

All of this is not very encouraging. The model of political change as uniquely determined by conditions is epistemologically flawed (as Elster put it, and Hempel much earlier, a theory limited to actual occurrences is not a theory but a description) and politically impotent. The orientation that views political transformations as a choice among possibilities satisfying the objective conditions *qua* constraints thus far has not produced a satisfactory way of asserting these constraints. Learning from history involves wishing, but whether this wishing can indeed be made "thoughtful," as O'Donnell and Schmitter suggest,[7] remains doubtful at this moment. Nevertheless, forced to choose between the two approaches as they stand, I opt for the second on pure grounds of utility. Even if we misjudge the possibilities inherent in a given historical situation, ignoring some that are in fact possible or mistakenly hoping for the impossible, we will at least have a chance to identify correctly some feasible ones and the paths that lead to them.

The Breakdown of Authoritarian Regimes

Let me first review some conditions under which the survival of an authoritarian regime may be threatened. Four kinds of factors are often put forward to explain why cracks begin to appear in an authoritarian regime and liberalization becomes possible:

1. The authoritarian regime has realized the functional needs that led to its establishment. It is, therefore, no longer necessary (or even possible), and it collapses.

2. The regime has, for one reason or another, with one possible reason being (1), lost its "legitimacy," and since no regime can last without legitimacy (support, acquiescence, consent), it disintegrates.

3. Conflicts within the ruling bloc, particularly within the military, for one reason or another, with one possible reason being (2), cannot be reconciled internally, and some ruling factions decide to appeal to outside groups for support. Hence, the ruling bloc disintegrates *qua* bloc.

4. Foreign pressures to "put on a democratic face" lead to compromises, perhaps through the mechanism of (3).

I deliberately emphasize that these explanations need not be strictly competitive, but I will discuss them one by one. I have nothing to say about the functionalist explanation and I do not believe that the effect of foreign pressures can be unambivalently assessed. Hence, I will concentrate on explanations that rely on the loss of legitimacy and on conflicts within the elite.

The "loss of legitimacy" theory is an "up" theory of regime transformation in the sense that it postulates that the regime first loses its legitimacy in the civil society; only when this loss is somehow manifested and recognized as such does the ruling bloc respond. From the empirical point of view, this theory has the virture of providing clear predictions: if this theory is valid, one would expect to observe mass unrest or at least mass noncompliance *before* any liberalization occurs.

The theory runs as follows: (1) any regime needs "legitimacy," "support" (with some Eastonian distinctions), or at least "acquiescence" to survive; (2) when a regime loses legitimacy it must reproduce it or collapse. I will immediately claim that, under any nontautological definition of legitimacy, this theory is false.

Why would survival of any regime require legitimacy, whatever it is? Clearly, by raising this question I do not intend to plunge into an analysis of Max Weber's complex and not-always-consistent intellectual patrimony. Let me merely note that Weber's first thesis—that "every system [of domination] attempts to establish and to cultivate the belief in its legitimacy"[8] or, even more abstractly, that there exists "the generally observable need of any power . . . to justify itself"[9]—does not necessarily imply that a system of domination cannot survive without this belief. Indeed, Weber did entertain the possibility that not "every case of submissiveness to persons in positions of power is primarily (or even at all) oriented to [by?] this belief. Loyalty may be hypocritically simulated by individuals or by whole groups on purely opportunistic grounds, or carried out in practice for reasons of material self-interest."[10] Moreover, to anticipate the point which in my view is crucial, Weber continued to assert that "people may submit from individual weakness and helplessness *because there is no acceptable alternative.*"[11] Hence, even for Weber, compliant, acquiescing behavior does not necessarily originate from beliefs in the legitimacy of a system of domination.

But the question is not whether legitimacy—in Lamounier's definition, the "acquiescence motivated by subjective agreement [*concordancia*] with given norms and values"[12]—is, as Lamounier formulates it, the *only* factor in maintaining a given political order. What such theories must defend is a stronger thesis—namely, that legitimacy is a *necessary* condition of regime survival. Stinchcombe's definition of legitimate power is of some help to these theories, since his conception has the virture of making one step away from mental notions of legitimacy by specifying a behavioral attribute of legitimate power.[13] Stinchcombe defines legitimate power as one that can call upon others for its own defense. But when Stinchcombe qualifies that this capacity to call upon stems from "the doctrines or norms which justify it [this power]," we are right back where we started. Could not the occupants of positions of power be able to call upon others for defense by virtue of something else rather than the belief in the legitimacy of this power?

The "loss of legitimacy" theories of regime transformation must make good two claims: (1) that legitimacy is irreducible to anything else, whatever it might be (self-interest and fear being the prime candidates), and (2) that legitimacy is a necessary condition of stable domination. If legitimacy is reducible,[14] as I have argued elsewhere,[15] then it cannot be the source of the dynamic of regime transformation. But more important, even if legitimacy is irreducible but not necessary, then the converse proposition does not hold: one cannot maintain that withdrawal of legitimacy is a sufficient cause for a regime collapse. If legitimacy is only sufficient (even if uniquely sufficient) for regime survival, then loss of legitimacy at most implies that some other mechanisms of regime reproduction would come into play. The inference to collapse is invalid.

The entire problem of legitimacy is in my view incorrectly posed. What matters for the stability of any regime is not the legitimacy of this particular system of domination but the presence or absence of preferable alternatives. Consider some situations. In one, the legitimacy of a regime is in fact increasing but some other political system is still viewed as more legitimate. This is not a farfetched case: many if not most authoritarian regimes face precisely this competition from democratic ideals. Examine Figure 2.1, in which the legitimacy of an authoritarian regime improves over time but the democratic alternative always hovers above it as more legitimate. Now, if it is indeed legitimacy that keeps a regime together, then this society should move to a more legitimate regime even if no loss of legitimacy is suffered by the authoritarian system.

In contrast, imagine that the authoritarian regime suffers a loss of legitimacy but no alternative regime is accessible, that is, no coherent alternative is politically organized. What would then happen? This is clearly a question open to and inviting an empirical investigation, but I do have a guess: nothing much. A regime survives when parents discipline their children and each other, when workers regularly turn out and leave factory gates, and when the handful of people not occupied with disciplining children or gaining a livelihood is prevented from organizing by repression or cooptation. A regime does not collapse unless and until some alternative is organized in such a way as to present a real choice for isolated individuals. Only when one has the option of not disciplining children, not leaving the factory but occupying it instead, not

Figure 2.1

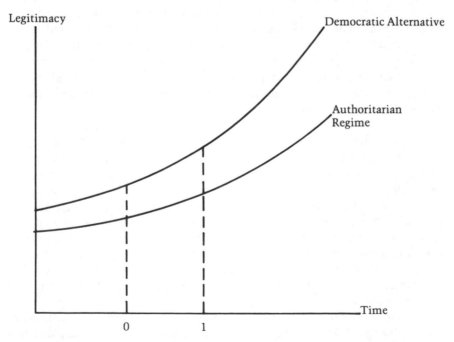

lowering the voice when speaking about politics but actively mobilizing others, only then is a regime threatened. If these options are not present, if one cannot engage in such behaviors without risking an almost certain extinction, one may believe that the regime is totally illegitimate and yet behave in an acquiescing manner. If legitimacy is in fact efficacious in maintaining a particular regime, it is precisely because it constitutes *organized* consent. If the belief in the legitimacy of the regime collapses and no alternative is organized, individuals have no choice.

Since I am never sure how one determines states of mind, I should be careful with making empirical statements. But let me put it this way: I can think of regimes that have lasted for tens of years and that must be illegitimate, whatever meaning one attaches to this term, and however one measures legitimacy. What reproduces consent is the threat of force, and short of moments of true desperation this threat is sufficient.

The Impetus for Liberalization

How do alternatives become organized? I do not want to tackle this question in such a frontal manner. Instead, I should like to focus on those explanations of the impetus for liberalization which see it as a result of power struggles within the ruling bloc.

One obstacle to understanding the processes of liberalization and democratization is the difficulty of identifying on a priori grounds the actors relevant to these processes. One way to approach this problem is to begin with interests, and classify the particular groups by imputing to them the interests that they may be expected to defend and promote in the face of conflicts. Another approach is to distinguish the actors directly by their strategic postures.

The overall structure of interests involved in the transition to democracy seems to be as follows. The armed forces have an interest in preserving their corporate autonomy; the bourgeoisie in preserving their ownership of the means of production and their authority to direct production; the state apparatus, particularly the technocrats and the police, in basic physical and economic survival. The working class has an interest in being able to organize itself in pursuit of its economic and political goals; other popular groups may have more narrowly economic interests. I have no particular attachment to this specific list, but something of this sort would have to be asserted in each concrete situation if one wanted to predict group behavior on the basis of class positions. The problem with this approach is that it appears to be of little predictive value, at least as one impressionistically surveys the dynamic of the situation in Spain or in Greece.

The other approach is to focus on the strategic postures directly and to distinguish the hard-liners (*duros*) and the soft-liners (*blandos*) within the ruling bloc, the moderates and the maximalists (and perhaps the principalists or moralists) among the opposition. The problem with this approach is that strategic postures may remain the same but the particular groups or important individuals that hold them may change, and we would clearly want to know why, and so we come back to the first approach.

In fact, neither approach seems sufficiently dynamic to account for the kind of volatility that seems to be characteristic of the processes of regime transformation, in which alliances are extremely shaky and particular groups and pivotal individuals at times shift their positions by 180 degrees. The difficulty, however, may turn out to be more apparent than real if we take into account not only interests but also perceptions of the likelihood of success in transforming the regime in a particular manner. Although interests may be quite stable, if calculations are made on the basis of expected benefits, that is, by taking into account not only the benefit of particular outcomes but also their probability contingent upon the actions of others, then strategies will be quite volatile. Indeed, one way to think of the strategic postures of different actors is to classify them by their risk aversion: the hard-liners and the maximalists, not to speak of the moralists, are risk-insensitive; the soft-liners and the moderates are risk-averse.

Figure 2.2

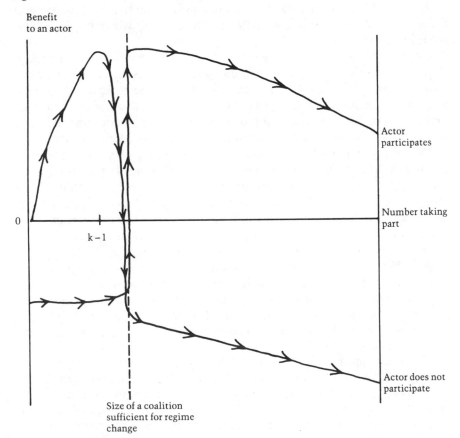

It may be helpful at this moment to engage in a Schelling-like analysis.[16] Figure 2.2 portrays the benefit to a particular member (individual or group) of the ruling bloc as a function of the actor participating in a move toward regime transformation and the number of others who go along. Let k be the number of actors necessary and sufficient to make a move toward liberalization successful. The strategic situation is then as follows. If I move and fewer than $(k - 1)$ others join, then I am likely to suffer unpleasant consequences. If I move and $(k - 1)$ others join, I will belong to a victorious movement and can expect to be rewarded appropriately. If I do not move and fewer than k others do, I will remain on the side of power and benefit from it. Finally, if I do not move, but more than $(k - 1)$ others do, I will again find myself on the losing side. Note that the value of the outcome increases as the number of actors making a move approaches k, from both sides.

Without making specific assumptions about the value of the particular outcomes, one cannot make any predictions about strategic behavior. But what is apparent is the importance of expectations of success. Neither position is safe under the circumstances: to make a precipitous move is as dangerous as not joining in a movement that is successful. What this analysis implies, therefore, is that interests may be quite stable throughout the process but that they will be a poor predictor of behavior when expectations of success shift rapidly. Consequently, group analysis may generate weak predictions when groups are identified only by their interests, and therefore particular strategic postures may be embraced at particular moments by the same groups.

Furthermore, this analysis implies that what matters most for the initiation of the process are signals: I would like to suggest that several factors that are often viewed as "causes" should be regarded precisely as such signals. These signals are of a twofold variety. Some are "objective," in the sense that all the relevant actors have good grounds to expect that some conflict within the ruling bloc will arise. Others are purely "putchist," that is, they consist of rumors that someone will make a move.

What are the likely candidates for the objective signals? An imminent death of the founding (and not yet succeeded) leader of a regime constitutes one such signal. The problem of succession appears, and if mechanisms of succession are not yet institutionalized, a conflict appears imminent. More abstractly, one such signal is given by an impending collapse of the authoritarian institutions, whatever the cause of this collapse. Another signal may consist of a forthcoming economic crisis. Yet another of a manifest loss of legitimacy, as evidenced by mass unrest or mass noncompliance. Still another may be given by strong foreign pressures to reform. All of these situations may produce cracks in the regime, precisely because they all make it the more likely that some move toward liberalization would occur and, therefore, make it unsafe to miss the opportunity of joining a movement in this direction. Note that a loss of legitimacy may indeed constitute a persuasive signal of this kind, if this loss consists of more than a change of the individual states of mind and is manifested in a clear message that something will have to be done.

A regime begins to crack if some members of the ruling bloc go outside for support. If the regime itself is cohesive or tightly controlled, then a compromise solution cannot emerge. Consequently most dictatorial regimes we have known fell only on the battlefield, in an external or civil war. Popular unrest in the face of a cohesive power bloc places the resolution of political conflicts in the relations of physical force. Where some perspectives of an "opening" (*apertura*, "thaw") have appeared, they have always involved some ruling groups that sought political support among forces until that moment excluded from politics by the authoritarian regime. This is not to say that once liberalization is initiated, only such chosen partners are politically mobilized: once the signal is given, a wave of popular mobilization often ensues. But it seems to me that the first critical threshold in the transition to democracy is precisely the move by some group within the ruling bloc to obtain support from forces external to it.

Characteristics of Democracy

For a variety of reasons, some of which will be discussed below, it is perhaps useful to think of transition from an authoritarian to a democratic system as consisting of two simultaneous but to some extent autonomous processes: a process of disintegration of the authoritarian regime, which often assumes the form of "liberalization," and a process of emergence of democratic institutions. Though both of these transformations are shaped by the particular features of the old regime, at some point specifically democratic institutions must be established. It is important, therefore, to analyze democracy as the final *telos* of these transformations.

Democracy is a particular system of processing and terminating intergroup conflicts. This system has a number of characteristics that distinguish it from other political arrangements.

1. The existence and the organization in pursuit of conflicting interests are explicitly recognized to be a permanent feature of politics. This norm implies specifically that (a) multiple groups can be organized to promote their interests, (b) these groups have an institutionally guaranteed access to political institutions, and (c) losers who play according to the rules do not foresake their right to keep playing.

2. Conflicts are processed and terminated according to rules that are specified a priori, explicit, potentially familiar to all participants, and subject to change only according to rules. These rules specify (a) the criteria for being admitted as a political participant, (b) the courses of action that constitute admissible strategies, and (c) the criteria by which conflicts are terminated. (Conflicts are "terminated" rather than "resolved" in the sense of Lewis Coser's *On the Function of Social Conflict*. Conflicts are rarely resolved, but under democracy some states of affairs are recognized as temporarily binding in the sense that they are alterable only by going through the same rules by which they were brought about.)

3. Some courses of action are excluded as admissible strategies, in the sense

that permanently organized physical force can be legitimately used if any group resorts to it. Such use of force is regulated by rules that specify the contingencies in which they can be applied universally and *ex ante*. Yet, since physical force is permanently organized in anticipation of such contingencies, the element of intimidation as well as the potential threat that this force might become autonomous is inherent in a democratic system.

4. As in any system, democracy constitutes a set of stable relations between the actions of particular groups and the effects of these actions upon them. Conflicts are organized in a specific manner and their outcomes bear some relation to the particular combinations of strategies pursued by various actors. Characteristic of a democracy is that each group has some choice of strategies and that strategies have consequences.

5. Since each participant (individual and collective) has a choice of strategies, and all strategies do not lead to the same outcome, the results of conflicts in a democracy are to some extent indeterminate with regard to positions that the participants occupy in all social relations, including the relations of production. Capitalists do not always win conflicts that are processed in a democratic manner; indeed, they have to struggle continually in pursuit of their interests. In a democracy, no one can win once and for all: even if successful at one time, victors immediately face the prospect of having to struggle in the future. Even the current position within the political system does not uniquely determine the chances of succeeding in the future. Incumbency may constitute an advantage in electoral competition, but it is not sufficient to guarantee reelection.

6. Outcomes of democratic conflicts are not simply indeterminate within limits. They are uncertain. Since any particular organization of conflicts constitutes an ordering of outcomes upon actions, associated with each institutional arrangement is a distribution of the probability that conflicts result in particular outcomes. Democracy thus constitutes an organization of political power in the sense of Poulantzas:[17] as a system, it determines the capacity of particular groups to realize their specific interests. Given a distribution of economic, ideological, and other resources, this organization determines which interests are likely to be satisfied, which are less likely to be satisfied, and which are almost impossible to satisfy.

The distribution of the probability of realizing group-specific interests—which is nothing less than political power—is determined jointly by the distribution of resources that participants bring into conflicts and by specific institutional arrangements. This point merits some attention since descriptions of democracy at times emphasize its formal character and the bias that results when resources are unequally distributed. Clearly, a universalist law that prohibits everyone from sleeping under bridges in fact prohibits only some people. Nevertheless, we can look at this relation inversely. The probability that a basketball team composed of players who are seven-feet tall will beat a six-feet-tall team by a number of points is determined by the height of the basket. Given a distribution of resources, the probability that any group will advance its interests to a definite degree and in a definite manner depends upon the way in which conflicts are organized. Electoral systems, judicial procedures, collective bargaining arrangements, laws regulating the access to mass media or land use all shape the prior probabilities of the realization of group-specific interests. Extensions of the franchise to workers did have consequences for the improvement of their material conditions, as did the right to organize, the legalization of collective bargaining, and several other reforms. Reforms are precisely those modifications of the organization of conflicts that alter the prior probabilities of realizing group interests given their resources.

To summarize this description, let me extract three aspects of democracy that are crucial for the process of transition. First, democracy is a form of institutionalization of continual conflicts. Second, the capacity of particular groups to realize their interests is shaped by the specific institutional arrangements of a given system. Finally, although this capacity is given a priori, outcomes of conflicts are not uniquely determined either by the institutional arrangements or by places occupied by participants within the system of production. Outcomes that are unlikely can and do occur: as *El Mercurio* put it in the aftermath of Allende's victory, "Nobody expected that a Marxist president would be elected by means of a secret, universal, bourgeois franchise."[18]

Uncertainty and the Transition to Democracy

It may have seemed strange to describe democracy in such an abstract, almost game-theoretic, way rather than simply to point out the institutional arrangements typical of democracy: parliaments, parties, elections, and so on. Yet such a point of departure is necessary to understand the transition to democracy as a process of creating specific institutions, with their effects upon the capacity of various groups to realize their interests.

The process of establishing a democracy is a process of institutionalizing uncertainty, of subjecting all interests to uncertainty. In an authoritarian regime, some groups, typically the armed forces, have the capacity of intervening whenever the result of a conflict is contrary to their program or their interests. Therefore the situation may be uncertain from the point of view of some groups—those that are excluded from the power bloc and that must consider the intervention of armed forces as an eventuality. But some groups have a high degree of control over the situation in the sense that they are not forced to accept undesirable outcomes. In a democracy, no group is able to intervene when outcomes of conflicts violate their self-perceived interests. Democracy means that all groups must subject their interests to uncertainty. It is this very act of alienation of control over outcomes of conflicts that constitutes the decisive step toward democracy.

Such a step was, for example, gingerly attempted in Poland in 1965 during elections to the *gromada* councils—the elected body of the smallest administrative division of the rural areas of the country. In a departure from previous practice, voters were allowed to reject during preelection meetings the originally proposed candidates and to replace them from the floor. Hence voters were given a chance to replace some of the local bosses and to make those elected more sensitive to popular pressures. The election took place as planned and a subsequent analysis showed that this process of replacement did not have any macropolitical content. (I had the doubtful pleasure of coauthoring this analysis, which was officially published and then almost simultaneously dubbed as Trotskyite, anarchosyndicalist, and revisionist.) The partisan composition of those eliminated and those who replaced them was almost identical; there was no movement whatsoever against the ruling party and certainly none that could be interpreted as directed against the regime. And yet the party leadership could not tolerate even this absolutely minimal degree of uncertainty. Though spontaneous protests have been tolerated at times and on some occasions have become uncontrollable, an institution that would contain uncertainty could not be tolerated in principle.

I mention this minor episode because it illustrates dramatically the political and psychological breakthrough involved in the creation of democratic institutions. If one set of policies is seen as superior for the welfare of the society and this set of policies is assumed to be known, then it seems irrational to introduce uncertainty as to whether this set of policies will be chosen. Even in an economic crisis, when the economic policy of a particular government is recognized to have been mistaken, some other policy always appears to authoritarian bureaucrats as uniquely destined to improve the situation. Recognition of past mistakes does not constitute a demonstration that the authoritarian system is inherently flawed but only that past mistakes must be corrected and a new, proper, policy must be followed. The only lesson authoritarian bureaucrats draw from past failures is that some additional repression is needed until things get straightened out. Rationality and democracy appear as mutually exclusive to authoritarian bureaucrats. The appeal to democracy cannot be formulated in terms of the values of authoritarian bureaucrats; they cannot be promised more of their kind of rationality; they are forced to contend with what, from their point of view, clearly appears to be "anarchy" in the sense described by Marx in 1851. For authoritarian bureaucrats, the introduction of democracy constitutes an ideological defeat, a collapse of their very vision of a world that can be rationally commanded to one's will. Uncertainty is what they abhor ideologically, psychologically, and politically.

This brings me to my principal thesis. Democratic compromise cannot be a substantive compromise; it can be only a contingent institutional compromise. It is within the nature of democracy that no one's interests can be guaranteed: in principle, workers endowed with universal franchise can even vote to nationalize the privately owned means of production, to dissolve the armed forces, and so on. Nobody can guarantee that the rate of taxation of highest incomes will not surpass 53 percent, even if the current leadership of the existing parties commits itself to such a compromise; this leadership could change its mind under more auspicious conditions, or be replaced, or a new party could appear and capture electoral support with a program of redistribution of income. Under democracy, no substantive compromises can be guaranteed. As Adolfo Suarez put it in a speech during the campaign of elections to the Constituent Assembly, "el futuro no está escrito, porque sólo el pueblo puede escribirlo. [The future is not written because only the people can write it.]"[19]

What is possible are institutional agreements, that is, compromises about the institutions that shape prior probabilities of the realization of group-specific interests. If a peaceful transition to democracy is to be possible, the first problem to be solved is how to institutionalize uncertainty without threatening the interests of those who can still reverse this process. The solutions to the democratic compromise consist of institutions.

One source for learning about the dynamic of this process is the experience of the introduction of democracy in Western Europe. For example, the package negotiated in Sweden between 1902 and 1907—a period of rapid industrialization, organization of the working-class movement, and popular unrest—involved the following issues: (1) whether to extend franchise and to whom (males with a certain income, all independent males, all males; at what age); (2) whether reforms should include the upper house or only the lower house; (3) whether parliamentary seats should be allocated to single-member districts or to multimember constituencies with proportional representation; (4) whether, if single-member districts were to be retained, there should be a first-past-the-post or a runoff criterion; and (5) whether the executive should continue to be responsible to the king rather than the Parliament. Each of these institutional details had an impact on the chances of particular groups and was perceived as having an impact. Conservatives, once they recognized that some extension of franchise was unavoidable, sought guarantees. As Bishop Gottfrid Billing put it, he would rather have "stronger guarantees and a further extension of the suffrage than weaker guarantees and a lesser extension."[20] The Conservatives' guarantee was proportional representation, which, they thought, would prevent Liberals or Social Democrats from winning a majority. Social Democrats would have preferred to extend the franchise as widely as possible and to stay with a single-member, first-past-the-post system.[21] They were willing to compromise on proportional representation but not on the single-member system with runoff, since this arrangement would have favored the Liberals, who as a Center party would have picked up second-round votes.

This, then, is the kind of compromise that is possible. The experience of democracies demonstrates that institutional guarantees are quite effective in preventing some interests from coming to the fore and in preventing certain interests from being politically articulated at all. It is possible to design democratic institutions in such a way that some basic interests, such as the private ownership of the means of production, are virtually guaranteed. Without being cynical and without exaggerating the importance of institutions, we do have to confront the fact that democracy—contrary to so many hopes and expectations—has never produced an electoral mandate for socialism. One is reminded of the words of one of the first Latin American democratizers, Roque Sáenz Peña, who said in 1913: "Some circles have viewed with disquiet the alternation in office of two polarized parties, fearing this could threaten social stability. . . . Of course both parties respect freedom and order, and their rival doctrines fall within the protection of the constitution. Their reliance on the vote means that they are not revolutionary parties, and those who dissent from their purposes have full use of the electoral process to oppose and restrain them by legal means."[22]

Class Compromise and Capitalist Democracy

As the recent history of Iran demonstrates, a breakdown of one authoritarian regime can result in the establishment of another. Ominously, the jocular reference in Poland is to Ayatollah Wyszyński: the forces of the opposition, led by the Catholic church, seem as authoritarian as the regime itself. As Andrei Sinyavski pointed out recently, an opposition is a product of the regime it opposes.[23]

All forces struggling to destroy a particular authoritarian regime represent specific interests and offer specific projects of social organization. In pursuit of these interests, they must not only dismantle the old regime but must create at the same time the conditions that would favor their interests in the newly established political system. Hence each group must struggle on two fronts: to dismantle the old authoritarian system, and to bring about such new institutional arrangements as will be most conducive to the realization of their interests not only against the forces associated with the old regime but also against their current allies. The problem of democracy, therefore, is to establish a compromise among the forces that are allied to bring it about, not only to provide safeguards for the forces defending the old regime. Once the anti-regime forces are successful, the crucial question becomes whether a democratic compromise can occur rather than a second phase during which the weaker members of the alliance are purged and a new authoritarian system established.

On purely commonsensical grounds, there should thus be a marked difference in the chances of establishing democracy in those countries where political parties have long-established traditions, still alive in the loyalties of the current generation. Greece and Chile would stand in contrast to Iran and perhaps Argentina. My confidence in this a priori argument is disturbed, however, by the cases of Portugal and, in particular, Spain. Spain seems to be the country to be studied: democracy was established there without a breakdown of the armed forces, without a purge of even the political police, without much apparent politicization, and with two major parties that sprang up almost overnight.

Rather than engage in a historical analysis, however, I would like to examine theoretically some rudimentary conditions of class compromise necessary to establish and maintain a capitalist democracy.[24] I have argued that capitalist democracy is a contingent institutional compromise, and that the willingness of particular social forces to enter and to adhere to this compromise depends upon the specific project that underlies it. I will now justify these assertions.

Capitalist democracy constitutes a form of class compromise in the sense that in this system neither the aggregate of interests of individual capitalists (persons and firms) nor the interests of organized wage-earners can be violated beyond specific limits. These limits have been specified by Gramsci:[25] profits cannot fall so low as to threaten reproduction of capital, and wages cannot fall so low as to make profits appear as a particularistic interest of capital.

Specifically, in a capitalist democracy, capitalists retain the capacity to withhold a part of societal product because the profits that they appropriate are expected to be saved, invested, transformed into productive capacity, and partly distributed as gains to other groups. Wage-earners are persuaded to view capitalism as a system in which they can improve their material conditions; they act as if capitalism was a positive-sum system; they organize as participants and behave as if cooperation was in their interest when they expect to benefit in the future from the fact that a part of societal product is currently withheld from them in the form of profit. For their part, capitalists consent as a class when they expect that they will be able to appropriate profits in the future as a consequence of current investment.

This two-class model of democratic compromise is obviously too schematic to be useful in analyzing concrete historical situations. Wage-earners are never organized as a unitary actor. Capitalists compete with one another, not only in the market but also in trying to push upon one another the costs of reproducing workers' consent. The coalitions that underlie particular democratic compromises rarely comprise capitalists and workers as classes; more often than not, they are based on particular fractions allied against other workers and capitalists. Nevertheless, the very logic of class compromise necessary to establish and maintain a democratic system elucidates the contents of economic projects that are likely to orient the formation of democratic institutions.

The typical democratizing coalition is likely to adopt a Keynesian economic project. A Keynesian orientation constitutes a perfect combination for guiding a tolerable compromise among several groups. It leaves the ownership of the means of production in private hands, and with it the authority to organize production. At the same time, it treats increases in lower incomes not only as just but also as technically efficient from the economic point of view. Moreover, it assigns an active role to the state in regulating the economy against cyclical crises. This combination of private property, redistribution of income, and a strong state seems like an ideal package for almost everyone.

Yet several experiences, including the second Peronist period in Argentina, demonstrate that the Keynesian program is extremely fragile. As long as private property is preserved, accumulation requires that capitalists appropriate profits and invest them. A redistribution of income, even if it increases consumption, aggregate demand, and supply in the short run, must eventually lead to crises of profitability and hence of investment. Indeed, if the economic structure is highly concentrated, rapid wage increases seem to result simultaneously in unemployment and inflation. And if wage increases are rapidly eroded by price increases and unemployment, the organizations that represent the poorer sectors of the population in the nascent democratic system are likely to lose their popular support. On the other hand, far-reaching demands for the nationalization of the means of production are likely to meet with immediate resistance from indigenous and foreign capitalists and the withdrawal of their support for the democratic transformation.

Keynesian projects may thus be more appealing from the point of view of building a democratic coalition than they are auspicious for establishing a stable democratic regime: a good net to catch allies, but one highly vulnerable to anyone with sharp teeth. It seems as if an almost complete docility and patience on the part of organized workers are needed for a democratic transformation to succeed. Here again it may be worth noting that the democratic system was solidified in Belgium, Sweden, France, and Great Britain only after organized workers were badly defeated in mass strikes and adopted a docile posture as a result.[26] Or, as Santiago Carrillo put it, "One must have the courage to explain to the working class that it is better to give surplus to this sector of the bourgeoisie than to create a situation that contains the risk of turning against us."[27] Indeed, a striking feature of the Spanish transition to democracy is that the political system has been transformed without affecting economic relations in any discernible manner. Not only was the structure of ownership left intact (albeit with a large public sector), but to my knowledge not even a redistribution of income took place. It is astonishing to find that those who were satisfied with the Franco regime are also likely to be satisfied with the new democratic government.[28]

We cannot avoid the possibility that a transition to democracy can be made only at the cost of leaving economic relations intact, not only the structure of production but even the distribution of income. Freedom from physical violence is as essential a value as freedom from hunger, but unfortunately authoritarian regimes often produce as a counterreaction the romanticization of a limited model of democracy. Democracy restricted to the political realm has historically coexisted with exploitation and oppression at the workplace, within the schools, within bureaucracies, and within families. Struggle for political power is necessary because without it all attempts to transform the society are vulnerable to brutal repression. Yet what we need, and do not have, is a more comprehensive, integral, ideological project of antiauthoritarianism that would encompass the totality of social life.

3 ·

Paths toward Redemocratization: Theoretical and Comparative Considerations

Alfred Stepan

In the course of our three conferences on redemocratization, the editors and I decided it would be useful to attempt to characterize in a systematic (but not ahistorical) manner the major alternative coalitional and institutional paths to redemocratization. What follows is a deliberate effort to use abstract analysis to highlight the political and policy implications of each path, taken by itself. We are of course painfully aware that no path to redemocratization is ever "taken by itself." However, in our efforts to arrive at new synthetic interpretations of redemocratization as an integrated process, we want to avoid undertheorizing the question of the radically different paths available for redemocratization in the modern world and the fact that each path entails a predictable set of possibilities, problems, and constraints.

The tasks of this chapter, then, are conceptual and historical. The goal is to explore the following questions concerning authoritarianism and redemocratization. How should we conceptualize the types of paths by which redemocratization can occur? What are the particular strengths and weaknesses of each path for the institutionalization of political democracy? What theoretically predictable implications does each path have for reactionary, status quo, progressive, or revolutionary policies? What can we learn from the history of the most important cases of redemocratization since World War II? And finally, what insights can we derive from our abstract and historical analysis that will illuminate instances of authoritarianism and redemocratization before us now?

Before I begin the analysis, some caveats are in order. First, some categories established on abstract grounds turn out to have no empirical referents; nonetheless, by indicating an apparently quite plausible path toward redemocratization, we can expand our conception of the empirically possible, or we can direct our attention to hidden obstacles otherwise not apparent. A second caveat is that any empirical case of redemocratization may well—and almost certainly does—contain features of more than one category. In fact, successful redemocratization, given the built-in limitations of certain paths taken by themselves, may well require the simultaneous pursuit of several paths.

Finally, I discuss only what appear to be the most important paths. Logic could derive and history provide examples of many other paths not discussed here. Parsimony and historical complexity rule out a textbook construction of "mutually exclusive and collectively exhaustive" categories. Instead my goal is to be suggestive and at the same time faithful to the realities of authoritarianism and redemocratization in the modern period.

On abstract and historical grounds, we can propose eight particularly plausible and distinctive paths leading to the termination of authoritarian regimes and the process of redemocratization. Obviously, as the rest of this volume makes clear, a complex variety of causes—economic, historical, political, and international—are involved in the outcome of the redemocratization process. Yet it is my contention that the actual route taken toward that redemocratization has an independent weight: serious comparative analysis must attempt the difficult task of isolating and assessing this distinctive contribution.

The first three paths are ones in which warfare and conquest play an integral part in the redemocratization process. The great majority of historical examples of successful redemocratization, most of them European, in fact fall into these first three categories. The balance between prior democratic strength, the political unity and disunity of the conquered country, and the role of external powers in the redemocratization process can be sufficiently different to warrant the identification of three distinct categories: (1) internal restoration after external reconquest; (2) internal reformulation; and (3) externally monitored installation.

For the last three decades, and for the conceivable future, the overwhelming majority of cases of redemocratization have been and will be ones in which sociopolitical forces rather than external military forces play the key role, though international and economic forces, as well as political blocs, play an important role. We can divide these paths toward redemocratization into two general categories. In the first category, the termination of authoritarian regimes and the move toward redemocratization could be initiated by the wielders of authoritarian power themselves. Authoritarian power-holders may attempt to relieve pressure on themselves while at the same time preserving as many of their interests as possible by: (4) redemocratization initiated from within authoritarian regimes. (This important path has three subtypes. Each subtype is differentiated by the distinctive institutional base of the power group within the authoritarian regime that initiates the redemocratization attempt. The initiating group can be drawn from the civilianized political leadership [4a], the military-as-government [4b], or the military-as-institution which acts against either the military as government or the civilianized political leadership [4c].)

In the final category, oppositional forces play the major role in terminating the authoritarian regime and in setting or not setting the framework for redemocratization. The following oppositional routes would seem the most important: (5) society-led regime termination; (6) party pact (with or without consociational elements); (7) organized violent revolt coordinated by democratic reformist parties; and (8) Marxist-led revolutionary war.

Internal Restoration after External Reconquest (1)

Internal restoration after external reconquest means that redemocratization takes place when a functioning democracy that has been conquered in war restores democracy after the conqueror is defeated by external force. Here the key questions seem to be whether the leaders of the original regime are deemed culpable for the conquest, whether there is an issue of collaboration by the democratic leadership, whether a resistance movement unconnected or antagonistic to the defeated democratic leadership becomes a competing center of national identification and authority, and whether, during the occupation, enduring changes occur in the social, economic, and political structures of the country. The more the answer is in the negative for all questions, the more likely it is that the outcome after reconquest will be the restoration of the previous democratic system, with full legal continuities between the old and new democratic regimes. Such restoration would entail few pressures or incentives for major socioeconomic change. The more the answer is positive for these four questions, the less likely it will be that restoration (Path 1) is possible and the more likely that internal reformulation (Path 2) or even externally monitored installation (Path 3) will be the outcome.

The obvious cases that fit Path 1 are the Netherlands, Belgium, Norway, and Denmark. The Netherlands and Norway are in fact cases of perfect fit. In both countries, crown and cabinet went into exile and there was no hint of the culpability or collaboration of the democratic leadership with the authoritarian conquerors, the Nazis. In both countries, the respective monarchs-in-exile became symbols of national unity and of resistance to the invader; the resistance movements did not challenge the legitimacy of the governments-in-exile, and the conquerors did not succeed in imposing any enduring socioeconomic changes.[1] In both cases, following the defeat of the conqueror, there was a complete restoration of the political system, complete legal and institutional continuity with the past democratic system, and no significant restructuring of the socioeconomic system.[2]

Denmark is a more complicated case in that crown and cabinet capitulated to the German "protective occupation" but continued to rule although the Germans controlled the press, radio, and economic policy. At first political leaders attempted to normalize the state of affairs through negotiations with the occupying forces, and relatively free elections were held in spring 1943. However, the growing strength of the resistance and a wave of sabotage led the Germans to demand that the Danish government introduce martial law. This demand was met by a firm rejection which precipitated a *Wehrmacht* assault on the Danish armed forces and the imposition of direct rule. The Danish cabinet retired and neither it nor the king were tarred with collaborationist label nor considered culpable. There was no fundamental questioning of the prevailing democratic structure or socioeconomic order. As in the Netherlands and Norway, no major resistance movement assumed significant claims to autonomy, and after the war there was complete restoration of the *status quo ante*.[3]

Belgium is even more complicated. In Belgium, the cabinet established a government-in-exile in England. However, King Leopold III disobeyed the cabinet's wish and stayed behind in Belgium. During the German occupation, the king did not rule but an ambiguous visit by him to Hitler raised doubts about his personal legitimacy. After reconquest, the Parliament declared Leopold III "unable to reign" but accepted his brother Charles as regent. In 1950, there was a closely fought referendum about Leopold's right to assume the throne. In the aftermath of a divided vote, with the Flemish in favor and the Walloons against, the king, faced with a Socialist-led general strike, assumed the throne briefly and resigned in favor of his son. For our purposes, the point is that neither the constitutional monarchy nor the institutions of democracy were questioned and constitutional and socioeconomic continuity was maintained.[4]

Internal Reformulation (2)

In this category redemocratization takes place after a conqueror has been defeated largely because of external force. However, the more internal circumstances cause the previous democratic regime to collapse, or the previous regime is deemed culpable for the conquest, or there is a perception of collaboration, or a powerful resistance movement unconnected or antagonistic to the previous democratic leadership emerges, or profound changes occur during the occupation, then: the more impossible simple restoration of the previous democratic system becomes, and the more likely that redemocratization will entail deep, constitutional reformulation. Further, the more the above factors (collaboration, autonomous resistance, etc.) are positive, the more likely the outcome will be civil war among the competing groups. This path toward redemocratization obviously has much greater potential for political instability than Path 1. It also has much greater potential for rightist reaction or leftist structural change than Path 1. Depending on the outcome of the struggle among the competing groups and classes, there is greater potential for popular forces to gain important changes such as nationalizations, legalization of popular control of unions, or the right to full participation in elections. On the other hand, there is also a greater likelihood that the outcome of the struggle could be repression, the exclusion of groups from the political system, and the denial of their rights to organize; that is, that there will be only partial redemocratization.

The two cases closest to Path 2 are postliberation France and Greece. Italy combines Path 2 and Path 3.

From a formal and legal perspective, the Pétain administration began as a legitimate democratic government. The president of the Republic, Lebrun, made Pétain prime minister on the understanding that he would make peace. However, as Paxton argues, "Vichy was not a band-aid. It was deep surgery. To an extent unique among the occupied nations of Western Europe, France went beyond mere administration during the occupation to carry out a domestic revolution in institutions and values." One could argue then that Vichy France began as a democratic emergency regime but rapidly became an authoritarian one.[5]

The resistance movements, three major groups of heterogeneous political persuasion—radicals, Catholics, Socialists, and Communists—in the South, and the National Front dominated by the Communist party in the North, all acknowledged, to a greater or lesser extent, the leadership of de Gaulle and his Free French forces. All the resistance movements also raised major questions about the culpability, collaboration, and legitimacy of the Vichy government.[6]

As Paxton demonstrates, France from 1941 to 1944 contained elements of a civil war mixed with a patriotic war.[7] The patriotic war was dominant, however, and the Gaullist forces, working with all the parties contributing to the resistance, and supported by Britain and the United States, reformulated the democratic constitution and founded the Fourth Republic after the war. The regime recognized the de facto configuration of power and the patriotic achievements of the resistance forces. De Gaulle accepted Communist and Socialist control of much of the trade union movement. The Communist party of France (PCF) was able to use the postliberation purges to eliminate opposition in the unions and in the Confédération Générale du Travail (CGT) in particular, and thus establish their overwhelming dominance over that organization.[8] The period 1944–46 also witnessed extensive nationalization of properties owned by collaborators. These included many of the major commercial banks and the major auto producer, Renault. Punitive expropriations were only one feature of the nationalization program as the French state extended its controls over key sectors of the economy, including the mines, electricity, and gas.[9] The French Communist party, though initially hurt by the Nazi-Soviet nonaggression pact of 1939–41, made substantial gains after 1941 because of its role in the resistance.[10] In 1946 the party polled an average of 27.4 percent in the two elections (its previous high had been 15.3 percent) and participated in the government of 1946–47.[11] In France, therefore, the path of redemocratization via reformulation resulted in extensive nationalizations and important organizational gains for the Left, substantially greater gains than occurred in any country following Path 1.

In Greece, by way of contrast, there was a very different constellation of forces, and the outcome, though one of formal redemocratization, was very different. Democracy was reformulated in a more unstable and exclusionary way than in any case following Path 1. Democracy broke down in Greece in 1936 but the authoritarian Metaxas government, though manifesting some sympathy for Fascist styles of government, resisted the Axis powers. After the occupation of Greece in July 1941 by German, Italian, and Bulgarian troops, the king went into exile in England and Egypt. However, the king and his cabinet did not actively support the main resistance movement, which developed into an increasingly autonomous, legitimate, Marxist, and republican force which in fact carried out a program of change in the territory it controlled. With a relative weight much greater than the French resistance movements, with open borders to Marxist partisans in Albania, Yugoslavia, and Bulgaria, and with no nationalist competitors such as the Gaullists, the Greek resistance movement at liberation had strong military and political claims to participate in, if not to control, Greek national leadership. Domestic power balances completely ruled out Path 1 restoration. However, Churchill and later Truman saw Greece as a key area of struggle against world Communism, and massively backed royalist and conservative forces. The 1944–49 Civil War was waged to determine the terms of constitutional, socioeconomic, and international alignments in Greece. In almost any civil war, regardless of the outcome, the losers lose much beside the war, and the country has normally a weak foundation for a successor democratic regime. In this particular Civil War over 80,000 Greeks were killed and 10 percent of the population were forced to move from their homes. In October 1949, when the remnants of the Democratic army of the resistance fled across the border to Albania, the resulting "democratic reformulation," which grew directly out of the civil war emergency powers, outlawed the Communist party, virtually excluded the Left from employment in the state apparatus, and gave great prerogatives to the Greek army, which was extensively purged of most leftists, republicans, and many centrists. This legacy of exclusion and military prerogatives within a democratic system contributed to the breakdown of democracy in 1967. The authoritarian regime that followed that breakdown was itself terminated in 1974 largely by the "military-as-institution" (Path 4c), which nevertheless retained some of the prerogatives of the 1949 reformulation, prerogatives that are being challenged only today by the Socialist government elected in 1981.[12]

Italy from 1943 to 1946 combined elements of Path 2 and Path 3 (externally monitored installation). As Gianfranco Pasquino notes, Mussolini was overthrown not by the allies but by a vote of the Fascist Grand Council on 25 July 1943, a decision that gave authority to the king to dismiss Mussolini from his office of prime minister.[13] The overthrow should also be seen in the context of the successful Allied attack on Sicily, the bombing of Rome, and Mussolini's failure to persuade Hitler to permit Italy to withdraw from the Axis war effort. The armistice signed by the new prime minister, Marshal Badoglio, in September 1943 provoked the full-scale occupation of North and Central Italy by Germany and the establishment of a puppet state under Mussolini. Italy was not fully liberated until April 1945.[14]

The armed resistance movement played an important role in the struggle against the German military, creating Committees of National Liberation with members from five political parties. In the North, the Left was particularly important. Pasquino notes: "While military actions in the Center and North of Italy were and remained of utmost importance, the resistance movement consistently attempted to create the foundations for a new, democratic, and republican State in the various zones it succeeded in liberating from the Germans."[15] There were thus some ingredients for polarization on the Greek scale, but the actual outcome in Italy was closer to that of France than Greece. Why?

Viewed strategically, the position of the Communist party was weaker in Italy than in Greece. In Greece, the resistance for much of the period between 1942 and 1944 was the strongest anti-Axis military force. In Italy, when the resistance became powerful, the Allies already had a military presence in the South.[16] In addition, the coexistence of four other parties in the Committees of National Liberation meant that the comparative weight of the Italian Communist party (PCI) within the resistance was less than in Greece. Finally, geopolitically, Italian Communists lacked extensive, open borders with access to Communist partisans as in Greece.

Partly because of this balance of forces, the Soviet Union gave diplomatic recognition to the royalist government under Badoglio in March 1944. Shortly thereafter, Togliatti returned to Italy promising to cooperate with the discredited king and prime minister and to postpone all questions of a social or institutional nature including even an anti-Fascist purge until after the cessation of hostilities. Even after the liberation the PCI used all its influence with the Socialists first to give the cold shoulder to the Action party's call in April 1945 for a revolutionary democratic republic and later, in December 1945, to cooperate with the Christian Democrats in bringing down the Parri administration, which had introduced measures favoring small business and a capital levy as well as stiff prosecutions of Fascists. By 1945, Togliatti could point to the suppression of ELAS in Greece in 1944, the Allied occupation of Northern Italy, and the impossibility of aid from the Red army in diverting the cadres from the revolutionary path.[17] In the judgment of Pasquino, "Togliatti put the Communist party at the service of the national cause: the war of national liberation took precedence in his strategy over the goals of sociopolitical reforms."[18] This strategy, unlike that in Greece, precluded any attempt to conquer state power, but, as in France, won for the Left legitimate claims to participate in the postwar political settlement. In the elections of 2 June 1946, the Communists and Socialists helped defeat the system of monarchy in the referendum and on the same day won for themselves 39.6 percent of the seats in the Constituent Assembly which drafted a progressive constitution.[19]

In contrast to France, however, purges of the state apparatus were less widespread and nationalizations were less extensive. It is tempting to assert the explanation that redemocratization in Italy contained an element of Path 3 (externally monitored installation). Certainly Churchill, until his electoral defeat in late 1945, was a strong force for continuity in the Italian state apparatus, and opposed extending participation to the Committees of National Liberation in local governments or factories.[20] However, a number of studies have also argued that neither the Communists nor the Christian Democrats pushed hard for sweeping postwar socioeconomic changes. For both parties, their insertion in the state apparatus and the attainment of a stable postwar institutional arrangement were paramount goals.[21]

Externally Monitored Installation (3)

This category includes cases in which democratic powers defeat an authoritarian regime and play a major role in the formulation and installation of a democratic regime.

The major political weakness of this path toward redemocratization would seem to be its foreign imposition. It would appear to have a problem of legitimacy not found in the first path. However, it does share with the Marxist revolutionary path, described later, the power to dismantle the military and political institutions and other features of the authoritarian state apparatus. Such dismantling removes an important obstacle to redemocratization, an obstacle that looms large in many of the other paths analyzed in this chapter. If the authoritarian regime has been severely discredited, nationalistic reaction against foreign imposition might be dampened. However, if imposition occurs by capitalist powers, the range of socioeconomic and political changes supported by the monitoring powers will fall within broadly predictable limits.

The purest case of this category is West Germany, followed by Japan.[22] Austria and Italy fall partially into this category, but Austria has elements of the consociational path described later, and Italy, as we have shown, had strong elements of the internal reformulation of Path 2. Rather surprisingly, especially in view of the element of foreign imposition, all four countries that redemocratized by this route have had an unbroken history of democratic rule since World War II. What explains this historical outcome, and why should we be extremely skeptical about the ease with which it could be reproduced?

The historically specific fact of worldwide repugnance against Fascism meant that the defeated regimes had almost no overt domestic political defenders. Also, because all four countries were part of the core of the world capitalist system, even though they had been defeated in the war, the successor democratic systems were the beneficiaries of unprecedented financial support from the United States. The United States emerged from the war as the unchallenged economic, political, and military leader of the world and used these powers—especially after the cold war began in 1947—to create economic and ideological allies against Communism.

The democratic imposition by the United States and other Western powers also helps to account for the consistency of the fundamental outlines of the supported model with the social and economic patterns of the conquering powers, though there were significant social changes and economic reforms during the reconstruction (especially the agrarian reform in Japan).[23]

Despite the concrete outcome in all four of the existing cases, it is virtually impossible—even with the advent of a war—for these conditions to reappear. Given the political and economic evolution of the world system, no single capitalist country today or plausible group of core capitalist countries is ever again likely to have the hegemonic power the United States had in the period immediately after the war. For countries outside the core of capitalism, instead of Marshall Plan integration, there is likely to be a much more complex set of factors, involving nationalism, dependency, North-South and East-West conflicts.

The first three categories are ones in which warfare and conquest played integral parts in redemocratization. The majority of historical examples of successful redemocratization (most of them European) fall into these three categories. The connection between successful redemocratization, World War II, and the legacy of democracy and capitalism is apparent. Equally apparent is that redemocratization today and in the future will almost always occur via very different paths.

Redemocratization Initiated from within the Authoritarian Regime (4)

By this category I do not mean a once-and-for-all decision to devolve power. Such a decision seldom happens. What often does happen, however, is that some major institutional power-holders within the ruling authoritarian coalition perceive that because of changing conditions their long-term interests are best pursued in a context in which authoritarian institutions give way to democratic institutions.

On the surface, it would appear that this path has at least three characteristic constraints and predictable problems that should be given special attention. First, the power-holders can attempt to reverse their initial liberalizing decision if—in Dahlian terms—the opening of the political system contributes to situations in which the costs of toleration are much greater than the costs of repression.[24] Second, the power-holders can attempt to construct formal and informal rules of the game that guarantee their core interests even in the context of the successor democratic regime, and thus yield only a limited democracy.[25] Third, more than in any other path, the security apparatus from the authoritarian regime can attempt to preserve its prerogatives intact.

The path of redemocratization initiated from within the authoritarian regime, however, is quite broad and for analytic and historic purposes it is useful to identify three subtypes, each of which has a somewhat different institutional base.

In any authoritarian regime, the security apparatus and specifically the military play a major role. However, there can be an authoritarian regime in which the political component (civilian or civilianized-military) is dominant over the military-as-institution.[26] In such a case it is possible to have a redemocratization subtype we could call "redemocratization initiated by the civilian or civilianized political leadership." The institutional base of such a redemocratization effort is thus the political leadership of the authoritarian regime.

Another kind of authoritarian regime is one in which a clear military government is the central base of power. If the attempt to redemocratize originates from within such an institutional base, we would call the subtype "redemocratization instituted by the 'military-as-government.' "

Finally there is a case in which the military-as-institution, though at one time a component part of the authoritarian regime, seeks to overthrow either the civilian political leadership or the military-as-government because it comes to believe that the continuation of the authoritarian regime is detrimental to its long-term core institutional interests. I call this subtype "redemocratization led by the 'military-as-institution.' "

In concrete empirical cases these three subtypes may be difficult to disentangle, but there are analytic gains for attempting to distinguish them. For example, in cases in which the institutional base of the redemocratization effort is the civilianized political leadership, there will tend to be a preoccupation on the part of the political leadership with potential vetoes from the military-as-institution and a corresponding preoccupation with obtaining nonmaximalist behavior from the democratic opposition. Likewise, if the institutional base of redemocratization is the military-as-government, the military-as-institution can play an important veto role which predictably can impede, slow, or severely constrain redemocratization. However, if the institutional base of the redemocratization effort is a highly threatened military-as-institution, which for its own preservation thinks it must terminate the authoritarian regime rapidly, there is a potential for a speedier process of redemocratization and greater purges against the authoritarian government than in either of the other two subtypes. Let us therefore examine each of the three major subtypes of redemocratization initiated from within an authoritarian regime.

Redemocratization Initiated by the Civilian or Civilianized Political Leadership (4a)

If one accepts as axiomatic that power-holders will retain power unless forced by circumstances to alter the power-sharing formula, then one would predict that (1) the more there are new socioeconomic and political demands from below or from former active supporters, (2) the more there is doubt or conflict about regime legitimacy rules (especially among those who have to enforce obedience), and (3) the more there is the chance that the power-holders will retain and ratify much of their power via competitive elections (or at a minimum be able to remain active in political life), the greater the chance that this path will be initiated and will arrive at redemocratization.[27]

What are the implications of this path for policy and democratic stability? The first point to consider is that even when civilians or civilianized leaders are in control of the state apparatus the military-as-institution is still a factor of significant power. Thus the civilian leadership is most likely to persist in its democratizing initiative (and not to encounter a military reaction) if the democratic opposition tacitly collaborates with the government in creating a peaceful framework for the transition. However, even if the initial transition is successful, much of the coercive apparatus of the authoritarian state will remain intact after the election. There is therefore strong potential for severe constraints against policies that might introduce greater control over the state apparatus via democratic procedures. The stability of the newly democratized regime is particularly vulnerable to an internal coup by the bureaucratic apparatus of the previous authoritarian regime, or an actual coup by the security forces, should members of the coercive apparatus come to believe that democratic procedures are creating security risks.

The clearest case of this path is Spain. A major factor in facilitating the internal transformation of the authoritarian regime was the death in November 1975 of the only chief excecutive the regime had ever known, General Franco, and before that the December 1973 death of the only potential heir apparent. Franco's death inevitably raised fundamental questions about the regime's legitimacy rules even for many of those charged with enforcing obedience. Very important, the pressures of demands from below kept the process of internal transformation of the authoritarian regime going forward. Juan Linz argues that, on the basis of the Spanish case, "the democratic opposition has to be involved in the process. . . . Successful completion requires the cooperation of the democratic opposition."[28] The Spanish opposition at strategic moments shrewdly alternated between pushing and compromising, and the democratizing process went from the initial modest "reform" (*reforma*), initiated by the government, to a reform worked out with the democratic opposition (*reforma-pactada*), to a rupture with the past negotiated with the opposition (*ruptura-pactada*).[29]

This cooperation between the government and the opposition in the transition decreased the chances of a military reaction. Also the agreement of the opposition to the system of electoral laws meant that leaders of the authoritarian regime like Suarez, whose careers had been made almost entirely within the regime's political organization, believed they had at least some chance of winning the first election; or, even if they lost, that they would have a chance to continue in political life. Despite these many favorable factors, however, Spanish democracy is fragile, and its fragility is in part a consequence of the path taken to redemocratization. The most sensitive issue is the Basque one. The consolidation of Spanish redemocratization has been greatly complicated because it has involved not only a change to democracy but also a change in the regional nature of the state. The security apparatus was left virtually intact by the transition, and views the Basque conflict as a major threat to order and a threat exacerbated by the style and context of democratic legal and electoral procedures.[30]

At times, Mexican leaders have talked as though they might take the path of internal transformation of the Mexican regime, but in the absence of continuing social pressures delegitimizing the authoritarian framework and pushing the system in the direction of redemocratization, the top political leaders of the party and state bureaucracies limit all such efforts to modest liberalizing measures.[31]

There are elements of internal transformation in Brazil, but ultimately, given the institutional base and the major power-holders in the regime, Brazil does not fit in this category. In Brazil, there are greater social, economic, and political demands for redemocratization from below than in Mexico, and much greater elite dissatisfaction with the original authoritarian formula. However, two factors are substantially less favorable to the path of internal transformation in Brazil than in Spain. The de facto executive body in Brazil since 1964 has been the military-as-institution and the leaders have never become "civilianized" as occurred in Mexico under Lázaro Cardenas or in Turkey under Mustafa Kemal.[32] As an institution, the Brazilian military has some capacity to renew itself periodically. Unlike Franco, no single military leader provides a self-limiting biological clock. Without such a clock, and with the perception that their chances of winning power in a fully competitive electoral system were much less than in Spain, the military power-holders had every reason to keep the liberalization process just short of democratization for the entire first decade of liberalization (1973–83). Redemocratization in Brazil therefore had to be pursued along additional paths.

Redemocratization Initiated by "Military-as-Government" (4b)
In this subpath, the primary drive for regime termination would come from the individual leaders of the military government. Since most modern authoritarian regimes are military regimes, this would seem to be a relatively secure and numerically predominant path. However, the important point to stress here is that if it is not perceived to be in the interests of the military-as-corporate-institution to extricate itself from power, and if there is not a strong societal demand for the termination of the authoritarian regime, this is an extremely precarious path. The redemocratization effort may falter because of military institutional resistance, and no actual transfer of power may occur.

Possibly because of these problems, I know of no pure empirical case in which redemocratization has been achieved by this path alone.[33] Indeed, on theoretical grounds, we can say that, though the leaders of a military government may voluntaristically begin a process of liberalization, the process cannot cross the threshold of redemocratization without the additional support of societal push or corporate pull. Let us explore the complexities of this assertion by assessing liberalization and democratization in Brazil.

The Brazilian opening began in conditions of voluntaristic fragility. In the months before they assumed office in March 1974, President Ernesto Geisel and his chief ally, General Golbery, the head of the Civil Household, virtually by themselves initiated a controlled series of liberalizing steps which by late 1974 were increasingly turned into liberalizing policies, including a less constricted right to contest elections, less censorship, and fewer arbitrary arrests and tortures. In terms of our eight paths, Brazil is a clear case of liberalization commencing under the aegis of the military-as-government. However, liberalization was sustained and broadened by a complex process involving governmental concessions and societal conquest. Despite the unquestioned growth of the power of civil society, the military-as-institution (particularly the security forces who are now an integral part of the institution) does not yet believe that devolution of power is necessary for the preservation of its institutional interests. Given this perspective, when the security apparatus concluded in November 1981 that the elections scheduled for November 1982 raised the possibility of crossing the threshold from liberalization to redemocratization, the military altered the rules of the political game to complicate this prospect greatly. Because opposition parties had only weak organic connections to the forces of civil society—the lawyers, the base communities, the church, entrepreneurs, and even the new unions—and because the November package did not threaten the fundamental achievements of liberalization (no one was tortured, no censorship was imposed), the parties were unable to rally sufficient support against the new barriers to redemocratization. In the first five days after the passage of the new regulations there was not a single political demonstration against them.[34]

Brazil is a clear example in which lack of support is not a sufficient case for the military-as-institution to yield power. The task of the democratic opposition would seem to be to forge more organic links between the new organizations in civil society and the political parties so that demands for redemocratization become a combined social and political force which raises the cost of rule for the military-as-institution and which presents at the same time a clear governing alternative. Should the strategy lead to success, redemocratization (notwithstanding the origins of liberalization in the military-as-government's policies) would have actually been achieved, not by Path 4b, but by a complex series of forces emanating from Paths 4c, 5, and 6, involving the calculation of the military-as-institution, the diffuse demands of civil society, and the more politically channeled pressures of the opposition parties.

Redemocratization Led by "Military-as-Institution" (4c)

In this category, the primary motivation for the termination of the authoritarian regime derives from corporate factors of the military-as-institution.

It is a peculiar category. If the military-as-institution wants to return to democracy in order to protect its fundamental corporate interests, this is an extremely powerful force for the termination of authoritarian rule. In cases in which the military-as-institution sees the leaders of the authoritarian government (be they civilian or military leaders) as carrying out policies that create a crisis for the military-as-institution, it may be willing to sacrifice many of its own fellow officers—especially the leaders of the military-as-government—in order to transcend the crisis and reequilibrate the situation. However, there are also special risks attached to this form of extrication. Unless this path is augmented by other factors such as societal pressure, the military may retain a number of emergency powers. Also, once the crisis is past, there may not be major obstacles to reentry. The institutional factor is so powerful that we should be aware that in cases in which there is military rule, if there is no reason why the military-as-institution feels it is in its interest to relinquish power, redemocratization, short of foreign imposition (Path 3) or opposition-led armed violence (Paths 7 and 8) will almost certainly not occur. I mean to stress that loss of civilian support alone is not enough for the government to fall. Authoritarian regimes, unlike monist regimes, do not have high active support requirements. Apathy and acquiescence will suffice. Loss of civilian support must somehow be transformed into a tangible cost or a direct threat to the military-as-institution.

The two sharpest examples in which perception of intense threat to the military-as-institution played a fundamental role in the termination of authoritarian regimes were Greece in 1973 and Portugal in 1974.[35] The Greek military government was born in 1967 as a colonels'—as opposed to a generals'—coup. But since the generals were never purged, the military government began with a relatively poor base in the military-as-institution. By 1973, the leader of the military government was politically isolated, possibly for this reason, and he became engaged in an extremely risky intervention in Cyprus. This intervention immediately put the military institution under the grave security threat of a war with Turkey, for which it was completely unprepared. Under these circumstances, with an acceptable civilian conservative alternative in former Prime Minister Constantine Karamanlis, the military institution negotiated an extremely rapid extrication. For those officers associated with the military-as-government, the military-as-institution accepted harsh terms. Over one hundred high-ranking military officers from the military government were still in jail eight years later. The combination of speed and purges would seem to be virtually impossible to achieve in either Paths 4a or 4b.

However, notwithstanding the unpopularity of the government and the university uprising in 1973, there was not much pressure from society for the military to withdraw from government. Under these conditions, the military-as-institution insisted that the military-as-government withdraw from political power, but retained substantial institutional prerogatives that only began to be challenged by the Socialist coalition elected in 1981. However, the Greek case is important because it illustrates that the rules of the game for extrication can be renegotiated if democracy endures and if a new political force mobilizes new sources of power in the electoral arena.[36]

The other case is Portugal. As a number of authors have documented, the colonial wars in Africa generated a series of what were perceived by Portuguese career officers as increasingly severe problems for their military-as-institution. The length of the war generated manpower shortages at the officer corps level. Conscripted university graduates and sergeants were more frequently made officers, and this practice was resented by the permanent corps of officers. The army, which was closest to the war, also saw the war in the long run as fundamentally unwinnable. The termination of the African colonial war, and of the Portuguese authoritarian government that persisted in waging the war, became a central goal of the Portuguese military institution. The Portuguese case is unusual in two respects. The colonial war radicalized a section of the army, and the Armed Forces Movement played an important role in the initial structure of the state after the overthrow of the authoritarian regime. Even after democratic elections in 1975, 1976, and 1980, the military retained sufficient power to warrant labeling Portugal a "dyarchial" system of government. The Constitution of 1976 gave the military's "Council of the Revolution" de jure veto power over the National Assembly in that its members had the power to judge the constitutionality of acts of that elected chamber. In conditions of conflict between the president and the prime minister, latent dual power conflicts in the 1976–82 period could have precipitated a constitutional crisis for Portuguese democracy. The dyarchy ended only in 1982.[37]

The Peruvian case is another example in which corporate, institutional factors in the military played an important role in redemocratization in 1980. As I have argued elsewhere, by 1977 the military-as-institution felt it faced external security problems on all its borders with Chile, with Ecuador, and with Bolivia (a Bolivia possibly backed by Brazil). It also felt that it had achieved much of its initial program (settlement of the IPC [International Petroleum Corporation] conflict, some agrarian reform, strengthening of state structures) and that the continuation of the military government created internal conflicts that further aggravated its external security position. More than in Greece or Portugal, societal threats were present in Peru in the form of general strikes and growing pressures from diverse groups and classes for the military to withdraw. In these circumstances, when the Peruvian military withdrew, it retained fewer prerogatives than its Greek or Portuguese counterparts.[38]

In all three cases, external threats played a central role in extrications led by the military-as-institution. Of course, a variety of internal pressures could become contributing factors in a decision by the military-as-institution to relinquish power. The most common of these are policy pressures and divisions that shake the internal unity of the military so that extrication is the safest path to internal cohesion. Sudden internal upheavals often initiate a "return to barracks" movement within the military. Also major reputational or budgetary costs borne by the military-as-institution can erode its support for the military-as-government. In most of these instances of internal pressures, society-initiated demands characteristic of Path 5 are vital.

Society-led Regime Termination (5)

The key phrase here is "society-led" as opposed to party-, pact-, or revolutionary-induced transformation of an authoritarian regime. In theory, such a transformation could be brought about by diffuse protests by grassroots organizations, massive but uncoordinated general strikes, and by general withdrawal of support for the government. However, upon closer analysis this is a path toward government change rather than a path toward full redemocratization. The most likely outcome of sharp crises of authoritarian regimes stemming from diffuse pressures and forces in society is either a newly constituted successor authoritarian government, or a caretaker military junta promising elections in the future.[39] In the latter case, the actual transition involves the extrication by the military-as-institution, and many of the elements of Path 4 obtain. The key factor is that despite societal resistance to authoritarianism, many of the rules of transition are set by the caretaker junta.

On theoretical grounds, therefore, one is tempted to argue that society-led upheavals *by themselves* are virtually incapable of leading to redemocratization but are, nevertheless, often a crucial, or in some cases an indispensable, component to the redemocratization.

Greece in 1973 had elements of this path, led by the student uprising, but the need of the military-as-institution rapidly to alleviate the security crisis with Turkey was the major reason for the rapid redemocratization. Argentina after the massive but uncoordinated revolt in Córdoba in 1969, a revolt that spread quickly to other parts of the country, and Peru after the general strike of 17 July 1977 also fall into this category in some important ways.

The power of civil society to create and channel social pressures is extremely important in successful redemocratization, particularly for all three subtypes of Path 4. Without demands from civil society, in Path 4a (redemocratization initiated by civilian or civilianized political leadership) and in Path 4b (redemocratization initiated by "military-as-government"), the soft-liners within the authoritarian regime will almost certainly not be able to convince the hard-liners that extrication or redemocratization is an institutional necessity: the best the soft-liners can achieve is liberalization. For Path 4c (redemocratization led by "military-as-institution"), the smaller the social pressures, the greater the prerogatives the military can demand in the postextrication period. Finally, for most paths, the politically organized strengths and weaknesses of civil society determine to a large extent the barriers to military reentry in the post-redemocratization period.

Party Pact (With or Without Consociational Elements) (6)

By this category is meant the internal construction of a grand oppositional pact, possibly with some consociational features. The pact members unite to defeat the authoritarian regime and lay the foundation for a successor democratic regime in which power is open to most opposition forces.

In theory, this path, especially in its full-blown consociational form, would appear to be one of great interest for strategies of redemocratization, because it simultaneously addresses two critical issues. First, the construction of such a pact helps erode the bases of the authoritarian regime, especially if the rationale for the authoritarian regime is that a bloody conflict would ensue in the absence of authoritarianism. Second, it helps lay the foundation for the successor democratic regime with elaborate formulas for power-sharing, mutual vetoes, and grand coalitions.

Despite its apparent attractiveness, a strict consociational path presents several problems of a political nature. Pact *creation* does not necessarily imply pact *maintenance*—pacts can fall apart. Also, even when the pact is maintained, social change may occur and important new groups that were not a part of the original pact will be excluded. This possibility would represent not a case of consociational redemocratization but an example of exclusionary consociational authoritarianism.

When we explore the predictable policy consequences of a strict consociational path toward redemocratization, it should be clear that the "mutual vetoes" and the "purposeful depoliticization" of some major substantive issue areas, which are a part of Arend Lijphart's classic definition of consociationalism, would appear to build in systemic constraints to rapid socioeconomic change. The recognition of such constraints may in turn explain why, if the fundamental conflict in society relates to socioeconomic issues, as opposed to religious, ethnic, or linguistic disputes, it will be difficult for warring classes to walk the consociational path together.

If we start our empirical examination with a reading of Arend Lijphart's *Democracy in Plural Societies: A Comparative Perspective*, we note the rather surprising fact that of the consociational or semiconsociational cases he fully discusses (the Netherlands, Belgium, Austria, Nigeria, Cyprus, Malaysia, and Lebanon), only Austria is a case of redemocratization of an authoritarian regime.[40] All the other cases are of consociationalism first emerging as a conflict regulation device to avoid democratic breakdown or of consociationalism in the process of the decolonization of new states. In the only case of consociationalism emerging for redemocratization, Austria, the defeat of the authoritarian regime is accomplished by foreign powers; this external factor played a role, along with consociationalism, in the creation of democratic institutions. Lijphart mentions Colombia twice in passing, but does not examine it in detail because he claims it is not a plural society. For our purposes, however, both Colombia (1958) and Venezuela (1958) were cases of redemocratization in which party pacts and even some consociational practices—mutual guarantees, vetoes, and purposeful depoliticization—were crucial.[41] Both Venezuela and Colombia are cases that conform to our theoretical expectation, in that, though pacts for a long time contributed to the stability of political democracy, these same pacts kept socioeconomic change within a narrow range.[42] In Spain, the negotiated agreements on economic policy contained in the Moncloa Pact of 1977 and the consensual working out of the constitution are evidence of the role of party pacts and some consociational practices in the redemocratization process.[43]

Pacts—with or without consociational elements—cannot be created in all political systems. Party pacts by their very nature have two indispensable requirements: first, leaders with the organizational and ideological capacity to negotiate a grand coalition among themselves; second, the allegiance of their political followers to the terms of the pact.

Let us briefly explore the possibilities and problems of party pacts and redemocratization in Chile and Uruguay to show how sharply political systems can vary in regard to these two requirements. In both countries, exclusionary authoritarian regimes came to power in 1973. In both countries, a plebiscite was held in 1980.

For Chile, throughout 1978–80, the original allies and supporters of the authoritarian regime still perceived that the regime had offensive and defensive projects that were desirable and feasible. No process of redemocratization initiated by the power-holders was foreseeable in this period. Some role for an oppositional party pact was seen as a possibility during the 1980 plebiscite. However, the problem of a party pact was clearly one of followers. If the party leaders made a Marxist-Christian Democratic party pact, both ideological components of the pact would have suffered serious erosion of their bases. Much of the Right and even part of the Center of the Christian Democratic party rank and file would probably have shifted to a position of passive support for the authoritarian regime rather than play an active part in a pact with the Marxist parties.[44] Likewise the left wing of the Marxist parties, particularly the Socialists, would probably have rejected party discipline in favor of violent action rather than carry out a pact compromise dictated essentially by the Christian Democrats. Since much of oppositional societal mobilization in Chile in this period was actually party mobilization, societal mobilization shared many of the self-isolating, mutually canceling characteristics of party mobilization.

In Uruguay there was much greater potential for a party pact than in Chile. For one thing, in 1978–80 the regime had weaker and less clear-cut offensive and defensive projects than the Chilean regime, and thus its claims to bourgeois support had lost much of their original power. In these circumstances, bourgeois disaffection from pacting parties was less of a potential problem than in Chile. Another crucial variable that differentiated Uruguay from Chile was the class base of the parties. In Uruguay, as in Colombia and Venezuela, the major signatories to any pact would be multiclass parties with a dominant bourgeois ethos. In Chile, the Marxist and the Christian Democratic parties have different class and ideological bases. Finally, unlike Chile, the two major parties in question, the Blancos and the Colorados, had always between them polled over 80 percent of the vote in all national elections in the twentieth century. For all these reasons there is considerably greater potential for a successful party pact path to redemocratization in Uruguay than in Chile.

Yet risks also exist. The very degree of culturally captive voting support the two Uruguayan parties have been able to count upon in the past makes them reluctant in the current authoritarian situation to seek out special support from trade union members. Any party pact must be able to count on both the active support and the mobilization potential of the unions. Without these, even if the military should withdraw from power, the barriers to military reentry would be quite low.[45]

Organized Violent Revolt Coordinated by Democratic Reformist Parties (7)

On theoretical grounds this path appears to have a number of advantages for the process of redemocratization. Because the revolt against authoritarianism has a party base, the parties can provide a continuous political direction unavailable to the diffuse society-led path. The political core is also one that is committed to democracy and whose most probable internal political allies will be drawn from democratic forces. If we ask how far this path can go in terms of socioeconomic change, it clearly has greater potential than a party pact with consociational elements because it does not have the mutual vetoes, depoliticization of key issues, and institutionalized power-sharing that are part of the consociational formula. Likewise, the fact that the authoritarian regime has been defeated in a political-military struggle gives some scope to the parties to restructure the state apparatus.

This path has predictable constraints, however. The most likely type of reformist parties, in Europe and Latin America at least, are Social Democratic or Christian Democratic parties. The range of international political and economic allies and role models of either type of party keeps socioeconomic change within the boundaries of the international capitalist system. Because Social Democrats, and especially Christian Democrats, do not have a strong tradition of clandestine, violent party activity, the most likely paramilitary formula appears to be one that coopts a wing of the military to its cause of overthrowing the authoritarian government. Even though the military is a junior partner, it still sets limits to the degree to which the military and security apparatus can be dismantled.

Historically, there are no successful examples of this path leading to redemocratization in Europe, Africa, the Middle East, or Asia. In Latin America, the closest case is the 1948 revolt in Costa Rica. Here a Social Democratic "National Liberation Movement" defeated an attempt to disregard election results. This victory, together with the Social Democratic goals of the movement, ushered in a period of important socioeconomic reforms—the complete nationalization of private banks and the nationalization of the oligarchically controlled coffee institute. It also provided the financial and political support to put into practice laws that were on the books but had never been enforced, such as the social security law and the labor code. These reforms were quite extensive by Latin American standards but fully within the parameters of Social Democratic capitalist reforms then developing in Europe. The paramilitary political base also enabled the victors to disband the military forces of the country and to create a smaller but loyal constabulary, which helped the new regime to weather two armed revolts, one supported by Somoza from neighboring Nicaragua. Only in the late 1970s and early 1980s did this formula come under challenge as Costa Rica became engaged in the more polarized revolutionary and counterrevolutionary struggles of Central America ignited by the Nicaraguan Revolution.[46]

In Bolivia in 1952 the National Revolutionary Movement (MNR) seized power, dismissed much of the army, and carried out a series of structural reforms, but by 1964 internal divisions, the failure to create political mechanisms for party alternation, and the persistence of economic problems, led to the MNR's increasing reliance on the newly enlarged military, a reliance that ended in the assumption of power by the military and inauguration of a cycle of authoritarianism and revolt that continues to this day.[47]

Venezuela in 1958 was also close to this path but it fell short in two respects. First, a wing of the military was an active junior partner in the party-led revolt and in the transitional democratic government. Second, there were many elements of a consociational pact. In this case, in addition to the two major parties (the Social Democratic Acción Democrática and the Christian Democratic COPEI), the Catholic church, the military-as-institution, and local industrialists participated in the consociational pact of mutual guarantees and vetoes. This overarching coalition, as Terry Karl documents, set limits to socioeconomic change in the postauthoritarian period, limits that were even more severe than in Costa Rica.[48]

Marxist-led Revolutionary War (8)

This path has the greatest theoretically predictable potential for fundamental socioeconomic change because the revolutionary forces come to power only after defeating the state apparatus and a sector of the social order is displaced without waiting for the results of elections. In theory, the revolutionary forces also have an ideology and a social base supportive of fundamental change.

Theoretically, there can be a space for democratic revolutionary Marxist reconstruction. However, the doctrinal and organizational tradition of revolutionary Leninism, which has been the most effective and prestigious modern revolutionary model, rejects two of the requirements of a minimalist definition of political democracy—the relatively unrestricted right to organize and the relatively unrestricted right to open contestation. The Leninist party model in power therefore virtually precludes the existence of other parties advocating alternative conceptions of society and having a legitimate chance to gain power through electoral means.

Historically, there are many cases—such as China, Yugoslavia, the Soviet Union, Vietnam, and Cuba—in which revolutionary Marxism has overthrown authoritarian regimes and introduced fundamental change. However, to date there has not yet been even one election with full rights of organization and contestation (and with the right to make the government accountable to the electorate) after a revolutionary Marxist triumph.[49]

Nonetheless, since the 1970s there seems to be greater doctrinal and geopolitical space for this option to be realized than before. There has been greater doctrinal space because the Leninism that dominated revolutionary Marxism from 1917 until the early 1970s began to have serious Marxist critics who drew on Italian Eurocommunism and the antivanguardist critique of democratic centralism, for example, Rosa Luxemburg's and Leon Trotsky's writing against *What Is to Be Done?*, and on some of the participatory themes emerging in Marxism.

There has been greater geopolitical space in the world for democratic revolutionary socialism because neither the functional equivalents of the capitalist encirclement that threatened the Soviet Union after World War I nor the Stalinist encirclement of Eastern Europe after 1945 seemed likely to be repeated. In the multipolar, post-OPEC world since the 1970s, new revolutionary regimes had greater opportunities than before for piecing together aid, trade, and security relationships with a variety of countries.

The country in the world with the greatest opportunity to arrive at revolutionary democratic Marxism was Nicaragua. Given its initial international support from the then financially strong oil powers as politically diverse as Mexico, Libya, and Venezuela, from the ruling Social Democratic party in Germany, good relations with the strong Socialist parties in France and Spain, as well as support from Leninist party systems such as Cuba and the Soviet Union, Nicaragua had the potential to maintain degrees of independence which would have allowed it to construct its own path to democracy within the revolution. International capitalist bankers accepted the new power relations in the region; and, under the aegis of Mexico, and with the initial tolerance of the Carter government, they entered into an unprecedented and creative debt-rescheduling process for the revolutionary government.[50] Domestically, in Nicaragua the participation of the post-Vatican II Catholic church and an important wing of the national bourgeoisie in making the revolution seemed to give the Sandinista regime the possibility of at least a loyal opposition to the construction of democratic revolutionary Marxism.[51] However, the triumph of President Reagan in the United States elections of 1980, the incorporation of El Salvador into the East-West struggle, economic difficulties, and the emergence (in a country without a rich tradition of Marxist debate) of classical Leninism as an important component of the core model of the Sandinista rule of organization have made revolutionary Marxist democracy problematic.

Regardless of the outcome in Nicaragua, some democratic currents within Marxism and new geopolitical realities have created somewhat greater theoretical space for a democratic, revolutionary Marxist alternative. The unfortunate way in which Nicaragua was caught in the East-West conflict reconfirmed capitalist hard-liners and Leninist hard-liners alike in their skepticism about the possibility of democratic revolutionary Marxism.[52]

4 ·

Liberalization and Democratization in South America: Perspectives from the 1970s

Robert R. Kaufman

Given broadly defined "internationalist" models of development in Latin America, what possibilities are there for the construction of stable constitutional democracies? Do the sociopolitical conflicts associated with efforts to consolidate such models imply unbreakable cycles of fragile civilian regimes and prolonged periods of "exclusionary" military authoritarianism? This chapter speculates on potential routes out of such predicaments in Argentina, Brazil, Chile, and Uruguay—four societies in which these conflicts have been linked to particularly severe dilemmas of democratic governance and to the imposition of especially repressive forms of "bureaucratic-authoritarian" rule.

Our analysis derives from a political-economic perspective that leaves some room for hope, but little for optimism. Following Cardoso, Faletto, O'Donnell, and others,[1] it presupposes a partial but systematic link between the formation of bureaucratic-authoritarian governments and a syndrome of issues associated with the post–World War II developmental setting: declining opportunities for "inward-oriented" import-substituting investment, the growing size and political independence of the "popular sector," and intensified struggles over the evolving role of transnational manufacturing and financial forces in new models of development. A turn toward authoritarianism has not, to be sure, been an inevitable product of these developments—there has been important space for choice. Even so, the South American societies that encountered these issues in the 1960s and 1970s *have* been engulfed by crisis and repression with a striking and depressing regularity—despite important cross national differences in party systems and historic patterns of civil-military relations. Our point of departure, then, is that the social-economic setting has significantly limited the kinds of options available to democratizing elites.[2]

The emphasis here, however, is on the kinds of nonrepressive democratic alternatives that *might* currently exist—even within the framework of contemporary patterns of accumulation and class domination. What are the opportunities for reducing or eliminating the control that military-technocratic elites now maintain over the political systems of southern South America? How can these governments be replaced by more durable, polyarchical alternatives? The first section of this chapter provides the background for a discussion of these issues by reviewing the concepts and empirical assumptions that underlie recent political-economic analyses of the origins, composition, and dynamics of existing bureaucratic-authoritarian governments.[3] The next section suggests a framework for analyzing the conditions in which the sociopolitical coalitions that underlie bureaucratic-authoritarian rule might decompose—impelling the military governments themselves to liberalize or to withdraw from power entirely. In the final section of the chapter, we offer some broad, strategic hypotheses about the types of new, democratic coalitions that might viably be reconstituted in this region during the next decade or so.

"Internationalist Economic Models" and the Limits on Choice: The Pattern of Political Constraint

Let me begin by specifying a bit more clearly the scope and limits of the political-economic approach adopted here. As noted, the "internationalization" of advanced, import-substituting Latin American economies provides the main historical-structural setting for the analysis that follows. The socioeconomic dimensions of this transformation, already extensively discussed in the literature on the region, require no elaborate description here.[4] The principal features include: a growing reliance on private external credit and technology; expanded exports of a variety of "nontraditional" manufactured and primary products; and, within the domestic social structure, the emergence of transnational(ized) oligopolies—banks, industrial firms, and agribusinesses—as major new poles of accumulation and growth. The specific form of these transformations has varied widely, over time and crossnationally—from diversified patterns of heavy industrial investment in Brazil and Mexico to the neoliberal emphasis on specialized agribusinesses in Argentina, Chile, and Uruguay. I am interested here, however, in the broad, common themes that underlie these variations: the proliferation of trade, financial, technological linkages to the world economy—linkages that have profoundly transformed local economies based previously on industrial production for protected home markets and on the foreign exchange earnings of "traditional" agroexport sectors.

The *political* implications of these transformations are difficult to define with scientific precision. Whether they in fact have produced authoritarian regime change has depended upon specific national configurations of institutional structures and class coalitions, and on the way these have been organized and articulated at critical "conjunctural" points of national development. Still, Cardoso and Faletto have argued persuasively that these contemporary forms of "dependent development" have produced far-reaching changes in the underlying organization of political power that would appear to diminish democratic prospects: the weakening of national-populist coalitions; the displacement or cooptation of local entrepreneurial elites; the concentration of income; and the emergence of new constellations of state and oligopolistic interests seeking to insulate from the pressures and uncertainties of mass electoral politics.[5]

The following propositions about the impact of such forces can be regarded as reasonably defensible building blocks for the analysis in subsequent sections.

1. The shift toward internationalist developmental models has increased the pressure on local states to initiate—over the political resistance of influential middle-sector, nationalist, and union groups—comparatively "orthodox" economic policies that conform more closely to the norms of the world capitalist system. Although the transnational banking and manufacturing firms that dominate this system do not normally insist on dogmatically imposed, "Chilean-style" free-market policies, they have pressed consistently for "sound" monetary and trade measures that attach the highest priority to controlling domestic inflationary pressures, establishing predictable exchange rates, and insuring the movement of necessary capital equipment and raw materials across national borders. In societies that have developed extensively under more populist and protectionist governmental orientations, however, efforts to implement such measures have implied extremely sharp political conflicts—even among middle-sector and local entrepreneurial groups that can, in principle, gain during periods of export-led growth. For sociopolitical forces with high stakes in less orthodox, import-substituting policies, the short-term risks implied by such policy shifts have frequently been perceived (not irrationally) as intolerably high. And given the strategic importance and enormous influence of the oligopolistic sector, the long-term benefits are at best uncertain. Thus, tense struggles and frequent stalemates over such issues have been an ongoing feature of the political process throughout most of the past several decades.[6]

2. Increased levels of income concentration have also been a consistent feature of internationalist development models. It may be the case that even within the framework of such models, it is "technically" feasible to design moderately redistributive tax and wage policies that can gradually alter global distributions of income without seriously threatening the investment capacity of the oligopolistic sector.[7] For a variety of reasons, however, such efforts have not in the past been successful. First, although transnational business forces might well accept more equitable *levels* of income distribution, they fear and have reacted negatively to the inherent uncertainties of the redistributive *process* itself. Contemporary manufacturing and financial oligopolies, moreover, possess important sources of bargaining leverage that make them far less vulnerable than older-style, enclave-based foreign companies. As customers, suppliers, creditors, and partners of most large-scale state and private enterprises, they are linked symbiotically to local forces of production, and are thus far more difficult to isolate politically.

3. A crossnational comparison of most of the advanced countries of the region suggests that the tendency for the conflicts over such issues to escalate to "crisis proportions" has varied directly with the competitiveness of the political system.[8] Mexico's comparatively mild, party-based authoritarian regime has been most successful in avoiding such crises. Elitist constitutional regimes, on the other hand, have been far less "successful," either economically or politically. Colombia's quasi-democracy, based on power-sharing agreements among the elite-dominated traditional parties, has survived precariously, in the context of guerrilla violence, states of seige, and increasing delegations of power from civil to military authorities. Brazil's Second Republic (1945–64), with its broad restrictions on voting and union activities, fared even less well. For a time, it was able to combine populist electoral politics with a major expansion of the oligopolistic industrial sector, experiencing extremely high growth rates during the late 1950s. By the early 1960s, however, stalemates over monetary and trade policies, mounting inflation and recession, increasingly militant union and peasant movements, and growing elite and middle-class anxieties about their security within the system, all contributed, in mutually reinforcing fashion, to an unprecedented polarization of Brazilian society and to the collapse of the regime in 1964.

Finally, it has been in Argentina, Chile, and Uruguay—the societies in which popular forces have been most able to challenge transnational economic interests—that stagflation problems have been the most chronic over the past two decades and that political-economic crises have eventually become the most severe. To be sure, the overthrow of elected regimes in each of these societies can be attributed to many factors—the "destabilization" and "antisubversion" policies of the U.S. government, the arrogance and paranoia of the local military establishments, and the tragic, perhaps avoidable, miscalculations by civilian political elites.[9] Nevertheless, in the comparative context sketched above, the intensity of the crises of the 1970s and the magnitude of the ensuing repression do indicate a systematic tradeoff between contemporary modes of internationalist development and the maintenance of broadly based political systems, in which unions and "popular" parties can compete effectively for influence in the workplace and political arena.[10]

4. Contemporary bureaucratic-authoritarian responses to these crises can be understood as exclusionary processes, in which military-technocratic governments, supported by shifting coalitions of capitalist, military, and middle-class interests, attempt to purge populist and radical forces from the political system and to reconstruct the socioeconomic foundations of civil society.[11] Although the authoritarian governments promoting these processes have varied widely in terms of stability, repressiveness, and precise policies, they share several core features.

First, the fear of the "threat from below"—activated during periods of political-economic crisis—is the lowest common denominator and the most important bond of cohesion within bureaucratic-authoritarian coalitions. In the context of antipopulist or counterrevolutionary fear, broad exclusionary policies have been accepted at least initially not only by the armed forces and "big business," but also by many white-collar, professional, and local entrepreneurial groups that otherwise suffer considerably from most aspects of bureaucratic-authoritarian rule. At the same time (often over the opposition of both middle-class forces and nationalist military factions), exclusionary bureaucratic-authoritarian governments have also attempted to "resolve" underlying problems of accumulation on terms defined primarily by transnational capital and upper layers of the local bourgeoisie. This approach is particularly true during the initial phase of bureaucratic-authoritarian rule, a period in which a high priority is attached to "restoring the confidence" of international creditors and investors through the imposition of austerity and "free-trade" policies. Even in the later phases, however, governmental development strategies have tended on the whole to encourage profound concentrations of oligopolistic power and to tie local economies far more closely to world market forces.

Finally, it is important to emphasize that these governments have seized office through military coups d'état; and although they must share the power de facto with transnational business, the local armed forces provide the principal institutional foundations of their authority. Consequently, notwithstanding their internationalist economic orientations, these bureaucratic-authoritarian governments are also accountable to highly chauvinistic factions of "hard-line" officers, who seek to establish an "apolitical" military state as a directive force of "national" development.

Table 4.1 summarizes the way in which the main political and economic objectives of bureaucratic-authoritarian governments tend to articulate with the interests of the underlying exclusionary coalition. Guillermo O'Donnell has argued that the political dynamics of bureaucratic-authoritarian rule can be understood in terms of the conflicts and alliances among these interests.[12] In the following pages, we will attempt to extend this argument to an analysis of the process of liberalization as well.

This rather lengthy introductory route brings me to the issues that provide the central focus of this chapter: under what conditions can we expect the collapse or liberalization of these repressive bureaucratic-authoritarian governments? What are the available democratic alternatives? Fully satisfactory answers to these questions, if one assumes they are possible at all, would require a far more extended discussion than is possible here of the historical and situational complexities of each of the societies and governments I am considering. Nevertheless, to the extent that the introductory generalizations do highlight significant dilemmas of democratic development and important components of contemporary bureaucratic-authoritarian rule, they should also provide useful clues about the patterns and possibilities of political transformation.

In the next portion of this chapter, I explore the dynamics of liberalization primarily in terms of the centrifugal forces that seem to exist within the exclusionary coalitions themselves; in other words, in the way in which the

Table 4.1 **Bureaucratic-Authoritarian Objectives and the Coup Coalition**

	Objectives of Bureaucratic-Authoritarian Governments			
Components of Coup Coalition	Exclusion of Radical and Populist Movements; Demobilization of Working Class	Implementation of Stabilization and Austerity Policies	Expansion of Trade-Investment Links to World Economy	Construction of an "Autonomous" Technocratic State
Hard-line officers	strong, unconditional support	support	acceptance contingent on perception of accumulation alternatives	strong, unconditional support
Soft-line officers	strong initial support	support		support contingent on perception of political alternatives and long-term interests of military establishment
International financial bourgeoisie	strong initial support	strong, unconditional support	strong, unconditional support	support contingent on perception of military reliability and political alternatives
International manufacturing bourgeoisie	strong initial support	support contingent on "success" of policies	strong support	
Small local producers	strong initial support	opposition	initial opposition	opposition
Salaried middle class	strong initial support	opposition	support contingent on "success" of policies	opposition

"defections" of middle-sector groups, and the erosion of military and capitalist support can contribute to the weakening and isolation of bureaucratic-authoritarian governments. In the Latin American setting, to be sure, external diplomatic pressures (e.g., the Carter human rights policies), or organized opposition from excluded working-class and peasant sectors may also be important for the timing, outcome, and success of such processes. Nevertheless, many bureaucratic-authoritarian governments have shown significant ability to survive prolonged periods of diplomatic isolation and a ruthless capacity to crush pressures from below; and in view of the coercive and economic resources of the forces that sustain them, these governments appear more likely to disintegrate than to be overthrown. My emphasis, therefore, is on the development of tensions and possible splits within these forces, as a necessary feature of the liberalization process.

The last section of the chapter considers the far more difficult task of reconstituting new governing (and opposition) coalitions that might provide the basis for more durable, democratic alternatives to bureaucratic-authoritarian rule. As I have already indicated, the prospects are hardly encouraging. Even so, for at least some of the cases I am considering, there may be roads that lead toward democratization. For reasons indicated more fully below, the most promising of these may involve only incremental changes in the existing accumulation framework, and a form of democratic legitimation based on "probusiness," Center-Right governments that seek their major source of support within the "middle sectors."

II. The Politics of Liberalization: The Disintegration of Authoritarian Coalitions

This topic subdivides logically into two separate issues. First, what are the conditions in which the question of liberalization moves onto the political agenda? Second, under what circumstances do such struggles acquire a momentum that can produce the transfer of authority to elected civilian regimes? This section provides a framework for an analysis of these issues in at least five instances of bureaucratic-authoritarian rule. In two of these instances—the post-1964 Brazilian case and the Onganía administration in Argentina (1966–70)—we can draw retrospectively on concrete historical processes of liberalization. In the Argentine case, the process led eventually (if temporarily) to the establishment of a new civilian government; and in the Brazilian case it has significantly eroded earlier patterns of exclusionary rule. However, I am also interested, obviously in a more speculative vein, in identifying factors that might sometime during the 1980s be relevant to a study of the liberalization of bureaucratic-authoritarian governments that now appear deeply entrenched in power: the juntas that have dominated Chile and Uruguay since 1973, and the military government that once again seized office in Argentina in 1976.

The analysis turns on the assumption, already suggested in the introduction, that although these governments may well be extremely powerful, they lack the organizational and political props that have buttressed their more institutionalized authoritarian counterparts in Spain, Portugal, and Mexico. There is no dominant party or movement, no conservative Catholic hierarchy to promote traditionalistic regional and ethnic loyalties, and (with the partial exception of Brazil) no elaborate bureaucratic-corporatist structures to channel populist impulses. The bureaucratic-authoritarians of South America have rested instead on especially transparent combinations of business, military, and some middle-class interests, which cohered initially around broadly perceived economic and political threats to the prevailing system of class relations.

It follows that the demise of bureaucratic-authoritarian rule can usefully be understood as the product of at least four kinds of changes in these relationships, each of which can be viewed as essential components of the liberalization process as a whole. The first is the decline of the initial sense of emergency and fear. The second is the attempt by bureaucratic-authoritarian governments to expand their links to civil society by tolerating broader institutional and political opportunities for "public contestation." Third, there is the formation of liberalizing oppositions—led or supported by some of the middle-sector groups that initially backed bureaucratic-authoritarian coups. Finally, there are changes in the interest calculus of the capitalist and military elites themselves, each of which must continuously assess the risks of supporting a potentially isolated bureaucratic-authoritarian government.

For the purposes of presentation, I have grouped each of these possible changes into three "phases," depicted schematically in Figure 4.1. These phases, it should be emphasized, should each be considered problematic and reversible; and they should not be presumed to unfold inevitably or necessarily in any precise chronological sequence. Figure 4.1 does, however, serve to identify analytically important subprocesses and relationships that warrant closer attention and empirical examination.

Phase 1: The Decline of Fear

The discussion of this aspect of liberalization is complicated somewhat by crossnational differences in the magnitude of the crises that prompted the initial formation of bureaucratic-authoritarian governments. In the case of the Onganía government, antipopulist fears were low, and served as a weak deterrent to the proliferation of centrifugal forces within the coalition. In all of the other cases, on the other hand, far more severe political-economic crises activated much more pervasive and deeply rooted fears which have been far more effective in sustaining support for (or acquiescence in) the exclusionary process. Although these fears are rooted in real experiences of "unrest" and political violence, they have typically exaggerated the extent of the dangers posed by radical or populist forces, and have persisted well after these forces have been crushed or exhausted. We have little systematic information about the sociopsychological mechanisms that sustain or reduce this sense of threat.

Figure 4.1 The Politics of Liberalization

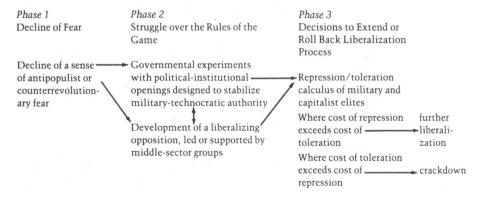

Phase 1 Decline of Fear	*Phase 2* Struggle over the Rules of the Game	*Phase 3* Decisions to Extend or Roll Back Liberalization Process
Decline of a sense of antipopulist or counterrevolutionary fear	Governmental experiments with political-institutional openings designed to stabilize military-technocratic authority	Repression/toleration calculus of military and capitalist elites
	Development of a liberalizing opposition, led or supported by middle-sector groups	Where cost of repression exceeds cost of toleration → further liberalization
		Where cost of toleration exceeds cost of repression → crackdown

For the purposes of this chapter, however, I proceed on the assumption that "declining fear" is a secular feature of bureaucratic-authoritarian rule, or at least that this fear cannot persist indefinitely with the same salience and intensity that it acquired during the crisis period itself. It is likely to diminish most rapidly among middle-sector forces which risk less and can gain more than their military and capitalist allies from a relaxation of authoritarian controls. As a degree of "normality" is restored to the daily rhythms of social life, a sense of security may also increase among at least some sectors of the military and capitalist establishment itself.

As time eventually blurs the memory of the acute conflicts of the crisis period, a new political situation is created in which other elements of the liberalization process can most effectively be set in motion. The politico-legal credibility of repressive "anti-Communist" military campaigns and "emergency" governments tends to decline in these circumstances; and the way is paved for broader struggles over the rules of the political game. At this point, two additional features of the liberalization process become especially relevant: governmental experiments with partial political and institutional openings to civil society; and the formation of liberalizing coalitions, led or joined by portions of the middle class. This destabilizing combination of concession from above and liberalizing pressure from below can produce harsh crackdowns as well as a further broadening of civil and political liberties. Either way, however, it creates new predicaments for the military and capitalist elites that remain as the principal supporters of the exclusionary process. It is in the context of these predicaments, finally, that I turn to the last phase of the liberalization process—the (re)calculation of military and business interests. The survival or demise of bureaucratic-authoritarian rule depends ultimately on whether significant portions of one or both of these sectors elect to jump on the liberalizing bandwagon.[13]

Phase 2: The Struggle over the Rules of the Game

Assorted Brazilian experiments with "guided democracy" and "decompression," together with the "political dialogues" initiated by the Argentine military in the early 1970s, are the main illustrations of the destabilizing consequences of governmental efforts to expand their links to civil society. Each of these initiatives can be understood primarily as efforts to stabilize the legal-political foundations of the military-technocratic incumbents, not as the planned first steps toward a withdrawal from power. But in each instance, such openings unleashed opposition forces that generated new choices for the ruling elites: either to acquiesce in still further liberalizing concessions, or to roll back existing ones through new acts of coercion. In Brazil's first experiment with "guided democracy" in the late 1960s, the choice was eventually for a crackdown in December 1968. On the other hand, the response to the liberalizing pressures that followed the 1974 decompression policies has been an uneven, but still extensive, pattern of new concessions. In Argentina, finally, the political relaxation intended to secure military authority and to isolate its Peronist targets ended, after only three years, with a previously "unthinkable" transfer of power to the Peronist coalition itself.

The "Pandora's Box" metaphor, which has sometimes been applied to these governmental "reforms," is clearly exaggerated, given the ever-present possibility of selective repression or the broad-scale use of naked coercion to deepen and extend the exclusionary process.[14] It is also possible, of course, that efforts to institutionalize this pattern of authoritarian rule may prove successful in the future. But at least so far, attempts to establish a new, more stable authoritarian equilibrium have failed. To understand this failure we must look more closely both at the orientations of the bureaucratic-authoritarian governments which seek to open new cooptive channels of participation and at the changing interests of the sociopolitical groups which tend to move into these channels.

Effective cooptation is impeded, on the one hand, by the inability of the generals and technocrats within the bureaucratic-association inner circle to define the political dimensions of their "revolution from above." The hard-liners are generally far more interested in closing preauthoritarian channels of participation than they are in designing new ones—indeed, they seem inspired primarily by the concept of an "autonomous" state that can function without the encumbrance of any operative linkages to the contending "political forces" within civil society. The more moderate governmental officials, on the other hand, may well acknowledge an "eventual" need to share authority with various combinations of parties and organized interest associations, but there is usually very little overall agreement about when such states should be instituted, about how authority should be shared, or about "how far" such sharing should go.

The typical response to such issues has been to ignore them for as long as possible after the bureaucratic-authoritarian coup, while the government concentrates "first" on its "war against subversives" and on its reorganization of the economy. But such issues, as I have already suggested, are difficult to suppress indefinitely; and when they do reach the surface of political life, they have tended to expose important divisions among governmental elites as well as within civil society. As the Brazilian case suggests, the result is not the establishment of clearly defined (and circumscribed) new arenas of representation and participation, but rather a shifting and ambiguous political space, characterized by constant reorganizations of the legal structure, shifting official definitions of "acceptable" political behavior, and unpredictable acts of "selective repression." This result may well, for a time, throw opponents off balance. It is not likely, however, to succeed in establishing an institutionalized framework for authoritarian rule.

The second major dilemma involved in bureaucratic-authoritarian efforts to define and institutionalize new authoritarian "rules of the game" is that once counterrevolutionary fears decline, even comparatively nonrepressive military-technocratic governments have little to offer to middle-sector groups that initially supported their rise to power (see Figure 4.1). In most cases, these groups have been forced to bear much of the initial costs of bureaucratic-authoritarian austerity and trade policies, and even when their economic situation improves, the emasculation of liberal-democratic channels of representation deprives them of much of their political leverage within the existing system. As the Brazilian authorities discovered in the 1974 congressional elections, material prosperity under these conditions may not be enough to secure middle-class electoral support.

The foregoing does not, of course, mean that the "middle sector" acts as a homogeneous unit within the political arena. On the contrary, there is typically a wide range of ideological and political diversity. But the "central tendency" within the middle classes does appear over time to involve shifts from support to neutrality or from neutrality to opposition. The cumulative impact of these shifts is pivotal for the formation of liberalizing coalitions.

On the one hand, even the conservative middle-sector groups that move most quickly into the political-institutional spaces opened by bureaucratic-authoritarian governments frequently seek to secure their own independence by expanding these spaces. In Brazil, the lawyers, journalists, academicians, and professional politicians within the "official parties" were all important forces in testing the initial limits of "guided" democracy, pressing with varying degrees of militance for greater legislative autonomy, a larger role for the parties, more freedom in the press and the universities, more opportunities for debate within the electoral arena. Not all such groups seek, of course, to dismantle bureaucratic-authoritarian governments entirely, or to establish mass democracies. Even so, they tend generally to add to the momentum for political change. Lacking the privileged access of military and business elites, they cannot accept the hard-line conception of an "autonomous state," a state in which they would have no meaningful place at all. And, as I have already suggested, they cannot depend on the ambiguous and shifting opportunities tentatively made available by more moderate elements within bureaucratic-authoritarian governmental circles. Despite their own ideological heterogeneity, therefore, they have a strong interest in attempting to insulate themselves from the arbitrary edge of bureaucratic-authoritarian rule by pressing for enlargements in the scope of civil and political liberties and for an expansion of the arenas of political debate. In this way, they tend to contribute indirectly, as well as directly, to pressures for greater liberalization.

At the same time, middle-sector support (or at least sympathetic neutrality) also seems to have been a crucial factor in facilitating the reentry of working-class and peasant forces into the political arena. As O'Donnell has suggested in the Argentine case, the alienation of local entrepreneurial and white-collar groups from Onganía's exclusionary coalition both preceded the *Cordobazo* (an insurrection in the industrial city of Córdoba in May 1969) and accelerated afterward, eroding the will of the armed forces to defend military governments from trade union and student pressures from below.[15] In Brazil, similarly, the diverse shadings of middle-class political activity and opposition that became publicly evident after 1974 seemed to pave the way for the strikes and peasant protests of the late 1970s.

Thus, despite their limited power capabilities and their political heterogeneity, the middle sectors are critical swing forces in the liberalization process. As the only major "nonelite" group backing bureaucratic-authoritarian coups, they occupy a strategic role in efforts by exclusionary governments to broaden their institutional and political links to civil society. Yet, as bureaucratic-authoritarian governments do relax their control, middle-class groups are also the ones most likely to have both the resources and the incentives to press for still broader opportunities for public contestation. Because the middle sectors do not themselves control the major levers of coercion or accumulation, these pressures in themselves do not ensure the collapse or overthrow of bureaucratic-authoritarian governments. Middle-class defection from the authoritarian coalition does, however, expose more fully the isolation of bureaucratic-authoritarian governments and places them more openly on the defensive.

Phase 3: The Repression/Toleration Calculus of Military and Capitalist Elites

We turn finally to the factors influencing the way such bureaucratic-authoritarian dilemmas are resolved. In situations in which governmental authority is so intensively concentrated, we cannot of course discount the importance of idiosyncratic responses by the military and technocratic incumbents within the "inner circle." The possibilities of crackdowns depend in part on the hard-line proclivities of a military president, his immediate advisers, and strategically placed personal rivals within the armed forces. From a more systematic perspective, however, the choice of crackdown or additional liberalizing concession seems to turn on the calculations of the most important pillars and beneficiaries of bureaucratic-authoritarian rule—the international(ized) bourgeoisie and the armed forces. With the broad backing of these sectors, repression from above can replace the threat from below as the principal mechanism for neutralizing middle-class dissent. Without such backing, effective governmental crackdowns are inconceivable.

We can plausibly assume that, for large numbers of officers and businessmen, the incentives to sustain or expand the exclusionary process have been extremely strong. The advantages offered by bureaucratic-authoritarian governments are, of course, considerable—economic opportunities, professional honor and security, and power. On the other side, there is the risk of the instability that might ensue from an "excessive" relaxation of authoritarian controls. Such considerations clearly underlay the strong military and capitalist support for the Brazilian crackdown of 1968, a period in which the memories of the turbulent Goulart years were still especially fresh.

But the commitments of the armed forces are not unconditional. In Argentina in the early 1970s, and in Brazil after 1974, serious frictions between nationalist military factions and the internationalized private sector contributed both indirectly and directly to a loosening of authoritarian controls. And in both cases, moderate sectors of the military-capitalist alliance began after a time to cooperate tacitly or overtly with opposition forces that had once been perceived as too weak to prevent new "left-wing" threats to the established order.

Under what conditions do significant portions of these sectors swing toward acquiescence to liberalization pressures? To highlight the kinds of considerations that seem to have been relevant in Argentina and Brazil, I focus on three strategic issues: (1) the military's perception of "accumulation alternatives" to international capital; (2) the capitalists' assessment of the "reliability" of the military establishment; and (3) military or capitalist perceptions of acceptable civilian political alternatives to bureaucratic-authoritarian rule.

Accumulation Alternatives. For military nationalists, a key issue is whether state or local bourgeois forces can provide the investment and technology necessary for the maintenance of a powerful state apparatus. The more viable such national alternatives are (or appear to be), the less likely the military is to be willing to deploy its coercive resources to defend the security and investment opportunities of transnational capital. I would hypothesize that such perceptions are influenced in part by specific economic conditions. The viability of economic nationalism may appear most limited in periods of extreme inflationary and trade crises, such as in the initial years of bureaucratic-authoritarian rule when military elites feel especially constrained to enforce the shock treatments urged by transnational banking sectors. Exceptional periods of economic expansion (i.e., Brazil, 1967–74) can also mute the frictions between nationalist and international investment forces. On the other hand, intermediate situations of only moderate growth, or mild "stagflation," may generate more opportunities for the military's economic nationalism to come into the open. In Brazil, for example, the slowing of the economy since 1974 has intensified the sharp public controversies over the growing role of military-backed state enterprises.

The political implications of these divisions are extremely complex. As the matrix in Figure 4.2 suggests, growing economic nationalism within the armed forces can imply two rather different courses of military action. If nationalist factions begin to perceive the availability of "acceptable" opposition forces within civil society, they may seek to reduce the influence of foreign capital by accelerating the search for civilian allies within the framework of a more liberalized political order. On the other hand, if such allies do not seem available, an alternative course is to attempt to reconstitute the economic base of military rule through increased reliance on state enterprises or the local bourgeoisie. The second option was pursued initially by the military governments that replaced Onganía in 1970, and it is a course that also seems currently attractive to at least some hard-line currents within the Brazilian military. Nevertheless for reasons that I will deal with shortly, this new, more nationalist authoritarian option is a risky one, which can work indirectly to increase the opportunities for an effective liberalizing opposition.

The Long-term "Reliability" of the Armed Forces. For international capitalists—the other major pillar of bureaucratic-authoritarian rule—this is, of course, a central factor in decisions about how to confront liberalizing pressures. If the military establishment as a whole is perceived as basically sympathetic to internationalist development models, the "business community" may actively urge it to take a "firm hand," as in Brazil in the late 1960s. And, of course, it is in a position to back a military crackdown with significant new inflows of financial credits and direct investments.

On the other hand, as I also suggest in Figure 4.2, capitalist uncertainties about the reliability of the military establishment can induce quite different sorts of responses, depending again on the "acceptability" of the civilian opposition. In Argentina during the early 1970s, both the nationalism of the post-Onganía military governments and business anxieties about a resurgent Peronist opposition movement seemed to close off most capitalist political options within the domestic political arena. The response by most sectors of international business was thus to reduce the level of investment, a process that, in turn, contributed to a marked deterioration of "economic conditions," and to the further isolation of the existing governments. In post-1974 Brazil, on the other hand, the growing perception of relatively safe and moder-

Figure 4.2 Repression/Toleration Calculus of Military and Capitalist-Elites

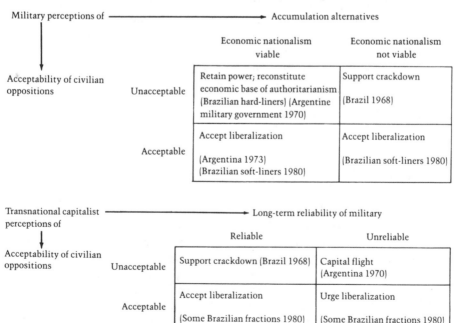

Military perceptions of ⟶ Accumulation alternatives

Acceptability of civilian oppositions		Economic nationalism viable	Economic nationalism not viable
	Unacceptable	Retain power; reconstitute economic base of authoritarianism (Brazilian hard-liners) (Argentine military government 1970)	Support crackdown (Brazil 1968)
	Acceptable	Accept liberalization (Argentina 1973) (Brazilian soft-liners 1980)	Accept liberalization (Brazilian soft-liners 1980)

Transnational capitalist perceptions of ⟶ Long-term reliability of military

Acceptability of civilian oppositions		Reliable	Unreliable
	Unacceptable	Support crackdown (Brazil 1968)	Capital flight (Argentina 1970)
	Acceptable	Accept liberalization (Some Brazilian fractions 1980)	Urge liberalization (Some Brazilian fractions 1980)

ate opposition forces has prompted at least some segments of international capital to press for an expansion of the constitutional framework, both as a defense against hard-line military nationalists and as a hedge against the possibility of an eventual collapse of authoritarian rule.

The Anti-authoritarian Political Alternatives. As has already been indicated, responses to liberalization pressures turn critically on perceptions of these alternatives. If opposition forces are viewed as too "radical" to be trusted, the prospects for liberalizing concessions are obviously dim. But experiences in both Argentina and Brazil do indicate that such perceptions can in fact change quite dramatically. On the one hand, views about the "acceptability" of civilian alternatives are related to the degree of friction between military and capitalist sectors. The greater these frictions, the greater the incentive for moderates within these sectors to redefine their connections with previously "disgraced" or "intolerable" opposition forces. At the same time, the "objective" character of these oppositions will also influence perceptions. Perceptions of acceptability are greatest (1) when such oppositions have (or appear to have) wide popular backing, and (2) when they are (or appear to be) capable of containing "extremist" attacks on the most salient military or capitalist interests.

The Argentine military's 1973 transfer of governmental power to the Peronists provides an illustration of the way new perceptions of acceptability can emerge. Even after one discounts for the initially low levels of fear, the possibilities of a détente between the profoundly antagonistic military and Peronist sectors of Argentine society seemed virtually inconceivable only a few years before it actually occurred. Yet from the perspective of the then-dominant nationalist military factions, the acceptance of a new Peronist government came increasingly to be viewed as the best of a number of unpalatable choices. On the one hand, the *Cordobazo* seemed to have proved the political bankruptcy of Onganía's internationalist model of development. Yet the more statist orientations of the post-Onganía military administration had also failed to deter a growing wave of middle- and working-class opposition. In this context, the Peronist alternative appeared more and more as a tolerable, if not a desirable, risk. The tragic epilogue of this story—Perón's death, the disintegration of his social pact, and the new, far more intense rounds of crisis and repression that followed after 1975–76—is irrelevant at this stage of my analysis. In 1973 the aged and "mellowed" Perón, with his wide personal following and his strong support within the union movement, seemed at least presumptively capable of constructing a new, centrist coalition between capital and labor.

The post-1974 Brazilian liberalization process presents a more complex and problematic picture. Nevertheless, from the perspective of the now seriously divided military and capitalist elites that continue to dominate this system, the range of "acceptable" forms of political action has also clearly expanded. The behavior and leadership of the opposition forces, it should be noted, have made an important contribution to these developments. In the initial years following the pivotal 1974 congressional elections, this opposition was dominated essentially by centrist and middle-class groups seeking to expand, rather than to bypass, the "official" channels opened by the Geisel administration. The reentry of working-class forces as an important political factor occurred only several years later, during the last years of the decade. Perhaps most important, finally, in contrast to the 1967–68 period, there has so far been no significant guerrilla activity that might furnish the pretext for a hard-line crackdown. In this new context, both military soft-liners and important segments of the business community have acknowledged the "need" or "inevitability" of a continuing liberalization of the political system. Even though the process is far from complete, an attempt to reverse the momentum would involve high political and economic risks for the hard-line proponents of a crackdown.

The Reconstitution of Democratic Coalitions: Accumulation and Legitimation Options in a Post–Bureaucratic-Authoritarian Political System

As authoritarian coalitions disintegrate, what are the opportunities for the (re)establishment of viable democratic systems? Two assumptions guide the inquiry into these issues. First, "democratization" implies movement toward a political system characterized by competitive elections, civil liberties, and the toleration of significant "loyal oppositions." Although a single-party Socialist regime might, in some cases, appear more consistent with demands for social justice, this form of Socialism is more usefully considered as an alternative to, rather than a version of, the kind of transition I am considering here. For my purposes, the concept of "democracy," whatever else its social content, must include the basic electoral and representative features of Western-style polyarchies.[16]

The second assumption is that the formation of durable polyarchies requires, at least in their formative periods, accommodation with the still powerful political and economic forces on which the old authoritarian order was based: not only the military establishment but also the transnational business sector. More equitable revisions of the extreme internationalist models typically promoted by bureaucratic-authoritarian governments will, to be sure, also be necessary. Nevertheless, in view of the strategic economic role now occupied by international business, a rapid and extensive attempt to displace this sector would imply levels of social conflict and political control that would be inconsistent with the concept of democratization as defined above. To remain both stable and democratic, newly elected governments like their bureaucratic-authoritarian predecessors, will have to maintain relatively open economies, with the emphasis on external credit and technology, on a dynamic export sector, and on political-economic security for international investment forces.

Given these "accumulation requirements," what are the chances that an electorally based system can avoid the kinds of crises that led initially to the imposition of bureaucratic-authoritarian rule? Notwithstanding the discouraging patterns reviewed in the introduction to this chapter, there may be some room for maneuver. The trauma of bureaucratic-authoritarian repression itself, for one thing, appears to have lowered the expectations of at least some of the excluded "popular sectors" and their political leaders, making them more amenable to self-limiting compromises over economic issues.[17] Conversely, in an era of declining U.S. hegemony, Latin American governments may now be more able than in the past to bargain with competing oligopolistic firms over the distribution of the surplus. Even so, the constraints on this process remain extensive. Although international business may be willing to accept electoral politics, it will not tolerate powerful political movements that overtly threaten its basic interests in control over the workplace or the capacity to accumulate profit within a market-based economy. On the other hand, if the population has already endured high levels of economic privation, there may be powerful redistributive demands.

Whether these problems can be resolved will, of course, depend on many factors that are beyond the control of political activists. But much may also depend on the way such activists organize the diffuse interests that reenter the political arena during the process of transition. Clearly, their chances for success will be maximized if they have realistic coalition-building strategies which anticipate some of the dilemmas just discussed. In the remaining portions of this chapter I concentrate particularly on the reconciliation of three key objectives—the construction of a governing electoral coalition, the organization of opportunities for political opposition, and the provision of "appropriate" guarantees for powerful economic elites.

Table 4.2 summarizes three broad approaches to these objectives. The first is a "national-populist" alternative, based on a governing alliance that cuts across the socioinstitutional structure of society, organizing middle-sector groups, workers, military nationalists, and some business groups around a combination of patronage benefits and broad nationalist appeals. In a second, "social-democratic" option, the government would be based more directly on the support of organized labor and the urban-industrial working class. The third option, finally, is a Center-Right coalition, rooted in an alliance between business and the middle sectors. Each of these options has its strengths and weaknesses, and each therefore must be assessed systematically on a case-by-case basis. But from the more general perspective adopted here, I will suggest below that the last of these options may hold out the greatest hope of reconciling the "accumulation" and "legitimation" dilemmas of newly established democratic states.

The National-Populist Alternatives. Venezuela since 1958 provides the most successful approximation of this legitimating formula. Under the leadership of the Acción Democrática political machine, this system was stabilized

Table 4.2 Legitimation Strategies in Newly Established Polyarchies

	Forces of Accumulation	Nucleus of Social Support	Nucleus of Social Opposition	Party Systems
National populist strategy	acceptance of transnationals, incremental emphasis on state investment and independent local bourgeoisie	urban poor and peasants unions salaried groups small business	upper middle class upper bourgeoisie	multiclass parties and party pacts
Social-democratic strategy	acceptance of transnationals; incremental emphasis on state investment	organized blue-collar workers some segments of peasantry and urban poor	middle classes	government: social-democratic "workers" party opposition: Center Right
Center Right	acceptance of transnationals and "associated" upper bourgeoisie, less emphasis on state investment	middle-sector groups some industrial blue-collar workers some segments of peasantry and urban poor	industrial workers unions	government: Center Right opposition: social democratic and/or populist parties

through power-sharing agreements with rival parties, guarantees to key institutional groups such as the army and the church, and the systematic isolation of political radicals.[18] As broad liberalizing coalitions evolve in opposition to bureaucratic-authoritarian rule, there will be strong incentives to move in similar directions: toward the formation of majoritarian "coalitions of the whole," in which class divisions are muted by shared nationalist and democratic aspirations, party pacts, and patronage. But although such arrangements may well prove useful in the initial establishment of democratic governments, there are serious questions about their long-term viability.

First, comparatively high rates of economic expansion are likely to be especially important to the stability of patronage-based governing coalitions. Systems organized more explicitly around the defense of class or ideological interests can presumably develop other bases of cohesion. But the capacity to extract and distribute material resources is the life blood of the more "pragmatic" political machines that form a central component of most national-populist alternatives.[19] Although raw-material export booms or upswings in the industrial business cycle may conceivably facilitate such distributive processes in the South American cases, increased inflationary pressures and slowing rates of growth are more likely to characterize the circumstances of a transfer of power from bureaucratic-authoritarian to civilian governments.

In this connection, we cannot discount the particular way in which the structure of the petroleum industry contributed to the bargaining leverage of the Venezuelan government. Oil companies were weakened considerably by the fact that they had already committed huge investments in Venezuela, and that petroleum was a scarce and nonsubstitutable natural resource in a situation of growing worldwide demand.[20] In the other cases, on the other hand, neither coffee, copper, wheat, nor meat (nor labor-intensive manufactured exports) seems to offer such extensive opportunities for the extraction of "export-led patronage."

Finally, though luck or political skill might still enable some new democratic governments to surmount these problems, the recent historical record is far from encouraging. Assorted versions of this strategy have failed repeatedly to provide a stable electoral base in Brazil (under Vargas, Kubitschek, Quadros, and Goulart), and in Chile, under Ibañez and Frei. The Uruguayan system of consociation and state patronage suffered increasing immobilism and decay throughout the 1950s and 1960s. And in Argentina, the Peronist social pact so carefully negotiated between capital and labor in 1973 disintegrated only three years after the withdrawal of the preceding military government. With lessons learned from the past, with more carefully designed pacts and organizational efforts, and with more finely tuned economic management, it is always possible that a new round of electoral populism might result in a more positive outcome. Even so, coalitional strategies that give greater emphasis to class and ideological appeals may provide firmer foundations for democratic legitimation. It is in this connection that I examine the two remaining alternatives.

The Social-Democratic Alternative. We have already ruled out the political viability (within a democratic context) of radical redistributive movements; but a system inspired by the more moderate European social democracies deserves consideration. Most social-democratic movements have tacitly or explicitly accepted many of the constraints implied by the rules of the market economy; and their capacity to alter "fundamentally" the inequalities of advanced capitalism remains limited. Within these parameters, however, they provide more or less humane models of legitimation in which union-based workers' parties have provided the principal source of electoral-legislative majorities, while quasi-official peak associations of big labor and big business negotiate within the state bureaucracy over welfare and planning issues.[21] Can similar systems of bargaining be worked out in Latin America?

Several similar structural and historical obstacles, emphasized in the sociological literature on the region, do seem to stand in the way. One is an industrial proletariat of limited size and considerable economic weakness—the outgrowth of "dependent capitalist" industrialization.[22] In contrast to the Latin American cases, moreover, European social democracies were institutionalized at a "historical moment"—the 1930s—when there were far fewer worldwide investment opportunities available to the upper bourgeoisie. Finally, in the Latin American context, it is not easy to conceive of labor, with its strong nationalist traditions and orientations, providing strong support for governments willing to negotiate pragmatically with the transnationals.

But despite the continuing importance of such obstacles, their weights in the contemporary context should be systematically reconsidered—especially in Brazil, where the size of the industrial work force has expanded enormously, and in Argentina, where a large proletariat has historically provided the basis for a powerful union movement. Ironically, the fierce exclusionary policies of the bureaucratic-authoritarian governments themselves may have provided new opportunities for the mobilization of these sectors on terms that need not be unacceptable to at least some portion of oligopoly capital. For by rolling back the trade union rights established during earlier decades, these bureaucratic-authoritarian governments may have reopened a "reform space" in which union and party organizers can capture worker loyalties by promising to restore basic collective bargaining opportunities and security provisions that have long been accepted in the advanced capitalist countries. For reasons already discussed, it will be much more difficult for such organizers to deliver quickly on economic as well as political payoffs, especially in the initial years of a democratic government; and the effort to induce self-restraint in wage and welfare demands of newly independent unions could well presuppose an insuperable task of political persuasion. Even so, a "workers' government" may still be more able than a populist one to convince its working-class supporters that economic restraint is in their best long-term interests.

In my judgment, however, the most serious problem that would face a prospective social democracy stems from political-ideological, rather than social-structural, factors. In almost every case (Argentina might be the exception), social-democratic governments would require the electoral and legislative support (and quite possibly the cabinet participation) of the Communist party—a political force that, despite its historic caution and moderation, has aroused profound ideological antipathy and fear among middle-class groups, capitalists, and the armed forces. Ironically, of all the parties that might round out a social-democratic coalition, the Communists have traditionally been most inclined toward the sorts of pragmatic approaches suggested above. Even so, hostility toward the Communists is deeply rooted and profound; and although it might be possible (indeed, necessary) to persuade established elites to accept them as legal contenders for power, these elites are almost certain to draw the line against any administration that seeks to incorporate them as a component of a post–bureaucratic-authoritarian governing coalition. So, whereas no social-democratic movement that excludes Communists is likely to be elected, no elected government that includes them is likely to last very long.

In view of this dilemma, as well as the others already mentioned, social-democratic coalitions can probably contribute more effectively to the democratization process as opposition, rather than as governing, forces. In opposition, many of the liabilities connected with such coalitions might disappear, or even be converted into assets. Social-democratic politicians, for example, could gain credit for the political concessions and opportunities wrested from a more conservative government; and by providing the leadership in a peaceful struggle for a broader distribution of economic benefits, they could contribute to the legitimation of the system as a whole. As one component of such an opposition, finally, the Communists would be in a far better position to provide a stabilizing influence on the Left—channeling protest, moderating the sectarianism of its more radical allies, and discouraging a turn toward guerrilla warfare or terrorism. Paradoxically, on the other hand, a "respectable" and secure Center-Right government, drawing on closer ties to military and capitalist elites, may be more able than a social-democratic government to open such opportunities for the Communists, and more likely to profit politically from their substantial potential as a moderating force.

Center-Right Alternatives. The third broad legitimating strategy is a governing coalition organized by centrist and "probusiness" segments of the political class (e.g., the Frei wing of the Chilean Christian Democrats), which relies on middle-sector organizations and voters as its principal nucleus of political support. This configuration of forces, parallel in some important respects to the sociopolitical coalitions that initially backed bureaucratic-authoritarian rule, is not without serious political dilemmas of its own. But versions of this strategy have worked reasonably well so far in Spain and Greece, two of the Southern European analogues of our cases; and although Latin American conditions are different and less favorable, this kind of coalition does offer some advantages over the others.

First, although Center-Right coalitions might well contain strong nationalist or statist currents, they would be least likely to divide sharply over internationally oriented trade and investment policies. There would be less dissonance about providing guarantees for transnational business and less reluctance about imposing fiscal and monetary brakes when such measures seem necessary.

Second, as I have already suggested, "safe" and "respectable" Center-Right governments may have the greatest opportunity to engineer the political and institutional integration of loyal Left-Center oppositions into the political system, since these governments would presumably be less vulnerable to the destabilizing attacks of the far Right.

Finally, a government that seeks to provide economic security for business and political opportunities for labor is perhaps in the strongest position to isolate and crack down on "disloyal" oppositions of the far Left and far Right, an essential aspect of the stabilization of new democracies.[23]

The most difficult issue raised by this coalitional alternative is whether the Latin American middle-sector, which constitutes perhaps one-fifth to one-third of the population of our cases, can actually serve as a sufficient electoral nucleus for Center-Right governments. Even in the best circumstances, these middle sectors offer a far smaller numerical base of support for a Center-Right bloc than do their counterparts in, say, contemporary Spain.

On the other hand, a number of factors work to offset these weaknesses. First, a Center-Right bloc would be able to marshal formidable resources—

financial backing from capitalist elites, ample access to the media, influence over the educational system, and substantial direct control over the major economic levers of power. Prior to the imposition of bureaucratic-authoritarian rule, the control of such resources allowed centrist and rightist politicians to dominate the electoral arena in most of our cases, supplementing middle-class constituencies with important support from the peasantry and the urban lower class. Even in Chile, for example, Allende's 1970 plurality victory was made possible by a split between centrist and rightist elites, and not by the mobilization of a new, lower-class majority. Second, in the aftermath of bureaucratic-authoritarian rule (and especially in processes of "controlled" liberalization such as Brazil's), centrist and rightist politicians may have important additional advantages. As the groups most likely to be the first to enter the new political spaces opened by soft-line military administrations, they have the opportunity to be the first and most visible public critics of authoritarianism and the first to start rebuilding party networks.

Finally, the comparatively high middle-class rates of organizational and electoral participation can offset its limited size and increase its potential for supplying an electoral plurality. The appropriate constitutional design, in turn, might convert such pluralities into rather commanding legislative majorities.

Of course, even in the short term, such arrangements are unlikely to be effective unless they are buttressed by many informal and partially self-denying "understandings" among contending political elites. From the perspective of a Center-Right government, the viability of its relations with a loyal opposition (including the Communists) will depend not only on the formal guarantees provided by a constitution, but also on the government's willingness to "consult" behind the scenes, and perhaps also on its effort to pursue to their maximum limits the "trickle-down" opportunities that may be possible within the technical-political parameters of broad internationalist development models. The stability of the system also presupposes considerable forbearance from opposition political elites. The success of a democratization effort would almost certainly depend on their circumspection and moderation in the articulation of potentially explosive redistributive issues, and on their explicit disavowal and condemnation of terrorist guerrilla activities. In some instances, finally, they might even be required to collaborate tacitly in maintaining the Center-Right in power, for example, by abstentions in legislative votes of confidence or by running rival opposition slates against the government coalition.

In view of the historic antagonism and profound mistrust that has so often divided these elites, it may, to say the least, be unrealistic to expect such heroic forms of restraint and cooperation. But then who in the early 1970s could have imagined the subtle patterns of cooperation that eventually evolved in Spain between the divergent sociopolitical forces represented by Suarez, Gonzáles, and Carillo? In the aftermath of a repressive experience of bureaucratic-authoritarian rule, the incentives for restraint and compromise expand; and however improbable they may appear, a mosaic of understandings rooted in such incentives will be a necessary condition for democratization of the Latin American countries I have discussed.[24]

The social underside of such understandings is not pleasant to contemplate. Although it is possible that Center-Right governments might find it in their electoral-political interests to seek ways to broaden the economic benefits of internationalist development models, they are unlikely to provide any fundamental solutions to the problems of poverty and alienation that have afflicted their societies for centuries. The prospects for genuine "economic democracy" are thus remote. For this reason, among others, my strategic hypotheses are advanced tentatively, and with the expectation of critical examination and rebuttal. But even the limited form of democratization envisioned here would represent a far from trivial advance over existing patterns of repressive military rule. At least governments that now openly employ coercion and torture would be replaced by ones that must compete in mass elections and respect civil liberties. Even when they are stacked explicitly in favor of capitalist elites and the middle classes, finally, newly established constitutional systems can (at least in principle) acquire an institutional life of their own which may eventually provide the chance for different, more progressive kinds of governing coalitions.

5 •

Demilitarization and the Institutionalization of Military-dominated Polities in Latin America

Alain Rouquié

Any assessment of the possible evolution of military-dominated polities in Latin America depends on the perspective used to explain their recurrent emergence in the past. If one believes that contemporary militarism is merely a culturally determined anachronism offering transitory resistance to the ultimate political good—that is, representative democracy—one assumes a unilinear evolution which is predictable and practically inevitable. Infrastructural interpretations of the appearance of modern authoritarian regimes likewise underline the latters' transitory nature. Functionalist determinism, by establishing a more or less instrumental correspondence between dominant economic actors and regime types, foresees an end to the authoritarian system when its supposed "objectives" have been fulfilled. The "necessary" or indispensable character of authoritarian rule for peripheral capitalism in its present phase will therefore assure with equal inevitability the disappearance of authoritarian regimes once they complete their historic role. These two contradictory perspectives have in common a facile and dogmatic certainty concerning the "exceptional" nature of authoritarian regimes. In effect, those who interpret Latin American history in terms of a protracted "struggle for democracy," like those who perceive the political arena as directly subordinated to the episodic necessities of capital, take for granted an inevitable outcome of liberalization.

The partisans of both of these theses generally ignore the strictly military dimension of the great majority of Latin American authoritarian regimes. The "liberal" perspective does so because its adherents have decided that armies as political forces are only an atavistic legacy of the past. Since modern politics is based exclusively on representative government and rational procedures of administrative specialization, obstacles to attaining this ultimate good must stem from some hangover from the past. Starting from these premises, one cannot envisage professionalized military institutions in terms of bureaucratic modernity, or analyze the political implications of this development.

The "economicist" perspective is equally neglectful of the martial component. Its mode of analysis omits the institution that is at the center of power since it is merely supposed to be the expression or instrument of exogenous socioeconomic factors. In short, the specific manifestations and particular processes of military organizations are treated as epiphenomenal by both approaches.

A less reductionist approach would focus the analysis on the real power-holders in political systems dominated by the military, take into account the specificity of the military corporation and of its pattern of alliances and civil support, and locate its extra-institutional political resources in the framework of structural constraints derived from each national society. It would not assume that the nature of postauthoritarian outcomes is known in advance. This is not to assume that military power is ineradicable, but that it has its own logic. The successive waves of militarization and demilitarization which the continent has experienced since 1945 should be enough to inspire caution on the part of those who would make predictions in this realm.

In effect, whereas in 1954 twelve out of twenty republics were being governed by military leaders who had come to power by force, by the middle of 1961, only one such leader was left: Stroessner in Paraguay. In seven years, revolutions and assassinations terminated ten military presidencies, and in Peru another withdrew "legally."[1] It is true that these military leaders headed diverse regimes, including some virtual democracies, and that the disappearance of the leader did not always change the regime's character, as demonstrated by the situation in Nicaragua after the assassination of the not-very-military dictator Somoza in 1956. These regimes were often military only in the sense of the president's profession and by virtue of their origin, but they evolved in quite different directions. Should one attribute to a burst of antimilitarism the deposing of Perón, who was a legally reelected constitutional president, or the overthrow of the personal tyranny of Pérez Jiménez in Venezuela, of General Magloire of Haiti, or of Colonel J. M. Lemus in El Salvador, even if all of these military leaders, like Batista in Cuba and Rojas Pinilla in Colombia, had been at least at a certain point the army's choice to occupy executive office? What should one say, after this ebbing of the tide, about the military wave which from March 1962 (Argentina) to November 1964 (Bolivia) and June 1966 (Argentina, again) put an end to civil regimes in nine of the continent's countries? Was it a prolongation or a phenomenon of another kind when, at the beginning of the 1970s, a series of coups d'état hit countries with solid traditions of civil government that some had estimated to have been "definitively" demilitarized (Chile and Uruguay), while in Argentina a new military intervention assumed a violent nature unprecedented in that nation's history?

As of 1976–77, democracy seemed to be making some headway once again. The time was apparently ripe for some liberalization of military rule and even the return of civilians to power. If one judges merely on the basis of figures, in 1978 twelve electoral consultations took place on the continent. This intense electoral activity seemed to augur a return to representative procedures. In fact, it ranged from authoritarian plebiscites to competitive elections, and included some ambiguous cases in between. The Chilean referendum and the fifth reelection of President Stroessner are far from indicating the termination of despotic systems. In Venezuela and Colombia, elections occur regularly and hardly constitute remarkable events. In Brazil, legislative elections took place in a framework of conditions and restrictions designed to assure regime continuity, but they were nevertheless unfavorable to the government. In Peru, Ecuador, and Bolivia, elections had the principal aim of preparing for the return of civilians to power, the free play of democratic institutions, and an orderly retreat of the military to their barracks.

This historical survey provides little support for unilineal and synchronic interpretations of military power, such as those described above. Nor do I believe that these movements in opposing directions condemn the states of the continent to an indefinite alternation between civil and military regimes. They indicate rather that the forms of demilitarization are complex and diverse, and that they may have their limits. Such an ebb and flow invites us to examine, without a priori assumptions and reassuring generalizations, the realities of demilitarization and, thus, the real impact of the militarization of the state. Does the phenomenon constitute a simple parenthesis without institutional consequences, after which, once the army returns to barracks, countries return to their previous regimes? Or, on the contrary, is it the case that the military do not withdraw until they judge that they have removed the political obstacles to a civil regime and created socioeconomic conditions favorable to the normal functioning of democratic institutions? I am inclined to be rather doubtful about either of these scenarios, and feel it necessary to examine empirically the outcome of postmilitarism in all its ambiguity.

The Exception and the Rule

Reference has often been made to the instability of concentrated power. Institutionally, military regimes—even when they appear to be the most common form of domination in a country—nevertheless remain "exceptional," paradoxical though this may seem. In effect, the official and dominant ideology throughout the continent is liberal and democratic. The incessant transformation of military regimes and the limited duration of noncivilian governments derive in part from their illegitimacy as perceived by the principal actors involved. In the Latin American normative and cultural context, those who hold military power know that, whatever they say, there still exists above them a superior legitimacy, that of the constitutional order. Not only can they not claim its support, but they also must ultimately pay lip service to it.[2] In fact, military regimes are only really legitimized by their future. If elected governments have legitimacy by virtue of their origin, de facto governments have legitimacy only by the way they exercise power, and almost, one might say, by the performance they ultimately accomplish. The past may be used to justify the arrival of the military in power, but customary references to political and social chaos, to the vacuum of power, and to menaces of every kind, still reflect objectives that must eventually be attained or outcomes that must finally be avoided. The military regime, therefore, always lives for the future. It is, in essence, transitory. A permanent system of military rule is almost a contradiction in terms.[3] The army cannot govern directly and durably without ceasing to be an army. And it is precisely the subsequent government, the successor regime, that legitimates the prior military usurpation.

Even if one makes a relatively arbitrary distinction between provisional (or caretaker) governments and constituent military regimes, in neither case has the historical experience been based on an explicitly avowed intention to create a new type of state, a definitive and durable mode of exercising political power. The democratic regime has been and still remains more legitimate in Latin America than this omnipresent state of exception. Contemporary Latin American military regimes differ notably in this regard from the dictatorships that Europe or other continents have known in modern times, precisely because of their constitutional precariousness. They do not pretend to create a new legitimacy, to construct a new system of political values on the ruins of the old. The European authoritarian regimes between 1920 and 1945 had the ambition of founding a "new order" in opposition to liberalism and democracy, of creating a "thousand-year Reich." The Latin American military dictatorships of today are first of all regimes without a stable justifying ideology. The "doctrine of national security" which in one form or another is shared by these institutionalized military governments provides a discourse or language that serves temporarily to disguise their illegitimacy, but it is incapable of generating a new and permanent source of legitimacy. Moreover, the doctrine has above all performed the internal function of forging and mobilizing a consensus within the military institution, around the alarmist image inherent to the profession of arms. Its hypotheses concerning internal war, by enlarging the specter of threats and by situating them inside national society, provide an institutional basis for the army's intervention, but they do not explain it. Such hypotheses may justify a more or less enduring occupancy of the posts of national leadership, but they do not establish a new basis of power. Briefly, the theory of national security cannot substitute for a legitimating ideology. Neither the consistency of the theory, nor the extent of its diffusion, nor the constitutive nature of its functions permits such a substitution.

Representative democracy always remains on the horizon for these regimes. They must invoke it for their own legitimation and in their own policy objectives, while at the same time proposing to improve, reinforce, amend, and even protect it, but never to annihilate or destroy it as has been the case elsewhere. Such an observation holds for the Brazilian *sistema*, which has always preserved (under careful supervision) parties, elections, and a legislative assembly—not to mention the archaic militarism of Stroessner, who, like all of the classic dictators on the continent, has himself regularly reelected to the presidency, and tolerates (under strict surveillance) a decorative multiparty system. In Uruguay and Argentina also, the proclamations, declarations, projects, and maneuvers of the ruling military refer to no political system and no source of legitimacy other than those identified with representative democracy. The justification is certainly superficial—a facade behind which quite different practices are promoted—but for all that, it serves to contradict martial messianism and undermine any idea of permanent military rule. No matter how central their position in the political system and how great their autonomy of decision-making, the governing military are constrained by the political culture of the dominant internal or external classes, whose self-interested liberalism constitutes a restraint on the organicist tendencies of the men in uniform. It is as if the dominant classes believe that the reestablishment of the market in economic matters cannot really be legitimized unless accompanied by a certain restoration of the market in political affairs.

Thus, in Argentina, all of the corporatist and antiliberal overtones of the military in power—from Uriburu in 1930 to Onganía in 1966–70—have only provoked a defensive rallying of the economic and social establishment, and the replacement of the "anticonstitutionalist" generals by more liberal members of the military.[4] In Uruguay, Bordaberry, the civilian president of a military dictatorship imposed by the "slow-motion" coup d'état of 1973, was dismissed by the high command in June 1976 for advocating "new institutions" in opposition to "the most cherished democratic traditions of the country." He had in effect pushed the logic of "military sovereignty" to the limit by proposing in a memo the suppression of the party system, and the introduction of a new authoritarian state in which the armed forces alone would assure legitimacy. Although they have militarized power, and have promoted the hypertrophy of the nation's defense institutions and an unlimited expansion of their responsibilities, Uruguay's generals will not for one moment renounce the fiction of a civil executive. Uruguay, the garrison state, has a nonmilitary president and a government from which officers are practically absent. The parties are only suspended, and the text of the constitutional referendum of 30 November 1980, although it made the participation of the armed forces in executive power official, also anticipated the legalization of the two traditional parties and a return to limited and purified representative procedures. The rejection by the electorate of this plan after the pretense of a campaign had the merit of showing that the military had been correct not to underestimate the vigor and appeal of the party system—even after seven years of prohibition and adverse propaganda. The strength of the party system was also demonstrated by the Peruvian elections of May 1980 and the Argentine elections of 1973, after twelve and seven years, respectively, of suspension of institutionalized political competition.[5]

The government presided over by General Pinochet since September 1973 in Chile figures among the most antiliberal military regimes in Latin America, and among those which concede the least to even the rhetoric of democracy. Indeed, the authoritarian discourse of the Chilean military—their insistence on the need for new institutions—is reminiscent of Franco's Spain. Corporatist inclinations are expressed without concealment by advisers and those responsible for the "hard" line of the regime—the "renovators," as they call themselves—who reject absolutely the parliamentary and partisan institutions in force until 1973. Immediately after the coup d'état, General Pinochet himself promised a new constitution that would "dispense forever with politicians, sectarianism, and demagogy."[6] The minister of the interior declared in September 1975 that "all political parties . . . act only to divide citizens, to favor demagogically their adherents and to cause the soul of the nation to deteriorate." The influential newspaper *Mercurio*, spokesman for the moderates (*blandos*) and partisan of a limited opening, commented on these remarks: "The government desires the annihilation or progressive disappearance of parties."[7] But although the constitutional debate on the aims and timetables of the Plan of Chacarillas (July 1977) may have encouraged the hopes of the "hard-liners" for the establishment of an "authoritarian democracy," the constitution submitted to a plebiscite on 11 September 1980, apart from the gradualism and the restriction of liberties that it imposes, nevertheless anticipates in the relatively distant future (1989) the establishment of a representative system, including parties, a congress, and a president elected by universal suffrage. Needless to say, this juridical structure is intended above all to justify the permanence in power of General Pinochet himself. But the reliance upon a constitutional text of noncorporatist inspiration and the fixing of a time limit to exceptional rule are sufficient to prove that, even in the Chilean case, the antiliberal temptation and the wish definitively to exclude the "vanquished" politicians of 1973 must be accommodated within the dominant democratic ideology.

These attempts to place representative practices under strong surveillance differ fundamentally from the ways and means adopted by dictatorships outside the continent to achieve the same objectives. If one compares the regime of General Franco with that of General Pinochet, the similarities may catch one's attention at first, but the differences are nonetheless important. These two counterrevolutionary systems both sought to break with the previous political situation, to deny open expression to political dissidents, and to exclude the "defeated" from power forever, by prolonging the victorious coalition (of the coup d'état or civil war) via the unlimited personal authority of the leader of the successful military operation.[8] But in the case of Franco, antipluralism made no concessions for forty years, except at the summit of state power and within his technocratic-bourgeois coalition. Liberal democracy was perpetually condemned without regard for internal developments or the international context. Franco, caudillo of Spain "by the grace of God," never tolerated even incidental questioning of his permanence in power. Neither the referendum of 1947 nor that of 1966 posed the question of choosing the chief of state, or of setting the length of his mandate. Furthermore, the opposition eventually accepted the idea that the dictatorship was lifelong and that a change of regime could only take place after the caudillo's death.[9] General

Pinochet, for his part, has stipulated the duration of his provisional regime (only after four years in power, it is true), whatever may be his real intentions for the future, and he has not excluded the revival of parties and of competitive elections, although tempering the possibility of such developments by diverse prohibitions designed "to protect democracy." This example is proof, in my view, that one cannot create a new legitimacy just as one wishes in an environment that is hostile to such ideological adventures. With this awareness of the limits of state militarization in Latin America, let us now examine the extent to which demilitarization is being accomplished, at what level, with what scope, and the kinds of regimes being established when the state is demilitarized.

The Postmilitary State and the Forms of Institutionalization

An analysis of the retreat of the army from power discloses diverse phenomena. Civilianization of the military state, however extensive, is by no means the same as a return to "democratic normality." For purposes of comparative equivalence, I will only examine the transformation of systems of extensive military domination—that is, regimes initiated by force in which the sovereignty of military institutions is exercised collectively and controls not only the selection of the executive but the making of all major policy decisions. I will therefore leave aside authoritarian regimes of other kinds, patrimonial or partisan, even though coercion and officer participation play large parts in them.

I also set aside, almost from the start, a first type of demilitarization—that brought about by force through a civilian *pronunciamiento*. In general, it is the military who overthrow regimes of their peers by violence (or sometimes, and indeed most frequently, by the threat of violence). Some personal dictatorships, patrimonial autocracies, and postmilitary tyrannies have been driven out by uprisings of civilians, occasionally allied with factions of the armed forces. I will not go back to Peru in the nineteenth century or to the civilian *montoneras* of Piérola. It was a combined civil and military revolution that overthrew General Ubico and his brief successor in Guatemala in 1944. That same year, in El Salvador, students and soldiers put an end to the dictatorship of Hernández Martínez. It was guerrillas and, therefore, civilians who fought Somoza's National Guard in 1979 and put an end to the dynasty in Nicaragua, repeating in different circumstances the Cuban precedent. But among institutionalized military governments, only that of Bolivia in 1952 was overthrown by civilians. The military junta that annulled the electoral victory of Paz Estenssoro's Movimiento Nacionalista Revolucionario (MNR) was in effect routed in the streets of La Paz. In this case, the relatively low level of effective militarization of power was followed by a drastic demilitarization. The Bolivian army was largely dismantled. Its officers were violently purged and, hence, rendered harmless to the new revolutionary civilian government.

The most common form of demilitarization, however, consists of leaving military structures in place while attempting to remove the armed forces from power. For reasons both external and internal to the institutions of the armed forces, direct military government cannot be made permanent, so that the continuity of martial power requires additional developments. We can group these into two dominant tendencies: personalization and legalization. Both of these models may, but need not necessarily, be linked to a democratic opening, which itself may be either real or a facade.

The transfer of power to a military leader who personally dominates the established hierarchy constitutes one means of subordinating the armed institutions to the executive and of returning the army to its professional tasks. The transition from the impersonal power of an institution to the personal power of a man, even a general, is never accomplished easily. This personalization of power is naturally less difficult the less bureaucratized the military institution. Somoza, *jefe director* of the National Guard of Nicaragua, and Trujillo, *generalíssimo* of the Dominican army, "personalized" the neocolonial military institutions that had been placed in their hands. This personalization had occurred before they assumed power. It was an act performed in their own name and not in the name of the military as such. Personalization occurred quite differently in Bolivia in 1964, when Barrientos had to prevail over his rivals by ratifying his power as "first among equals" through an electoral mobilization in which he appropriated a specific historico-military legitimacy (the Chaco tradition) and created a basis of popular support that was partly personal in character (the military-peasant pact). The eventual establishment of Barrientos as constitutional president served to prolong the military junta at the same time as it represented an extension of the preceding legal regime in which the "putschist" general had served as vice-president. General Banzer had less success than his predecessor when he attempted to repeat the operation. Having come to power as a result of a coup d'état in 1971, he governed until 1974 with a section of the political class at the head of a conservative coalition. When, in 1974, he reshuffled his government and replaced the civilian politicians of the MNR and the Falange with military officers, he seemed to have emerged with enhanced personal power, but in practice the army had once again taken over the state apparatus.[10] After having announced presidential elections at various intervals from 1974 onward, General Banzer had to resign in 1978 when the army insisted that he not be a candidate in the election he was organizing. He then supported Juan Pereda, his former minister of interior, and the hopelessly divided armed forces proclaimed their neutrality. The ensuing elections of July 1978 were immediately followed by a coup d'état led by the "official" winner, a weakly legitimated and fraudulently elected successor of a military power structure that had been incompetently institutionalized.

Democratic procedures may also enable a military regime that has fallen into an impasse to find a legal means for self-perpetuation in power. In Argentina in 1945, the regime born of a coup d'état in 1943 was caught in an apparently fatal crossfire between internal and external oppositions strengthened by the defeat of the Axis powers. Nevertheless, one officer among their ranks, the "workers' colonel," was at the height of his personal popularity. Ill-regarded by one part of the army, which rejected his prolabor stance and opposed his political ambitions, Perón still presented his candidacy for the presidency in free elections, and thereby offered an honorable way out to the institution that had brought him to power and that he sought to represent. The "revolutionary" officers of 1943, even though hostile to Perón, had no choice but to accept the return of the traditional parties and the candidacy of the man who had used the vice-presidency in the military government as a stepping stone to elected office. Moreover, Perón, throughout his first presidency, took great care to draw attention to his military investiture, and sought to appear as the successor to the "Revolution of 4 June 1943." Thus, by an electoral sanction favorable to the candidate of the army or to one who presents himself as such, the military institution can recover its coherence and cease in principle to be directly responsible for policy. Vertical discipline can impose itself once again, reestablishing internal unity after a period of deterioration. Demilitarization may stop here, or it may, on the contrary, be pursued and extended as a result of alternative political resources which become available to the elected military leader, to the point that he can sometimes end up cutting himself off dangerously from his support in the armed forces. This is what happened to Perón after 1951.

The transfer of power to a military head of state may permit demilitarization without immediately leading to dangerous and uncertain electoral procedures. Usurpation by the military institution can culminate in the dictatorship of one man. This outcome is what seems to be evolving today in Chile. Since 1977, there has been a prolongation of the military regime, reflecting the tutelary role in which the armed forces have found themselves, and confirming the absolute power of General Pinochet. His irresistible ascension, which has relegated the junta to a merely legislative and constituent role, was skillfully promoted by the success of the January 1978 referendum, whose text, imposed on the other members of the junta, stipulated: "I support General Pinochet."

In the Chilean case, it may be argued that the high level of professionalization and the limited political experience of the armed forces are not unrelated to this process of personalized institutionalization of the military regime. Hierarchical discipline has substituted for political consensus. Fear of a return of the "vanquished" has cemented cohesion around a single leader who symbolizes a counterrevolutionary policy questioned by no one in the army. This fear may explain the feeble response to the criticisms made by General Leigh, the air force representative in the junta, with regard to General Pinochet's political projects, and the subsequent lack of response to Leigh's dismissal in 1978, which was accompanied by the early retirement or resignation of eighteen of the twenty-one air force generals. The slowness of the "constitutional itinerary" and the persistence of international isolation have had the effect of reinforcing military support for an "institutionalization without opening" that, nevertheless, gives the army essential guarantees. The army may no longer govern Chile, but it is still not very far from power, and above all it continues to regard itself as an integral part of the power structure.

Most often, what is called the institutionalization of a military regime involves its legalization within the constitutional framework. This transformation, which has certain features in common with a return to democracy and which may be associated with a certain liberalization of political practices, signifies that the political power of the military is embedded purely and simply within an institutional framework which is presumed to be legitimate. The military then uses that framework to dispose of the major sources of uncertainty inherent in the democratic process. These processes may lead— as, for example, in Guatemala—to "military governments which are at the same time elected, constitutional, and anti-democratic."[11] This legalization generally takes place according to two modalities: either a controlled and coercive multiparty system or the creation of a dominant military party.

This last formula is well illustrated by the system in operation in El Salvador from 1950 to October 1979, the date of General Carlos Humberto Romero's overthrow by a civil and military junta. The military in power in 1948 attempted to imitate the Mexican Institutionalized Revolutionary Party (PRI), but without its popular base, by creating an official party, PRUD (Revolutionary Party of Democratic Unification), a true party of colonels.[12] The Party of National Conciliation (PCN) which succeeded it was both the partisan expression of the military institution and its electoral prolongation.[13] But it was also the party of the state, in which, under the aegis of the army, transactions between civilian or military bureaucracies and the dominant class were carried out. With alternations between political openings and restrictions on political competition, notably whenever the PCN lost ground, this "military party" subsequently controlled political life, obtained a parliamentary majority, and caused a colonel or a general to be elected to the presidency—although not without occasional resort to visible fraud, as in 1972. PCN's defeat by the opposition in 1972 revealed the decline of this partially open electoral system. The resort to fraud, repression, and limitation of electoral competition which followed revealed the importance and decay of the machinery created to assure the legal continuity of the military-controlled state.

The institutionalization of General Torrijos's nationalist military regime in Panama seems to have followed a parallel path to that of the Salvadorean colonels—despite differences in political orientation. The Democratic Revolutionary party (PRD), launched by its partisans nearly ten years after the national guard's 1968 coup d'état against the traditional oligarchic parties, seemed also to aspire to transform itself into a Mexican-styled institutionalized party. Its success in the legislative elections of 1978 permitted the new civilian president, elected by the Assembly, to democratize the regime without taking great risks.[14] Will the renaissance of competitive political life eventually take place at the expense of PRD, and will the process of democratization extend to acceptance of an eventual defeat of the official party? By retaining personal command of the national guard, General Torrijos remained the strong man of Panama in the classic Central American tradition of military *caudillismo* and *continuismo*, and such outcomes seemed quite unlikely. It was whispered in Panama that the new president, Aristides Royos, was no more than the transitory occupant of a six-year term conceded by Torrijos.[15] The latter's unexpected death in 1981, of course, may have upset these calculations.

The fluid politico-military situation in Honduras offers us a singular case of an attempt at institutionalization within a traditional two-party arrangement. As in Peru, the reformist military officers who came to power in December 1972 found themselves confronted by conservative demands for a return to normal political practices. After the eviction of General López Arellano, and then of his successor, Melgar Castro, in August 1978 the government of the armed forces entered a third stage which put an end to the cycle of reforms. The conservative National party, which supported the new government, offered to play the role of a "military party, that is to say, a civilian organization through which the military could continue to exercise power."[16] For this, elections were necessary. They took place on 20 April 1980, but gave an unexpected victory to the traditional Liberal adversaries of the National party. Thanks to Liberal goodwill and international circumstances, this vote of protest against the military did not have the predictable consequence of provoking a coup d'état to annul the "unwelcome" results. Liberal and Conservative deputies joined forces to elect General Paz García, head of the military junta, to the provisional presidency of the Republic until subsequent elections could be held after the drafting of a new constitution, and the winning party accepted a minority position in the intervening government.[17]

In Guatemala, the state has been profoundly militarized. The army not only occupies power but also fulfills numerous civilian functions, and constitutes a veritable bureaucratic bourgeoisie. The military high command supervises nominations to all posts of responsibility.[18] In spite of more or less regular competitive elections, there is no single and distinctive military party. But in 1974 all three presidential candidates were generals. Since the overthrow of Arbenz, the progressive civilian president, by Castillo Armas in 1954, "anti-Communist" governments supported by the army have occupied power with or without popular ratification. Since 1970, in a climate of increasing violence, generals have regularly acceded to the presidency as a result of elections which the army always manages to win. The same scenario is repeated with variations: the armed forces choose a candidate who will necessarily become the chief executive. They then negotiate with one or two parties on the Right or extreme Right which provide the incumbent with his label and his electoral base. Pluralist competition is limited to a "constitutional arc" from which the parties of the Left are banished by definition.[19] In 1970 General Carlos Arana Osorio was elected president with the support of the Movement of National Liberation (MLN), "the party of organized violence" and of counterterrorism; in 1974 General Kjell Laugerud was the candidate of a coalition of the MLN and the Institutional Democratic party (PID); in 1978, the ironically named Revolutionary party allied itself with the PID in order to elect General Romeo Lucas García. It seems that only Arana Osorio really won any of these elections. His successors owed their accession to power to fraud or to strong-arm measures by the previous government. For example, in 1974 General Laugerud certainly obtained fewer votes than General Ríos Montt, but the government had his election ratified by Congress.[20] Ríos Montt, having insufficient support in the army, had to leave the country. These legal and constitutional governments are therefore really the expression of an institutionalized military state in its "controlled and coercive multiparty" mode. But simultaneously they represent a type of demilitarization that may alternatively close or open in the direction of establishing less exclusionary systems.

The evolution of Brazil illustrates both the ambiguities and the opportunities of a redemocratization controlled by military power in which the military have not suppressed formal democratic procedures, even if they have emptied them of much of their content. The policy of "decompression" and "opening" undertaken since 1974 by General Geisel and pursued by his successor, General Figueiredo, has provoked an undeniable liberalization, involving the suppression of dictatorial powers given to the president by Institutional Act No. 5, the suppression of censorship, an amnesty, a return of political exiles, and the reestablishment of direct elections for governors and senators. These were all stages of a "gradual" democratization managed by the government at a rhythm of their own choosing. The reactivation of civil society and the enlargement of the arena of political tolerance (as demonstrated by the proliferation of extreme Left publications which now circulate legally) may nevertheless be perceived as forming a new strategy of institutionalization following the failure of the compulsory two-party system installed after 1965. The continual electoral progress of the tolerated opposition (the Brazilian Democratic Movement—MDB) and the poor showing since the legislative elections of 1974 of the official party, ARENA (National Renovating Alliance), created a delicate and potentially uncontrollable situation for those in power. Some strategists of the regime thought that a well-regulated opening could assure continuity by limiting from the outset the "plebiscitary deadlock" which the regime had created for itself because of its identification with ARENA and the existence of a clear two-party choice offered to the electorate.[21] Some observers have argued that the return of the pre-1964 leaders to political activity and the restoration of a multiparty system are measures calculated to split the MDB and, thus, to weaken the opposition while ostensibly freeing it.[22] Although the new law on parties has not succeeded for the moment in completely isolating the Left by provoking profound political regroupings, it has favored the formation of two more conservative parties—the Social Democratic party (PDS), party of the president, and a moderate, centrist opposition, the Brazilian Popular party (PPB). This new range of parties could make possible an alternation in power without risks, acceptable to the military on condition that the more militant opposition was divided or, even better, atomized. But the prohibition of "electoral alliances" designed to prevent the formation of a united opposition compelled the PPB to merge with the MDB, thus complicating the regime's calculations. The continued good showing of the MDB (now transformed into the PMDB), was not part of the plan, and the rise of an unexpected "Workers' party" (PT) complicated the intended opening even more.

Such an opening of the electoral arena constitutes a novel legitimation tactic by an isolated regime that is in crisis, and that is looking for an enlarged base of support. According to this scenario, "slow and gradual" democratization would in no way be the prelude to a transformation of the "system," but would prolong the existing practice of changing the rules of the game when the previous ones had become disadvantageous. This new manifestation of *casuismo* and flexibility by a regime which is a past master in elections at the game of "whoever loses, wins," could produce, in spite of all its built-in safeguards, certain unexpected consequences which could in the longer run affect its very nature.[23] As Fernando Henrique Cardoso so rightly points out, until now "it was the system which legitimized the parties."[24] Now the parties have become essential elements in the functioning of the regime, to the point at which the head of state is regarded as a party leader. Within this framework, liberalization could have its own dynamic. The utilization of authoritarian measures to contain a tolerated democracy could become unfeasible—it is only by playing the electoral game that the project can result in something, and bring the regime what it needs: legitimation. An eventual authoritarian regression would cause the political dividends of the strategy to be lost. Restricted political liberalization may not remain compatible with a potentially uncontrollable social opening now that long-repressed and delayed popular demands have burst spontaneously into view. The repression of major strikes in April–May 1980 and of free trade unions seems to indicate that the regime does not intend to modify its control over the "dangerous classes" bequeathed by Vargas's *Estado novo*, which had hardly been modified during the "democratic experience" of 1946 to 1964. Will this authoritarian resource remain in reserve, and does it indicate the limits beyond which liberalization will not be allowed to go? Is this, indeed, the social price to be paid in order to make the political opening irreversible? Whatever the case, it would seem that the regime does not intend to hold back, or to lose the initiative. It holds all the trump cards, and seems to assume that democracy will work in its favor. What is being created, then, is not so much a restricted democracy but rather a democracy in which those in power cannot lose.[25] The key test evidently remains the presidential succession. The renaissance of civil society and the reactivation of the parties and of parliamentary life, by reducing the scope of authoritarianism, also reduce the space for military sovereignty. The regime is changing its nature, but to whom will power ultimately belong?

Civil Government and Military Power

While one can see the ambiguous character of controlled liberalization without rupture, one must also be aware of the opportunities provided by the conservation of even a democratic facade. Both imply a certain degree and form of demilitarization. In the recent history of Latin America, noninstitutionalized military governments have generally agreed to withdraw from power only in the context of certain guarantees. They have endeavored, to the best of their ability, to fix the subsequent rules of the game. What is more, they have not hesitated, when the situation permitted it, to demand a place for the military institutions in the constitutional structure of the emergent democracy and, hence, a permanent right to supervise ensuing political decisions. The plan for a constitution proposed by the Uruguayan military in the referendum of 30 November 1980 was intended to provide just such a juridical basis to their de facto power, by stipulating that the National Security Council (COSENA), made up of senior officers, would have the right to challenge the conduct of members of both the executive and legislative branches of power, without itself being responsible to any higher authority, and that it could intervene in "matters relating to national security" and even (with the president) declare a "state of emergency" without reference to Parliament, except a posteriori.[26] As we know, this tutelary democracy was rejected by the electorate after having been condemned by a spectrum of parties ranging from the Broad Front on the Left to the traditional *Blanco* and *Colorado* organizations.[27]

In 1972, the Argentine military, in power since 1966, faced a climate of crisis. In order to avoid an uncontrollable social explosion, it was decided to organize elections without proscriptions for the first time since 1955. But the military wanted to avoid an electoral "leap in the dark," which, according to them, could allow a return to the "disastrous errors of the past." To this end, General Lanusse, president of the government of the armed forces, sought to obtain a series of guarantees from civilian political forces which would have given the army the upper hand. The military, in search of an honorable outcome, even made the holding of elections conditional on a "Grand National Accord" of all the political groups under their aegis. A military candidate of transition and national unity would have suited the high command. When the political groups rejected any institutionalization of military participation in the reestablished democracy, and the attempts at generating an official candidate had failed, the military, *in extremis*, insisted on a double guarantee. They reformed the electoral law to institute two rounds of voting for the presidential election if a majority was not obtained the first time, and imposed a residence clause which effectively would have prevented Perón from becoming a candidate. This accumulation of safeguards and stratagems imposed by the de facto regime hardly elicited much support from the political forces. Finally, the junta of the commanders-in-chief issued a declaration, in the absence of an agreement, which recorded the principles that the military wanted to have respected. This text foresaw that the armed forces would oppose, among other things, an "indiscriminate amnesty" of subversives, and it anticipated that the armed forces would have to "share governmental responsibilities."[28]

In reality, the regime had already lost the initiative. The massive electoral victory of the Peronist candidate swept away the restraints placed by the departing government. The slogan "Campora to government, Perón to power" rendered ridiculous the proscriptive clause imposed by the generals. In spite of their own electoral law, the military declared the Peronist candidate, Campora, elected, even though he had received only 49.5 percent of the votes, in order to avoid the humiliation they would have faced in a second presidential round, in all likelihood even more agitated and more massively hostile to the holders of power. The two political parties against which the coup d'état of 1966 had been directed (the Peronists and the Radicals) together received 70 percent of the suffrage. The semiofficial candidate of the armed forces did not even get 3 percent of the votes! The group of candidates who collectively represented continuity scarcely surpassed 18 percent.[29] What is more, the new government promulgated an immediate general amnesty, and the elected president refused all institutional suggestions regarding the choice of men charged with representing the armed forces. Command over the army was even disrupted by the nomination of a commander-in-chief who did not come from the cavalry, the branch that had dominated it since 1960.

In Ecuador, *mutatis mutandis*, the military (which had come to power in 1972) withdrew while trying to impose conditions analogous to those of the Argentine army. The Ecuadorian military, having decided to return the government to civilians after a palace revolution in 1976 which removed General Guillermo Rodríguez Lara from office, announced their wish to give the country a truly representative democracy. Nevertheless, the junta took its own precautions, or rather tried to establish a democratic system which would conform to the military's image and interests. The transition process was thus marked by a stately slowness: it would last not less than three years and began by excluding from the election the three most representative candidates considered by the army to be dangerous demagogues. As an added precaution, an electoral law was promulgated in February 1978, providing that the future president must not be a previous incumbent. This restriction deprived both Velasco Ibarra, an eternal caudillo who had already been elected president five times, and Carlos Julio Arosamena of any future. Yet another ad hoc clause stipulated that the future president must be an Ecuadorian and the child of an Ecuadorian. This requirement was specifically directed against Assad Bucarám, head of the Concentration of Popular Forces and one of the leading potential candidates, who was the son of a Lebanese. This populist leader, who enjoyed great support among the subproletariat of Guayaquil, was the heavy favorite in the election, as he had previously been in 1972 at the time of the coup d'état.

This use of the veto and control over candidacies, contrary to democratic norms, augured poorly for the reestablishment of a legitimate and constitutional regime. The imposition of voting in two rounds, on the French model, leaving only the two leading candidates in the competition at the second stage, was apparently intended to promote a united front of conservatives. The interlude of nearly ten months between the two rounds, and the numerous incidents that accompanied the campaign, hardly gave grounds for hoping that the results would be respected if they did not correspond to the wishes of the military. More especially, the military's support for Sixto Durán, the conservative candidate, was almost visible, while Bucarám, excluded, was represented by proxy, through his nephew by marriage, Jaime Roldós. Eventually, after an obstacle-ridden process as difficult as it was uncertain, it was Roldós who won the election and who became the constitutional president of Ecuador in August 1979, without the military attempting to question the result of the vote.

It does not always work out this way. The military appear not to accept withdrawal unless the civil government that replaces them is similar to their own policies or preferences, or unless the elections produce a victory for their own candidate. In any other cases, the result may be invalidated either immediately or eventually, after a period of observation, when circumstances are more propitious. According to the formulation of François Bourricaud, the multiplication of "contentious elections" expresses this *continuista* behavior. The agitated political life of Bolivia from 1978 to 1980 illustrates this tendency well. General Banzer's official candidate in the election of 9 July 1978, General Pereda, was the author of a coup d'état on 21 July designed to assure his "victory"—a victory whose legality was strongly contested, notably by the moderate left-wing candidate, Siles Suazo. In November 1978, the constitutionalist sector of the army, led by General Padilla, overthrew General Pereda and organized new elections, which were held in June 1979. Since these elections did not yield a clear majority, the president of the Senate became head of state. The process of constitutionalization pursued its course until 1 November 1979, when Colonel Natusch Busch seized power but was compelled to resign after a fortnight. He was replaced by the president of the Chamber of Deputies, Mrs. Lydia Gueiler. New elections were held on 29 June 1980, and marked a clear shift to the Left. Siles Suazo, who was ahead with a Center-Left coalition, would have been ratified by Congress as head of state on 4 August. General Banzer, who had presented himself as a candidate in these elections, had obtained only 15 percent of the votes. However, on 17 July 1980 a bloody and overpowering coup d'état installed General García Meza as president of the Republic. The "putschists" no longer speak of elections. Their primary stated objective, to "extirpate the Marxist cancer," postpones any form of institutionalization to a nebulous future.

Unable to impose their preferred form of government and prolong their ascendancy, the armed forces may qualify their withdrawal by insisting on corporative defense measures which would impede the reestablishment of civilian supremacy in all domains. Thus the "postmilitary" civilian regime may rule only if elected authorities agree not to exercise control over military appointments. Such an affirmation of military autonomy is a frequent legacy of the militarization of power, and a standard price paid for the return of the military to their barracks. In Peru, President Belaúnde, elected after the military interlude of 1962, was required in 1963 to designate as commander-in-chief of each branch of the army the highest ranking officer and to nominate military ministers, in accord with the wishes of the high command. In Ecuador, shortly before the first round of presidential elections in July 1978, the military reformed the organic law of the armed forces and decreed that the future president would have to name as minister of defense the officer occupying the highest position in the hierarchy.[30]

A military defeat at the polls accompanied by a veritable rout in the face of exasperated public opinion, such as occurred in Argentina in March–May 1973, may not guarantee a return to full representative democracy, even if the army respects the results of the elections. The demilitarization of government need not signify demilitarization of power if the military have entrenched themselves as quasilegitimate actors in the political game. Thus from 1973 to 1976, Argentine military leaders, apparently routed by Peronism and swept aside by the electoral landslide, in fact "accompanied" the evolution of the political situation step by step. It was only after the high command restored Perón to his rank of general and gave him the green light that Perón deposed his proxy, Campora. Under subsequent commanders-in-chief, the army was still a force in public life, regardless of its more or less strong inclination toward neutrality when faced with a regime that rapidly fell apart after the death of the "leader." The effort by Mrs. Perón's government to attract military participation, and therefore legitimacy, provoked a serious crisis in August 1975, and was a prelude to the eventual collapse of civilian power. The ostentatious political neutrality of the Argentine high command was revealed in March 1976 to have been a mere facade behind which they were preparing the way for a subtle form of "putschist" intervention. Their theory of the "ripe fruit," and the military's complacency about allowing the situation to worsen, contradict any suggestion that the uprising of 1976 was either accidental or spontaneous.

These mock withdrawals from government by the Argentine army in no way signify that countries that have once known military power in the contemporary period are condemned to inevitable repetitions of it.[31] With its half-century of martial domination, Argentina is without doubt the extreme case of a militarized political system. Nevertheless, who would deny that the return to barracks is never definitive, and that the postmilitary state, whatever its degree of democracy, continues to live in the shadow of the barracks? This reality conditions the conduct of civilian actors. They always face the alternatives of discouraging a putsch or attempting to provoke one. No one knocks on the barracks doors who is not sure there is some chance of being asked to enter. But there is nothing inevitable about the outcome. To defer a military intervention is to affirm civilian power and to make militarist usurpation more and more difficult, thereby serving to demilitarize the political system. On the other hand, the permanent menace or fear of a putsch is a real form of intervention, as has been evident recently in Spain. Since Franco's death, allusions to military "tolerance" continue to fill political life, while the specter of Pavia's horse still haunts the Parliament.[32]

Demilitarization therefore has its degrees. The return of civilians to power is not automatically equivalent to the "civilianization" of power, even after free and representative elections. One may ask why, under what influences, and in what conditions the military hand over office to civilians, but one may also ask what explains the limitations on the process of "extricating" militarism from politics. We will first of all consider the reasons for the formal opening of systems dominated by the military, and then the causes of recurrent "praetorian" militarism.

The Moment of Civilian Politicians

The multiplicity of hypotheses that one might put forward with regard to the causes of transition from military authoritarian rule to civilian representative regimes in Latin America complicates all attempts at explanation. The political, social, and economic conditions generally listed as explanatory factors apply in fact to all sorts of authoritarianism, not just to the martial variety. Besides, a certain number of them seem of little explanatory value by reason of their reversibility, and even their "mythological" nature. It is by this latter term that Wanderley Guilherme dos Santos critically evaluates the contradictory economic interpretations of authoritarianism:

> It is thus that economic recessions are presented sometimes as an explanation of the erosion of authoritarianism, given that it would be impossible for these regimes—according to these theories—to coopt the masses and/or the elites via the distribution of advantages; sometimes the same recession is presented as an explanation of the survival of authoritarianism, given that only authoritarian procedures may be possible if one has to suppress popular demands, in a context of acute penury. Inversely, high rates of economic growth and accumulation have been used both to explain the continuation of authoritarianism, since the regimes can thus anesthetize the population, and particularly the masses, via the distribution of new advantages, *and* to explain the erosion of authoritarian systems; on the argument that the social groups benefitting selectively from the growth will begin to demand a greater political participation. The erosion, just as the permanence of authoritarianism—political phenomena—are thus "inferred" as much from economic growth as from economic recession. When contrary processes simultaneously explain inverse results, they belong to the mythology of conventional classification.[33]

Deterministic hypotheses of closer and more immediate bearing seem at the same time both convincing and of little operational use. This is true of those interpretations of the recent "hesitations" of Latin American military regimes and of their tendencies toward liberalization and institutionalization which rely on the assumption that they have accomplished the process of "authoritarian restructuring of capitalism" which necessarily gave rise to them.[34] If one considers that Pinochet's Chile is the most accomplished example of such a transformation, to the point at which it has been possible to speak of a veritable "capitalist revolution," the recent evolution of the Chilean situation would seem to contradict the validity of this thesis. Both officials of the regime and a number of its more crucial civilian supporters have stated that there are still "objectives" to be attained rather than a timetable to be followed, even if in practice some not very restrictive timetable has been adopted. But the future prospect of the "seven modernizations," concerning the privatizing and "modernizing" of the essential sectors of national activity by denationalizing them (so as to establish the ascendancy of the market and to change mentalities), has not prevented the fixing of a calendar for the progressive construction of an institutionalized and representative polity.[35]

If it is evident that such factors as the behavior and expectations of the different actors, the range of political resources at the disposal of martial power, the duration of its ascendancy, and the initial justification for its emergence should be taken into consideration, the international hemispheric conjuncture and the processes internal to the military institutions also seem to merit serious consideration in any explanation of political changes occurring within systems of martial domination. Two sequences that appear contradictory, but are most often complementary, help to illuminate these transformations. One concerns the voluntarism and intentionality of the military actors, and relates to the overarching question of legitimacy which we have already discussed, as well as to the necessity of avoiding or obviating the risk of democratic uncertainty. The other, involving multiple social determinants as well as the particular functioning of "factions" and "parties" within the military, underlies the difficult, unprogrammed, and undetermined nature of the demilitarization process, the result of a series of perverse and accidental influences, of misunderstandings or errors by the protagonists.

It does not require much argument to demonstrate the importance of the hemispheric conjuncture as a factor affecting the diffusion and fluctuation, as well as the orientation, of martial power.[36] The hemispheric policy of the United States—the alternation after 1945 between anti-Communist vigilance and democratizing preoccupations of successive U.S. administrations—imparts a rhythm to the phases of autocracy and the waves of demilitarization which follow with only short time lags. Such policy does not diminish the role of internal dynamics in the more autonomous Latin American states, but does imply formal and other "cosmetic" adaptations in their case. If the overthrow of President Frondizi in Argentina in March 1962 was a response to strictly national conflicts dating back to 1955, the military "putschists" borrowed their justification from the defensive perspective outlined by the Pentagon in the framework of post–Cuban-Revolution strategic objectives, but disguised their illegitimacy with a legal cloak—by making Vice President Guido the president—in order to satisfy the criteria of respectability inherent in the

Alliance for Progress. In this case, the contract between the civilian reformism of Kennedy and the counterinsurrectionary antireformism of the hemispheric defense inspired by the Pentagon permitted a double reading of the politico-military process and resulted in a policy operating at two levels.

More recently in Bolivia, the failure of the 1 November 1979 putsch and the success of the 17 July 1980 coup d'état are not unrelated to the continental conjuncture and, hence, to U.S. policy. Colonel Natusch Busch was compelled to resign after a fortnight under pressure from the Carter administration, which was supporting the process of democratization. The member countries of the Andean Pact, forming a veritable democratic bloc, reinforced the stand of Washington by not recognizing the usurpers.[37] In July 1980 President Carter, at the end of his term and in mid-electoral campaign, could condemn only morally and feebly a determined and brutal military intervention which, itself, was anticipating the victory of his opponent. Observers have in fact remarked that General García Meza's coup took place the day after the Republican convention's nomination of Ronald Reagan, who was (and remains) the hope of all conservative forces on the continent.

More generally, it is appropriate for a martial regime to demilitarize and legalize itself somewhat—both by reason of the global ideology I alluded to earlier and by virtue of the specific nature of the military apparatus in its relationship to power. Not only do the internal tensions brought about by the tasks of government weaken corporative cohesion and thus the defensive capacities that provide the foundation for the (provisional) legitimacy of the military's usurpation of power, but they also reduce the political resources of the institution. In power, the military suffer a dangerous "desacralization." Furthermore, the overt, unconstitutional form of military governance is neither a necessity nor even a good solution for military power and those who support it. Such direct rule corresponds rather to a stage, to a moment of political domination. Legalization is the next stage. In terms of a cost-benefit analysis, the choice for the military involves a difficult equilibrium between the political costs deriving from the risks of democracy and the institutional costs required by martial authoritarianism. Consequently institutionalization only rarely implies the withdrawal of the military from power, and legalization does not often have complete and unrestricted democracy as its objective. On the contrary, the military withdrawal contains an element of continuity, and represents the accomplishment of the mission invoked to justify the initial intervention. The calling of elections, even if pluralism is not limited by the authorities, does not ipso facto entail the restoration or installation of an authentic democracy. If one adopts the definition of democratic procedures proposed by Schumpeter, according to which "it means only that the people have the opportunity of accepting or refusing the men who are to rule them," the postmilitary state is more likely to organize elections without surprises and without effects.[38] The true holders of power are not affected by them.

Moreover, the key figures in conservative military systems and their ideologues and allies explicitly reject the uncertainties of the democratic game. Their avowed ideal, of "protected democracy," reflects the search for an absolute guarantee against the risk of a legal advent to power by the adversaries of the status quo. One of the ideologues most listened to by successive Argentine military regimes wrote, after the overthrow of the civilian government in 1976, that the new governments of the Southern Cone were in the process of founding "future democracies on a bedrock of order and development."[39] The "hardliners" of the Chilean regime aspire, for their part, to put in place definite remedies against democratic subversion since, in the words of one of them, "one cannot always live on one's guard."[40] But the best "protection" of democracy is in fact the use—perverted, denatured, controlled—of democratic procedures to legitimize authoritarian rule. The well-established and stable postmilitary state gives rise, like all durable authoritarian regimes in Latin America, to semicompetitive political systems—that is, to systems in which open and uncontrolled competition is restricted to the periphery of power, while the real holders of power keep out of the way of the electoral contest.[41] This system presents its users with the legitimizing advantages of representative regimes without the risks of alternation or massive shifts in coalitional strength. It is clearly in this direction that military-dominated systems move when they have the opportunity and when they have not lost the initiative. The conservative military do not have a monopoly on this strategy, as demonstrated by the experience of Panama, which under populist Torrijos moved smoothly toward an exemplary semicompetitive system.

General Figueiredo's Brazil, with its gestures toward "decompression," seems to be tending toward such an outcome. Certainly the development of forces favorable to the liberalization of the regime, as well as the convergence of the tolerated political opposition with the industrial bourgeoisie and of the new middle class with the old political class, have played a role, but the system controlled the choice of instruments and the timing of initiatives. Moreover, Geisel's project consisted not only of splintering the opposition front by abolishing the two-party system but also of rendering the army politically autonomous. General Figueiredo was chosen by Geisel as a successor against the wishes of the military apparatus. The army lost its role as decisive elector. With the legitimacy of the military presence being contested by civil society,[42] as illustrated by the electoral results, it was undoubtedly opportune to provide a legal base for the system without recourse to the army. Demilitarization without risk is also evident in the care subsequently taken by General Geisel and the "palace group" surrounding him to separate within the army those with institutional responsibilities from those with military leadership roles (*chefia* against *lideranĉa*, to apply Rizzo de Oliveira's distinction),[43] in order to impose a bureaucratic hegemony on the armed forces and, most notably, in order to prevent the appearance of politico-military leaders possessing their own legitimacy and following.[44] This nondemocratic plan could, of course, escape the control of those who put it into operation. The "perfect political crime," in the words of an opposition deputy, could fail to be consummated. There is a narrow margin between risk and legitimacy. The maximum of uncertainty, and thus of electoral fair play, produces a maximum of legitimacy. Thus in Brazil the outcome is still uncertain despite the precautions taken by the regime. The direct election of state governors for the first time in November 1982 took place within the framework of liberalization as promised, but it did nothing to increase the legitimacy of those in power. The undeniable victory of the opposition in the richest and most populous states of the country's Center and South made even more ridiculous the pretense of a presidential election based on an ad hoc electoral college in which the regime is guaranteed a majority if its official party does not split under the pressure of public opinion massively demanding direct elections and substantially disaffected by the growing economic crisis. If the opposition obtains a majority in this rigged electoral college and defeats the government's candidate, then the limited democracy *(democradura)* will have been defeated. If not, what sort of legitimacy would such a badly elected president have to govern such a crisis-ridden country? In this case, tensions within the military establishment in the face of a revived civil society so buffeted by policies of economic austerity could provoke rather unexpected reactions.

In fact it is frequently the case that processes internal to the military apparatus shape the phases of demilitarization and open the way to eventual democratic alternation. A failure in the martial apparatus, a grave conflict within the officer corps, can condemn the project of institutionalization. An appeal may then be made to civilians and to democratic sanctions in order to escape from the impasse or to overcome further destabilizing splits. We do not wish to imply that the behavior of other actors is unimportant, or that the outcome of the processes of demilitarization-institutionalization is unaffected by other factors such as the duration of the noncivilian government, the circumstances of its installation, and the level of violence that it introduces into the society. But the return of the military to barracks is above all a military problem, and it would be somewhat paradoxical to study it without considering this decisive angle. It is evident that the erosion accompanying the exercise of power is more demoralizing for the military establishment as a state institution than for a political party, and that economic and social crises amplify its internal conflicts around military issues.[45]

A civilian restoration, accomplished by unconditional elections and without proscriptions, frequently comes about as the result of a change in the inner circle produced by a palace revolution. The project of the military which initially justified their seizure of power is thus overwhelmed after several years of uncertainty and indirection (three years in Argentina after 1970, three years, too, in Ecuador after 1976, but five years in Peru from 1975 to 1980). Then, the military have only to prepare their retreat in good order and with "honor." Military refusal to sustain a political orientation or to endorse a caudillista attempt often gives rise to intervals marked by multiple coups Thus, in Peru and Honduras in 1975, and in Ecuador in 1976, the conservative sector of the army opposed the military reformists in power, provoking the fall respectively of Velasco Alvarado, Rodríguez Lara, and López Arellano. But a second factor was the refusal, in the name of the corporative functioning of military power, to give a blank check to a man brought into government by the army. This factor has the same consequences. The two courses sometimes coincide, as in Peru. In the name of institutional rotation of the members of the executive—such as occurred in Brazil after 1964, and in Argentina after 1976—the Peruvian high command deposed Velasco Alvarado, who wanted to hold onto power beyond the time prescribed by military regulations and who had attempted to acquire a personal following. The changed alignment of the "military party," explicable according to certain observers in terms of the economic crisis and the urgency of negotiating with resurgent social forces, led to the restoration of democracy.[46] In the absence of charismatic resources and given the refusal to attempt any partisan mobilization, a bureaucratic system without support or project could only retreat or collapse. The regime of General Morales Bermúdez, bereft of partisan support and of the will to obtain it, nevertheless lasted five years, certainly representing an unprecedented case of "political levitation," but also illustrating the difficulties inherent in an orderly transfer of power when the internal military situation is so lacking in consensus.

In Argentina, after the overthrow of General Onganía, who had not fixed any limit on his power and who intended to place the army outside the government, General Lanusse, commander-in-chief and kingmaker, brought to power the ephemeral General Levingston. The latter broke with the liberal economic policy of his predecessor without having the means to do so and without specifying alternative goals for his government. It only remained for the high command to acknowledge the failure of the "Argentine revolution" by preparing the withdrawal of the army. The acute internal cleavages and the intensity of social tensions hardly permitted them anything other than to transfer the government to civilians or to throw themselves into a repressive assault, which internal conflicts within their ranks would scarcely allow.

In such cases, the resort to civilians and the opening up of free democratic competition without guarantees for the incumbents of government seem like the only outcome that would reconstitute the internal cohesion of the armed forces. An electoral consultation eases tensions and reunifies a military apparatus torn between contradictory tendencies and faced with the danger of the splintering and decomposition of their institution. It is not out of a taste for the paradoxical that, parodying the martial rhetoric, one may say that on such occasions, civil intervention puts a limit on military dissension. In the absence of a minimal consensus, let alone a coherent program within the armed forces, formal demilitarization by the democratic route comes to seem inescapable. But in order for the tactical withdrawal to be effective, it is still necessary to have a minimum of agreement on the neutrality to be observed, if the military politicization is not to lead to a cascade of coups and countercoups in the Bolivian style. Furthermore, since the military disagreements are not unrelated to civilian conflicts, such an outcome is only possible if the majority of the political forces have accepted the need for a demilitarization, and if the military do not perceive any direct peril or intention of seeking revenge on the part of returning civilians.

The Future of Military Rule—or How to Keep Them in Their Barracks

There are numerous obstacles to the departure of the military from the political scene—that is, from command over government—that slow down or prevent the return of freely elected civilians to public affairs. They derive for the most part from a logic internal to the military corporation. The permanence of the threat which justified the army's coming to power obviously represents the most frequently mentioned obstacle. A blaze of urban terrorism or an incompletely extinguished focus of rural guerrilla activity will engender militarist twitching scarcely propitious for a democratic relaxation. The abstract invocation of the "Communist danger" or the "Marxist cancer" which must be extirpated before returning to normal institutional functioning only has validity insofar as the specter of subversion remains a concrete threat for significant sectors of opinion. The counterrevolutionary logic cannot but nourish itself on the memory of the revolutionary menace. The recollection of three years of Popular Unity government is still the surest foundation of the Chilean dictatorship. But in Brazil, sixteen years after the overthrow of the Goulart regime and the rout of the populist forces, those responsible for the "system," although they are the authors of the Manichaean doctrine of "ideological frontiers," have played down this worn-out and, henceforth, ineffective legitimation. In Argentina, on the contrary, the chaotic condition of Isabelita's government and "subversive aggression" so undermined the value of democratic coexistence that the counterterrorist regime installed in 1976 has acquired a far-from-negligible stock of political capital.

The level of official violence constitutes another decisive variable. A weakly repressive military regime enjoys much greater freedom of maneuver. A terrorist government, on the contrary, risks being eventually called to account by the people. Violations of human rights, the problem of those who have "disappeared" in the course of the antisubversive fight, will require at least illumination, if not the establishment of penal responsibilities when the situation becomes normalized. In Argentina, the specter of Nuremberg haunts the barracks and explains the *fuite en avant* into the Malvinas/Falklands adventure, as well as the uncertainties that have attended the surrender of power to civilians until the last moment on 10 December 1983. "Argentina does not confess except before God," proclaimed General Videla's minister of the interior only recently.[47] The demoralization and defensive reflex of an army that has carried out the "dirty work" of a revolutionary war explain the multiple and feeble guarantees promulgated by the military in power before their return to barracks (e.g., the Self-Amnesty Law, the Anti-Subversive Law). This situation makes more understandable the "prudent audacity" of the newly elected President Alfonsin in dealing with the military question. He has sought to reestablish the sovereignty of law and of civilian authority, and to avoid all measures that could provoke a corporative reflex that might unite all officers against the democratic government. In Brazil, despite a skillful amnesty which whitewashed the "dark moments" of the repression, public revelations and the denunciations of the officers' responsibilities in the assassination of opponents provoked a vigorous response by the military ministers in February 1981. They warned against any "revanchist" attempt, saying that it might put brakes on the process of decompression. "The honor of the barracks is above the rights of man" was the headline of an opposition weekly.[48] The liberalization seemed at least to be hostage to that necessity.

It is with regard to this question in particular that the strategies of the civilians enter into play. Their margin of maneuver is narrow. The search for compromise and their acceptance of the "law of silence" imposed by the military may permit the political forces and supporters of democracy to make some gains.[49] Avoiding direct confrontation, dissipating any personal or institutional disquiet among the officers most compromised in the repression, can, curiously, facilitate progress toward the rule of law and representative procedures. But doing so also means restoring legitimacy by an act of weakness, underwriting the impunity of the usurpation—in a word—placing the military apparatus in an arbitrary and irresponsible position, thus demilitarizing the government while maintaining the militarization of the political system. This problem raises the eternal dilemma of the skillful and the pure—foxes and lions, Machiavelli would say—of accommodation and intransigence. But it is also a fundamental difference between a conceded transition and democratic rupture, and perhaps takes into account the evolution of the balance of forces.

The nature and the duration of the military government, tied to the preceding characteristic, condition the processes of eventual demilitarization. If democracy restores both the competitive procedures for the choice of rulers, and that substratum of freedoms which makes them possible and regular, certain Latin American military systems only suppress the former while but feebly restricting the latter. The restriction of party or union freedoms and even to a certain extent restrictions on the freedom of expression were not in fact major features of the Peruvian or Panamanian military regimes after 1968, or of the Ecuadorian between 1972 and 1979. The Argentina of Generals Onganía, Levingston, and Lanusse, in comparison with neighboring or subsequent authoritarian regimes, allowed a remarkable level of tolerance vis-à-vis the opposition. The sustained vitality of civil society no doubt facilitated the diverse forms of demilitarization undertaken by these regimes.

By contrast, the persistence of noninstitutionalized military power and the corruption caused by an absolutist exercise of authority make political alternation more improbable. The case of Bolivia, and of an army fractionalized into cliques, in which the accession to officer grade seems like a path to social advancement, perhaps best exemplifies this phenomenon. It has even been possible to venture the hypothesis that the refusal on several occasions in

1979–80 to recognize the results of elections that did not assure military continuity had to do both with the fears of numerous officers that they would have to reveal, before public opinion or the tribunals, the origin of their enrichment, and with the wish of more junior officers to take part in the feast of the corrupted. But it is true that besides these psychologistic and anecdotal explanations one can find a deeper significance in the Bolivian case which touches on the militarization of the whole political system.[50]

If, in Bolivia, the defense of the institution that thought itself to be threatened by the return of civilians, and notably by the victory of a moderate Left, blocked the transition, it was also and above all because in this case the army has provided the terrain and the arena in which all political struggles occur. In this "praetorianized" system, civilian political sectors have always been implicated in the military interventions. A military clique rarely launches a "putschist" adventure without a sectional endorsement or without an alliance with civilian groups. The civilian-military overlap, the permanent articulation of the two spheres, makes the "extrication" of militarism and the "civilianization" of power difficult. Contrary to a view marked by liberal ethnocentrism, in a system so militarized, there do not exist two worlds entrenched like two camps prepared for battle, with civilians on one side and the military on the other. Far from provoking a sacred union of the political class or of the social forces organized to defend democratic institutions in danger, any military uprising will enlist the public support of certain civilian forces competing with their rivals. It seems that in Bolivia this "praetorianization" of political life is not unrelated to the absence of a political majority, as indicated in the last elections. Also in Argentina, where the army has dominated political life for fifty years, the demilitarization of government does not necessarily change the system for all that, and sets no real limit on the likelihood of a "praetorian inversion." Elections are not synonymous with democracy. The disengagement of the armed forces from executive power and the lasting return to a liberal-constitutional model of civil-military relations is a difficult and lengthy task. It must confront models of behavior that have been strongly internalized. This sort of blockage cannot be overcome in Argentina without a profound societal and cultural transformation.[51] The choices and behaviors of political actors are not insignificant or inconsequential, but attitudes and tactics are not programmable and are themselves conditioned by social and cultural reality that recurrent military intervention contributes to forming and deforming.

By Way of Conclusion

Without doubt, it is easier to demilitarize the government than the centers of power. Many instances of opening up or of legal institutionalization represent merely tactical withdrawals that will allow subsequent interventions once the military apparatus has reconstituted its political resources. If not that, withdrawal may only be a question of assuring the juridical bases for the continuity of a system established by force. The objection can be raised that there have indeed been successful cases of demilitarization. Without having the cruelty to recall the precedents of Chile or Uruguay, let us examine these illustrative democracies of today, sheltered for twenty years or more from the military storms that have periodically or consistently shaken their neighbors. If one examines the civil-military relations of Mexico, Costa Rica, Venezuela, or Colombia, leaving aside what might happen in any of these countries tomorrow, one may inquire into the means adopted for establishing civilian preponderance and the steps required. The initial question, however, is whether these countries hitherto experienced protracted phases of militarization and, if so, how they overcame it. In fact, only Venezuela and Colombia emerged from a military dictatorship to a restoration of civilian power. But in the Colombian case, the brief interlude of General Rojas Pinilla in 1953 was based on the support of almost all political groups, which called him to power in order to put an end to the violence tearing the country apart.[52] The *rapprochement* of the two traditional parties in 1957 sounded the death knell of the military government, just as their dissension had presided over its birth. In Venezuela, which had only recently emerged from decades of caudillo dictatorship, the army in 1948 ousted from government the civilian reformists whom they had previously helped install, but the ascension of General Pérez Jiménez to supreme and absolute power drew together the dispossessed officers and the democratic opposition. The putsches by opposing factions which punctuated the presidency of Rómulo Betancourt after 1958 underline the difficulties of civilian supremacy. Nevertheless, the Acción Democrática party's influence within the military helped to reinforce the democratic party all the more surely since Pérez Jiménez had so discredited army intervention in political life.

In Mexico, the generals of the revolutionary armies formed part of the power elite, and then of the dominant party. The stabilization of the revolutionary order in their collective interest facilitated the containment of spontaneous and predatory forms of military caudillismo. The "generals" had in some sense to recognize the civilian power in which they participated in order to assure their political preeminence. In Costa Rica, which has not experienced true military intervention since 1917, the army was suppressed in 1948. Even before its legal abolition, the permanent military apparatus was already on the road to institutional decline.[53] Thus, there has not been a transition from military domination to civilian preponderance there either.

Do all these examples mean that the extirpation of militarism can only occur by some miracle, or under exceptional historical conditions? Could it be, as certain sympathizers with the Cuban or Sandinista revolutions think, that only "the total politicization of the military . . . will in future exclude all militarization of politics"?[54] Certainly, an army emerging from and guarantor of a revolutionary process and staffed with political commissars, selecting their cadres on the basis of extramilitary merits,[55] presents few risks for established power. The maximization of civilian power imposes a sort of "subjective control"—according to Huntington's distinction—which is secure.[56] But one should not confuse contexts, for we are here not considering the prospects for liberal democracy marked by pluralism and alternation. Thus suppressing the civilian/military distinction can and often does result in militarizing the whole of social life. The civil/military fusion in the ruling elite of Cuba seems to have overridden the distinction in a way that has tipped the balance toward military preoccupations. Even there, the model of the "civic soldier" which, according to Jorge I. Domínguez, results from this fusion is not without its own forms of role conflict.[57]

If one reverts to the capitalist societies of the continent and to outcomes framed within the pluralist constitutional context, it is evident that there are no preestablished scenarios for democratic reconstruction. Outside the revolutionary scheme just mentioned, which is founded on the liquidation of the state army, only limited precedents can give merely a first approximation to a possibilistic model of demilitarization. One should, however, observe that the path to "civilianization" through armed struggle is not identical with the repudiation of capitalism in the short or medium term. Civilian supremacy in Mexico has its origin in the dissolution of the Porfirista army and its replacement by revolutionary armies, closely linked with the emergence of the new regime. But the same schema applied to Bolivia in another international context was a failure. The 1952 Revolution purged the army to the point of practically annihilating it, but instead of creating a popularly based and politicized army, the government of the MNR, alarmed by social agitation and the workers' militias that they did not control, strove to reconstitute the classical army with the help of a U.S. military mission.[58] In Bolivia, far from favoring demilitarization, the specter of the dissolution of the military institution is today one of the unifying sources of military intervention.

The liberalization of military regimes often gives the impression of a stratagem, of bending to the wind in order to survive. Underlining the provisional nature of power may serve to disarm the opposition. The latter is often faced with a difficult choice: accepting the marked cards of the regime and thereby legitimizing its activities, or refusing to participate and thereby paralyzing the institutional process. In fact, the distinction between an electoral farce and an opening that would be usable by civilian forces does not depend upon the degree of competitiveness of the elections. Elections without surprises, or won in advance by those in power, may advance the process of subsequent demilitarization—first, by sanctioning the competitive system without the aid of the military, and above all, by giving the right of self-expression to the forces of opposition. But the decisive test occurs not at the level of the electoral competition but at that of constitutional liberties. Organizing apparently pluralistic elections may procure a facade of legality, which does not modify the authoritarian nature of power. Accepting the political game requires opening up a space of freedom which may, in turn, entail a "qualitative jump." The logic of these two outcomes is different; the risks are not the same. In the latter case, if the opening has a content, and even though it may not lead immediately to a "democratic rupture," the tactic of adopting a "low profile" by forces that are politically moderate (but not moderately democratic) and that are capable of temporary compromises, can be effective and may allow them to ameliorate the balance of forces.

In this case, the precarious character of a civilian regime under close military surveillance implies first constructing democracy *before* changing society.[59] It means limiting the stakes in order to permit a political agreement on noninvolvement of the military so as to resolve subsequent political conflicts. It is the accord to which Venezuelan and Colombian parties subscribed in the 1950s. It is also what has underlaid the behavior of the parliamentary political forces of both Right and Left in Spain since 1976.[60] From here, several stages may be envisaged without prejudging their order. One of them consists of democratizing the institutions and notably the apparatus of the state (army, police, tribunals), and another, virtually contradictory with the first, consists of creating, in a less dramatic climate, the condition of alternation which is the very expression of real pluralism, and which thus constitutes, without any fireworks, the true "democratic rupture."[61] This long and uncertain path to democracy involves a gamble: one has to accept the game proposed by those in power, in order to beat them at their own game. For this to happen, it helps if the whole of the political class and the majority of social sectors participating favor democratic values and procedures, and accept the uncertainties of the polls, and if the civilian social and political forces can say a definitive farewell to arms—before their military brethren have.

6 ·

Entrepreneurs and the Transition Process: The Brazilian Case

Fernando H. Cardoso

This chapter analyzes the role of entrepreneurs in the recent liberalization of Brazil's political regime. It deals particularly with the way in which industrialists (for it is they who have played the prominent role) have rethought their policies to suit not only their own interests but also the concept of society that seems best to guarantee "economic development" and promote political coexistence among social classes.

The opening pages briefly summarize the bibliography on the role of the "Brazilian bourgeoisie" and its relationship with society and the state. The ensuing analysis of the subject itself records the instances when the private sector partially fell out with the bureaucratic and authoritarian military regime, in order to demonstrate in what ways and how far the business community has distanced itself politically from the state. Finally, an attempt is made to describe how entrepreneurs have been trying to reestablish their links since the period of the Geisel government (1974–78) up until the present Figueiredo administration (which began in 1979). In this process, although groups of entrepreneurs have formed diverse relationships with other social and political forces in the country, the business community as a whole is faced with a problem that, in Antonio Gramsci's terminology, would be the equivalent of an attempt to overcome the state's inherent crisis by searching for new forms of bourgeois hegemony.

Entrepreneurs in Politics, Yesterday and Today

It has been a long time since one has been able to believe that the "Brazilian bourgeoisie" plays a determining role in elaborating policies that favor democratization. Before 1964 the private sector wavered between consolidating its alliance with the masses and becoming part of a feudal state. This hesitation has led many authors to believe that the socially innovative and democratizing role of the country's business community was evanescent. They saw it as the result, not so much of the Latin American situation, as of an analogical interpretation which considered that the patterns of political behavior of the "conquering bourgeoisie" of previous centuries in Europe could be repeated in emerging industrial countries.[1]

Several researchers, notably Luciano Martins,[2] have studied this subject in great detail and have put the expectations that might be entertained about the progressive role of the so-called national bourgeoisie into their proper perspective.[3] The studies mentioned, and a number of others, have indicated the limits of such an interpretation.[4] Thus, since the role of entrepreneurs has been redefined, the notion of "populism" has been put into its proper perspective, the meaning of the state has been redefined, and integrated views of development have been rethought so as to get away from the idea either that an alliance between popular forces and industrialists came about to control the state, democratize it, and put it to the service of economic development, or else that stagnation and disguised colonialism would be the inevitable result.

The basic idea of the post-1964 critical review was to delimit industrialists' political action in the context of a dependent economy and of a society whose history had imbued social classes and the state with characteristics that could not be "deduced" from the abstract model that reconstructed the relationships between bourgeoisie-state and capitalism in the "Center" countries. Schmitter's contribution to this review was both singular and enlightening: he demonstrated that "corporate" links were also at work in the tissue of "civilian society" and that ipso facto one could not reasonably entertain expectations of entrepreneurial-bourgeois behavior based on the values of liberal-democratic individualism.[5]

It was not, therefore, a question of underestimating the political action of industrialists, but of placing it in a particular historical context. The industrial bourgeoisie was obviously *not* excluded from the system of alliances that came into being after 1964.[6] It was simply that the emergence of a new state of affairs—economic, political, and social—redefined the role of the private sector in the system of dominant alliances.[7]

However, the prevailing theory, especially in party-political literature—remotely but persistently echoed in academic circles—insisted that "external dependence," which now took the new guise of the presence of multinational enterprises, was restricting the freedom of action of local entrepreneurs, except perhaps in the state manufacturing sector. It was now felt that industrial development, undeniable in countries like Brazil and Mexico, had been brought about by foreign enclaves. At best, there was a belief that this kind of industrialization would not provide "development." Instead, there was talk of "growth," "perverse accumulation," and even of a tendency toward stagnation.

The picture was complete when certain countries that had undergone industrialization and were taking an increasingly active part in the international manufacturing system, notably Brazil, suffered the political effects of coups which saw the armed forces taking over the corporate body of the state. Industrialization came under the control of international monopolies, aided by an economic infrastructure set up by the state, with all the trappings of an authoritarian, if not fascistic, regime.[8]

There are considerable difficulties in rethinking this analysis in terms that are neither simplistic nor mechanical. The presence of the military and of multinational corporations is a fact. The autonomy of the country's economy—understood as an autarchic-bourgeois-state economy—has become more problematic. This reality all too easily leads many into siding with the other extreme which emphasizes the fact that Brazilian society is dominated by external forces and controlled by the state, a state linked with foreign interests, trying to revive the nationalism of the 1950s, which has become an anachronism in the context of an internationalized economy.

However, as political history does not conform to the logic of mental constructs, regimes that had earlier seemed inexorably set to suffocate civilian society through overbearing domination, have begun to change, most noticeably in Peru and Brazil. The local business communities have had a not inconsiderable hand in these transformations. Even their action does not follow the scheme that presumed that the "momentum of monopolistic state accumulation" would lead the bourgeoisie permanently to reinforce the coercive aspects of the military regime.

The renewal of party-political activity and the emergence of pressure groups and social classes, however, demands new approaches to prevent a return to thinking that one is faced with the revival of the "national bourgeoisie," as conceived by populist-nationalist theories; or that one is faced with a return to democracy of the kind that took place after World War II, when the system changed from the Vargas period to the period of the 1946 Constitution.

The following points must be explained in this chapter: what does the action of the present entrepreneurial class in Brazilian society consist of? What kind of regime is emerging with the compliance of the entrepreneurs' political action to replace military authoritarianism, *without severance from the state*, that is, bringing about a gradual transformation under the control of the authoritarian regime, but without changing either the social complexion of the regime or even the armed forces' direct control of basic decisions?

As far as the first point is concerned, discussion is based on the most recent bibliography on entrepreneurs, revising some primary sources in order to define the nature of entrepreneurial action in the phase of political liberalization (*abertura política*) from the beginning of the Geisel government (1974–78). The second point is dealt with at the end, in terms of the way the regime relates to the private sector and of a possible emergence of a "bourgeois hegemony" and its limits.

The Reencounter with Politics

At the same time as it was becoming apparent to the general public that groups of entrepreneurs were forming, favoring the liberalization policies and a renewal of the balance in the distribution of responsibilities between the public and private sectors of the economy, social scientists had begun to correct the distortions that attributing a subordinate role to the business community in social and political activity had caused.

This review meant a reconsideration of the role of the bourgeoisie in the Vargas Revolution in October 1930 and of its ability to influence the state[9] and, more recently, a structural analysis of the relationship between national industrialists, technobureaucrats,[10] and multinational corporations. It has been given a more concrete form in empirical studies. Though they do not deny the structural characteristics of a dependent society or the role of the technocrats, they still insist that the private sector must not back down when it comes up against state bureaucracy[11] and though the business community does not have the characteristics of a hegemonic elite and has to adapt to the peculiarities of a bureaucratized authoritarian regime, it must play its own hand.[12]

Nowadays it is clear that the private sector was sheltered behind the state during the most repressive years of bureaucratic-military authoritarianism (until about 1976, with a brief interlude in 1974), keeping a low profile, seeming not to be the agent of political activity. As a certain amount of liberalization became apparent, sectors of the vanguard of the industrial bourgeoisie strategically began to take up positions that would increase their relative power.

It is also obvious that at the height of the bureaucratic-authoritarian period industrialists tried to exert corporate rather than political influence on the state. The term "bureaucratic spheres" attempts to describe this kind of association between the state and the business community, which sought to exert pressure without recourse to the independent mechanisms of civilian society, digging itself into defensive positions in the state system from which it could defend its economic interests. These "spheres" are at the core of the state apparatus and are usually run by civil servant allies and it is through them that entrepreneurs exert political influence in authoritarian regimes.[13]

Authoritarianism does not, of course, eliminate the entrepreneurs' play of interests and political activity, even when overall policy is grounded on the "state enterprise–multinational enterprise" setup. It does, however, affect the way entrepreneurial interests are expressed and limits their influence.

Therefore, to what extent does the growth of a politically prominent "new industrial elite," such as has emerged in recent years, require a rethinking of earlier analyses of the role of the industrial bourgeoisie in peripheral or dependent economies? In order to answer this question it is best to examine in detail how and when entrepreneurial pressure surfaced and what its guiding principle was.

From the interpretative point of view, there seems to be agreement both as to when industrialists reemerged in politics and as to the political and economic objectives they set themselves. The best synthetic consideration of this subject is by Carlos Lessa.[14] His study suggests that certain palpable changes in economic strategy occurred at three separate times:

1974, the Médici government comes to an end. The second National Development Plan—hitherto referred to as PND II—is presented at a time when

Brazil is seen as an "island of prosperity" in the context of a worldwide crisis. "A new development strategy has been proposed in the light of the priority given to heavy industry as a positive means of prolonging the [economic] miracle";

1976, the strategy is abandoned (one should remember the removal of the minister for industry and commerce, Severo Gomes, who was in favor of protecting Brazilian industry and supported an alternative form of development, less subject to the international division of labor, fomented by the multinationals, and the subsequent strengthening of the position of the more "orthodox" minister, Simonsen);

1979, proposal to reduce the rate of growth and emphasis on agricultural policies.

Lessa argues that, given these changes, it would be easy to derive a mechanical analysis that indicates the coincidence of entrepreneurial dissent with the points at which their objective interests diverged from proposed policies. However, before these palpable changes in economic policy, which took place from 1976 onward, when industrialists' plans could no longer find realization by adherence to official recommendations, the private sector was already actively opposed to the authoritarian regime's "nationalization" of the economy. But there was no awareness of any economic crisis. One should remember that in the five-year period 1975–80 the economy grew at rates of 6 percent and 7 percent per annum.[15]

In order to avoid a purely mechanical economic analysis, but without going to the other extreme (subjective interpretation at a purely political level), Lessa proposes a more sophisticated interpretation: from 1974 onward the private sector discovered that the state was a Leviathan, especially when it realized that PND II had triggered off an irreversible process of bringing the economy under state control. Therefore, the antinationalization campaign and support for a "free market economy" should be understood not so much in literal terms as the defense of thwarted economic interests, but rather as a "code" (a set of principles), a sort of political discourse whose aim was to make openings in the authoritarian state system. The defense of Lockean liberalism by entrepreneurs who know that state action is inseparable from contemporary forms of society and accumulation, and the return to the idea of the inseparability of "the two freedoms," economic and political—an image that was used and abused by entrepreneurs from 1974 to 1977 in speeches, interviews, seminars, and so on—can only be regarded as "a kind of coded language which prudently proffers . . . the argument for economic liberalism as a vector for the expression of demands for other freedoms."[16]

Assuming Lessa's interpretation is correct, we are looking, then, at a business community that is demanding freedom. It is true that some industrialists have been explicit on this point. José Mindlin, for instance, was categorical: "If it is a fact that a strong political regime tends to intervene in the economy, this intervention in turn strengthens the regime and leads to the consolidation of a strong technocratic state. It is a short walk from there to arbitrary rule."[17] At the assembly of the National Manufacturing Sector Congress (CONCLAP) in 1977, Mindlin defended the workers' right to strike action. Cláudio Bardella, elected as leader of the private sector in the "Forum" of *Gazeta Mercantil* by 5,000 entrepreneurs in 1977, added—in opposition to Geisel's slogan about a "responsible and possible democracy"—that he wanted an "unqualified democracy and qualified economic liberalism."[18] Bardella progressively called for closer links between the business community and other sectors of society and demanded participation in decision-making processes: "We, the business community, like all other sectors of society, each according to its ability, have and wish to participate in this process and so we have and wish to participate in the definition of the course that the country is to take."[19] Taking the private sector's demand a step further along the road to politicization, Severo Gomes, removed in the same year from his ministerial post and elected in second place in the Forum as a representative of the private sector, declared: "What matters is that society can control the state and not vice versa, as is the case at the moment. And if this is to happen, there is only one way out— political correction. Democracy is the only solution."[20]

In this respect, Lessa's interpretation of entrepreneurial discourse would seem to be correct. Lessa does not presume that the business community's enthusiasm for democracy came about independently of its interests.[21] On the contrary, he shows that the Geisel administration proposed a continuation of the "economic miracle" by means of a new pattern of accumulation which would be based on the growing demand for capital goods and basic inputs. The latter would expand as a result, above all, of the acquisitions made by state enterprises. Industrialists in the capital goods sector gave the PND II policy an enthusiastic reception. The private sector did not perceive official directives (state enterprises were required to sustain the capital goods sector by buying from the home market) as a dangerous threat of state control. Instead, leading lights in the sector expressed optimism. The president of ABDIB (Associação Brasileira das Indústrias de Base, Brazilian Association of Base Industries) officially accepted the challenge of PND II at the end of 1974, but the association demanded:

special finance (BNDE, National Economic Development Bank, charged 40 percent interest per annum);

a price policy that would allow for the absorption of labor costs, which were rising faster than the rates established by collective arbitration;

control of competitors, by the introduction of restrictions on the entry of new producers.

Private initiative and state action (direct intervention in the market through the buying of local products on the part of state enterprises and control of investments by the Industrial Development Council (CDI) seemed mutually indispensable.[22]

This response was not the private sector's only one to the plans of the Geisel government, though. To many industrialists, the attempt to weld together the interests of economic development (firmly anchored in the multinational-state enterprise setup) by creating a local capital goods manufacturing sector (and thus a rapid assimilator, if not a producer, of technology) looked unrealistic and dangerous: unrealistic because it required excessively onerous investment for the country (PND II spoke of a savings rate of 35 percent between 1975 and 1981) and dangerous because it not only increased the role of state enterprises in the dynamics of development but also enlarged the area of the economy regulated by the state.

This "threat," viewed by the private sector associated with multinationals as restricting their action led some entrepreneurs to express attitudes of misgiving and criticism. They were influenced too by the fact that the development plan was of a voluntary nature and did not meet the demands of social bases that had formerly supported the regime, by the policies that the Industrial Development Council were implementing, by the centralization of PIS-PASEP resources in the National Economic Development Bank [translator's note: PIS-PASEP is a participation fund set up in 1970 to which firms were supposed to contribute on behalf of their employees], and so on. Thus, while the Geisel government encouraged the growth of private industry, and in particular national private industry, it emphasized economic policies that led to discontent among the sectors connected with the manufacture of durable consumer goods and, in 1974, began the mandate that dealt somewhat harshly with the financial-speculative sector. Furthermore, it allowed Fiat to set up in the state of Minas Gerais, causing discontent in the unpromising São Paulo automobile sector. With its policy of "regional balances," encouraging the decentralization of the petrochemical industry and the creation of industries in other regions to supply the São Paulo car assembly plants, the government instilled an even deeper feeling of insecurity in the São Paulo business community.

It was against this background that the private sector discovered "democracy," and some industrialists even rediscovered the constitution: "It [a Geisel measure] would have a prejudicial effect on the factories already in existence, as well as ignoring rights acquired and guaranteed by the constitution."[23]

Thus, the Geisel government's industrialization policy—which followed the lines of what Guillermo O'Donnell in his writings on the "bureaucratic-authoritarian state" calls "deepening" of the economy—unsettled the linchpins of the system of alliances that sustained the authoritarian military regime, the international enterprises involved in the manufacture of durable consumer goods and the importation of equipment or the controlled transfer of part of their production process to Brazil, and also the enormous national sector dependent on them, structurally dependent on the internationalization of local production, and the local enterprises, even the larger ones, which had initially supported PND II.

On the other hand, the evolution of the international economic crisis and the pressure from international partners to place their equipment in Brazil's industrial projects (as occurred with the Italian Fisinder company, the Japanese Kawasaki company in the case of the Tubarão factory, and even the atomic power plant project) made it difficult for the Geisel government to keep its promise to sustain the national capital goods sector. Worsening foreign debt, fueled by the importation of foreign equipment until at least 1976, left the government even less room for maneuver in maintaining the goals of autonomy declared in PND II. They became untenable. State enterprises could not (and certain sectors of state enterprise bureaucracy did not wish to) sustain the local capital goods manufacturing sector.

Given this state of affairs, it was not long before leading industrialists in the national heavy equipment sector became disillusioned with official promises and fiercely critical first of economic policy and then of the regime itself.[24] They had embarked on an expansion policy that was no longer backed by official recommendations. Being highly dependent on official policies, as they are, their "politicization" was immediate and clamorous.

In this context, it hardly mattered that the aim of PND II and the Geisel government had been to sustain growth and encourage the private sector; it also hardly mattered that practical measures had been taken to counter nationalization. The way entrepreneurs read the overall changes and the authoritarian practices of a government that, even when it wanted to better the economic lot of the private sector, took decisions without consultation, made it plain that "something was rotten in the state of Denmark."[25] Points of view—ideology—became as important as the hard facts. The government that had most wanted to favor the interests of the national sector and that had already lifted restrictions, at least in the press, became the object of irate criticism from industrialists who began by attacking the government and ended up calling the regime itself into question.

This criticism went so far as to consider the question of democracy as a political demand and was limited to the more progressive democratizing sector alone. Statements were repetitive but it is a fact that in 1976 and 1977 the more politically outspoken industrialists lent their voices to the chorus of leaders mentioned above, demanding liberalization.[26] In the year 1977 industrialists closed ranks to criticize the government; in order to do so they began to speak of democracy.[27]

The Demand for Democracy: Its Penetration and Limits

Criticism consisted of a sort of general acceptance of the opposition's standpoint in terms of the social and economic "distortions" of the prevailing "development model," of an emphasis on the need to control direct state intervention in the economy, of an insistence on the participation of the private sector in the decision-making process, of the reiteration of the importance of democracy and of opposition to measures proposed by the government. This last aspect highlights the business community's position far more than the overall tone of entrepreneurial discourse, though it is important to reaffirm the significance of its general prodemocratic tone (which remains to the present day).

In a public declaration in 1978, entrepreneurs elected to the Forum of *Gazeta Mercantil* in 1977 summed up their position: "We wish to express our view of the path to economic development, based on social justice and promoted by democratic political institutions, convinced that these are essentially the general wishes of Brazilian society."[28]

In tune with the government's emphasis, they reiterated their belief that industrial development should be based on heavy industry; they demanded a better balance in the "tripartite system of development" ("Brazilian private industry was in a fragile condition, state enterprises were not controlled by society, and foreign companies were not subject to clear or adequate norms of conduct"); they criticized the financial system and growing foreign debt, demanded adequate policies on technology, requested the regulation of foreign capital, became the standard-bearers for small- and medium-sized businesses, and so on. If these demands were to be put into practice, the "active participation of the private sector" in the elaboration of policies naturally became a necessity.

Still in general discourse, the private sector adhered to opposition theories about a "just incomes policy," freedom of trade unions, modernization of the organization of unions, employers and employees; they called for the state to "face up to the howling shortcomings in terms of health, basic sanitation, housing, education, urban public transport and environmental protection"; they demanded a review of the tax system which would "make income tax more evenhanded for private individuals, taxing capital earnings on a sliding scale"; they criticized regional imbalances, and so on.

One might think that one was reading a manifesto of the opposition party of the period, the MDB (Brazilian Democratic Movement), or a U.N. document. In political terms, in like manner, they demanded "across-the-board participation for everyone." "And there is only one regime that can provide for the full expression of interests and absorb tensions without channeling them into undesirable class conflict—the democratic regime."

Note that this document was published before the 1978 elections, at a critical stage in the battle for the presidential succession, when Geisel was facing opposition from within the armed forces, and the MDB was running a political campaign with a general as its presidential candidate.

The tone of the entrepreneurs' declaration is one of general opposition to authoritarianism.[29] It does not pinpoint "enemies" nor does it name "allies." Two years later, the entrepreneurs elected to the Forum began to express themselves differently. The object of their criticism was now energy policy, along with the development of agriculture and increased social expenditure. Without actually mentioning it, they went along with Delfim Netto's recipe for avoiding recession: "The path to progress, social justice, and democracy must circumvent the dangers of recession. This would be the worst outcome." "And in an atmosphere like the present [one of crisis] the enemies of democracy would find it easy to put abroad their totalitarian designs."[30]

The earlier demands for better social conditions, independence for trade unions, and public freedoms were endorsed. Now, however, they begin to portray the "enemy": "any kind of political backsliding is inadmissible. Those who are dedicated to plotting covertly the downfall of the return to democratic rule—and, even worse, who dare use abominable terrorist tactics—will not prevail against the will of the overwhelming majority of the population." They reacted, then, against the state terrorism of the special security services. Moreover, just *how* the fight was to be carried forward was made clear: "Under the firm and well-intentioned leadership of president João Figueiredo we have already begun the march."[31]

The president of the Rio de Janeiro Federation of Industries supported the document, as did the vice-president of the Association of Commerce of São Paulo. Minister Delfim Netto rejoiced at it and, eventually, so did the president of the republic: "Gentlemen, I am most satisfied because what is written here, in the summary of your document, is what I have been saying in my speeches.(. . .) I am pleased to see that those in private business (. . .) are, in general terms, if not almost entirely, in agreement with the ideas that I have proclaimed."[32]

One of the most vociferous industrial leaders commented on the president's declaration: "Now we must wait to hear from the president how he intends to put this participation into effect."[33]

This "arabesque," which went from abstract criticism to concrete support, from aversion to the state to begging for a definition from the state, from ideological oppositionist discourse to a position of support for João Figueiredo's liberalization program, did not attract industrial leaders. A 1980 opinion poll among entrepreneurs provided the following results:[34]

1. In terms of the government's political program, do you think *abertura* [liberalization] is:

successful?	27.86%
exaggerated?	7.35%
doubtful?	64.79%

2. Bearing in mind the present political scene in Brazil, do you think the government should:
   a. act prudently, staggering the final stages of *abertura* in order to guarantee the stability of the democratic regime? 57.44%
   b. consult the newly formed parties to establish a consensus with government regarding the most adequate timetable for the completion of *abertura*? 29.4%
   c. call on politicians, independently of their parties, to support the *abertura* program? 12.62%

The idea of a "slow, gradual, and stable" liberalization, as the Geisel government slogan expressed it, reappeared in other questions. The search for political stability based on strong parties was given greater support (57.53 percent) than the idea of holding elections before parties were properly established (23.72 percent) or that of completing liberalization and giving the Left a chance to run (18.75 percent).

In 1981 the leaders of the business community made another declaration. This time their basic economic concerns were foreign debt (which, according to the business community, should have been negotiated without recourse to the International Monetary Fund), high interest rates, the control of credit, agricultural policy, diminishing public expenditure; in sum, the climate of recession. With the exception of the bankers, entrepreneurs criticized the handling of credit and monetary policies sharply. As far as liberalization and social policies were concerned, however (for example, entrepreneurial leaders who were consulted agreed that the government's wage policy was not responsible for inflation, which was true but still surprising), attitudes remained the same.

Bourgeois Hegemony?

At this point it is convenient to return to our initial questions and Lessa's interpretation of the private sector's "democratizing code."

One cannot properly apprehend the meaning of the pressures the private sector was applying without an explicit reference to the fact that it was the Geisel government itself that (from 1974 onward, though not continuously) had instigated the debate on the subject of liberalization. It is unnecessary to repeat the sequence of events in this process, which others have dealt with. From 1976–77 on, when the business community decided to take part in the debate on liberalization, meetings of professors and researchers at the Brazilian Society for the Advancement of Science, protests against the use of torture (as in the case of the death of the journalist Vladimir Herzog) organized by the Catholic church, some trade unionists, students, journalists, lawyers, and so on, already constituted the backdrop to Brazilian politics.

Industrialists' voices were added to the chorus. If the business community did not take the initiative, it did add weight to the movement of civilian society; the press itself "used" the leadership of the private sector to increase the clamor for liberalization.[35] Even so, it is true that the more active and outspoken industrial leaders had already moved to support liberalization. It is probable that the majority of the private sector initially found the positions of some leaders rather perplexing.[36] With time, as the results of the opinion poll I have reproduced show, most entrepreneurs were pledged to the same position.

Entrepreneurial pressure, however, was not responsible for the liberalization strategy. It was added, rather belatedly, to the political changes proposed by the Geisel-Golbery group and to the chorus of protests from civilian society.

In this light, would it be correct to suppose that the criticism of increasing state control was a means of deepening the criticism of the regime? In terms of effect, this was certainly the case. It was hardly so in terms of intentions.

Liberal, anti-state-control emphasis was given to entrepreneurial declarations only after Geisel had repeatedly allayed suspicions of increased state control in economic policy and once the government had begun to look favorably on liberalization. This emphasis may correspond to an "ideological delay," which the more intellectually articulate industrialists and those who had closest links with the state (normally from the largest companies) themselves frequently criticized. It may also correspond to the private sector's desire to oppose bureaucratic pressures in the political game. However, it has as much to do with the failure of the Geisel government to carry out its plans to sustain economic growth to the benefit of local sectors as it has with the subsequent economic crisis, which led the government to treat its preferred allies less benevolently. As I have already discussed, the interregnum in which "liberal" entrepreneurs appeared to represent themselves as an "autonomous social group" that should fight to obtain political power and control the state in civilian society was shortlived. More recently, in the face of strong and more general pressures for democracy from other sectors of society industrial leaders began to talk again about a democracy "managed" by the state.

After liberalization, entrepreneurs seem to have been attracted by "democratic liberalism" in the same way that other social sectors had been. The pressure for the autonomy of social groups and for the breaking of state ties was encouraged (among other classes) by the church, openly supported by intellectuals, and adopted as a policy by trade unionists. Entrepreneurs, for their part, came out in favor of severing the corporate ties between state and society. There is even a degree of similarity between the private sector's view of the kind of society emerging and the views among labor leaders, intellectuals, and the clergy. One can detect a similar tone of general political discourse among these separate social groups.[37]

So there seem to be structural elements, derived from the formation of a mass, industrialized society, which lead to the search for a social model that values civilian society more highly than the state. Just as authentic labor leaders had enlarged their spheres of influence, taking over unions and inter-union movements, liberal-minded industrialists won greater influence in their class organizations and succeeded in controlling the powerful Federation of Industries of the State of São Paulo.[38] Once in this position, they simultaneously strengthened their contacts with the government and with opposition parties. The dynamics of personal interests (both economic and social) and differing views about the future will probably rearrange the alignment of these forces, drawing them closer to the government on the one hand or (in the case of certain individuals) closer to the opposition camps.

Nevertheless, I believe it is not possible to sustain the idea that there is any real possibility of the emergence of a new "bourgeois hegemony," made up of national leaders of the private sector, dedicated to creating a democratic society.

As the Figueiredo government began to outline the time and space in which the liberalization process would take place, industrialists began to assume the role of guarantors of the president's intentions. More important still, the very notion that industrialists should independently put pressure on the government and the regime began to change. Repeated declarations show that the business community once again expects the process to be officially "directed"; political action should be carried out by competent "social entities." There is a renewed recognition that there can be no salvation beyond the bounds of the state.[39] The business community must get organized and apply pressure. However, this effort should be done more as a group defending corporate interests than as a class that is politically organized to occupy the state.

The long debate among the leaders of the more prodemocratic entrepreneurial group, which the press transcribed, shows frequent perplexity over party-political participation versus the safeguarding of entrepreneurial independence, enterprise economy versus state economy, "classical" democracy versus democracy of the masses, the ability of unions to put pressure on the state versus their corporate integration in the state, and so on. An analysis of the discourse of entrepreneurs, politicians, and union leaders would probably demonstrate that the oppositions that constitute the tissue of ideological discourse take a similar form. But one cannot detect the code of a new hegemony in the babble of industrial leaders. Rather, one can make out an abstract identity brought about by issues that unite one and all against the state, as if the state were not the reflection of a domination that exists in society itself.

This general, abstract, ideological identity naturally disappears in the concrete clash of interests. The rebirth of the union movement and the outbreak of strikes (above all the metal workers' strike), beginning in 1978, established the limits of society's generalized good conscience. When the flames of wage claims began to singe the direct interests of enterprises, the enchantment of a consensus of liberal attitudes evaporated. In the 1980 strike, faced with an onslaught from the workers, industrialists, some rather shame-faced, others in haste, again resorted to using the state as a shield. The employment minister acted harshly, prohibiting "direct negotiations" between management and the work force and, to my knowledge, not a single manager defied the state dictum. Instead, managers kept silent and stepped aside, leaving the state to act, to intervene in unions and break up their leaderships. It is undeniable that from this moment onward the private sector began to view the Figueiredo government as, if not an ally, then a necessary barrier for containing the avid manner in which pressure for liberalization, stirring among the masses, was being transferred from an institutional to a social arena. As a result, working-class democratization was shattered: the country would certainly become a democracy, but without a social contract of the Moncloa Pact type agreed in Spain in 1977. Democratization was to proceed at a slower pace, under the president's baton.

In saying this, I am not in any way trying to diminish the private sector's role in "transition." The business community has firmly rejected a possible reversal in the liberalization process and has opposed any threat of right-wing terrorism at any rate. The private sector "bought" the liberalization process. And in this respect Lessa is right: entrepreneurial ideological articulation is more than just the simple transposition of immediate economic interest into abstract discourse. But the project which in the end has the backing of industrialists (and their bases) is none other than the government's. We are not dealing with the emergence of a hegemonic democratic movement which sees civilian society as its source of power, political parties as its instrument, and a democratic regime as its objective, although there are individuals in the private sector who think this way. We are dealing, rather, with the equivalent in the private sector of a policy of controlled liberalization.

Without business participation, however, the experiment with "enlightened-authoritarian transformation" would have been difficult: just as before 1964 and in 1968, the more hard-line sectors of the military needed business support for their resistance to any attempt at liberalization (even controlled from "above") for fear that the political process might get out of hand. In this phase of transition to democracy the position of the business community in support of liberalization has undoubtedly been a favorable factor. Favorable, one should make clear, for a transition model which was not brought about by entrepreneurial pressure and whose center of gravity is the government.

Is not this blending of an authoritarian regime with a hierarchic society, both demonstrating a degree of sensitivity toward social problems (at least in theory) and toward vocal protest, precisely what characterizes transition in Brazil? And is not the aversion toward sudden changes in political attitudes, including those that may cause leaders of professional groups in civilian society to take political action, what distinguishes this transition in political terms? Does not the constant complaint about the ineptitude of political parties go hand in hand with an attitude that strongly disapproves of leaders of social groups "sullying" the arguments by making them political rather than social? And is this not the meaning of sectors of the public and ideologues of certain social movements, using another code, when they say that the right moment for political action lies in the future and when they restrict it to distant parts of the state and the decision-making process?

Why, then, should we expect the private sector to be the harbinger of the good news of democratic society? Only if it is in the name of a specific conception of society and of the hegemonic role that the "Brazilian bourgeoisie" should play in it. These suppositions, though, are as dead as before. Without this (unnecessary) ideological premise one can only recognize that the private sector's role in the Brazilian transition process has been strategic and demonstrates the importance of the business community in the new system of alliances, without it being necessary or convenient to assume that we are witnessing a "hegemonic" resurgence of the liberal bourgeoisie.

Conclusions

The transition from an authoritarian regime in Brazil tells us something about the dynamics of authoritarian regimes.[40] It is true that in Brazil one is dealing with an "authoritarian situation" rather than a regime of this nature, as Juan Linz has pointed out. Even so, much of the discussion of authoritarian-bureaucratic regimes, if it has not actually been based on the Brazilian case, has at least considered it an expressive example of this form of political regime and this kind of state. The connection between the internationalization of the economy (the consequent presence of multinational enterprises) and the active role played by the state is flagrant in the Brazilian case; just as, borrowing O'Donnell's apt expression, the formation of the "trio"—by the addition of the Brazilian private sector's action to that of the other two partners—was perhaps more evident in Brazil than in other authoritarian-bureaucratic regimes. The very intention of strengthening the national capital goods manufacturing sector, embodied in PND II, set in motion, as mentioned earlier, something that O'Donnell called a process of "deepening" of the economy, under the aegis of an authoritarian state.

The foregoing has shown how, and how quickly, this marriage of convenience fell apart. One has the impression that the local business community is a sort of Delilah, ready to entangle the Samson-state in a web of perfidious love, only to betray him and call in the Philistines of the private sector to rebuild a pagan democracy which does not light candles to an authoritarian god.

However, this chapter has also tried to show that an interpretation too closely based on the liberal idea that civilian society, once strengthened under the aegis of the industrial bourgeoisie, would resist state action and permit public demands and protests to control the excesses of public power, is, to say the least, precipitate.

Indeed, what is specific about the Brazilian "transition policy," when viewed from the limited angle of the realignment of the business community, as has been the case in this chapter, is the increasing demands for political participation from civilian society, *without severance from the state*. In this respect, Brazilian transition is progression as it is in Spain:[41] there is a sort of move toward change from a nucleus of authoritarian power because of pressures from groups within the regime which register the changes in society and in the international system and which tend to open valves and use their influence to include parts of social sectors, which were formerly excluded, in the decision-making process; at the same time, these social sectors put pressure on the nucleus of the state and try to win over some segments of society formerly implicated with authoritarianism to their way of thinking. Entrepreneurs have become more politicized through this pincer movement, which puts pressure on both sides in the correlation of emerging forces.

Apparently—at any rate until the present—the state has not been "weakened," nor has the—real—strengthening of civilian society allowed political parties and social leaderships to develop a strategy for making inroads on the nucleus of power. It is as if society has opted for a prolonged seige because there was disagreement among the troops over which strategy to adopt. If it eventually launches an attack to rupture the authoritarian nucleus and reestablishes democracy (changing the social bases of the state), that is one thing. If, on the other hand, it speeds up the transformation of the state, causing a fusion of the "old" and the "new" which will force concessions from the state, it will broaden the class alliances that constitute the system of domination; it will provoke considerable alterations in the regime, but it will not jeopardize the control of the state exercised by the authoritarian nucleus, which sprang from the armed forces, and especially from the so-called information community, both fully persuaded that the interests of national security are only served if there is economic development and that such development can only be effected by large production units, both state and private, in association with multinational enterprises.

The analysis in this chapter has shown that the business community—as is only natural—opts for the second alternative. Consequently it simultaneously adopts a stance that is critical of authoritarianism and another that supports controlled transition—not by "mistake" or through "weakness."

The simultaneous strengthening of the state's decision-making capacity (which, given the pressures from civilian society, requires an alteration in social policies and an opening up, even if only symbolic, of regulated channels of participation) and of civilian society's demands for autonomy (which, as we have seen, requires the reinforcing of horizontal valves, within classes, and vertical valves, between classes, which affects the church, the mass media, universities, and so on) is what makes the Brazilian transition unique. It neither leads, purely and simply, to a return to liberalism and democratic values, nor is it limited to the contrivance of a formal facade of democratization. It is not a game, then, in which the authoritarian state loses what society gains or vice versa.

This form of transition requires compromises and calls for tolerance. (Once again, Spain is the most similar case, though Brazil does not have regions demanding autonomy or socially ingrained Fascism, nor, on the other hand, does it have such a strong working-class, or Socialist and Communist "class" parties.) The opposing parties know that, for the moment at least, they do not have the power to impose their rules on one another. They also know that retaliation will not help them win ground. For this reason, terrorism (especially right-wing terrorism) is no sooner attempted as a means of persuasion than it peters out as a focus for political action and becomes counterproductive.

In this context, it is not difficult to realize that the role of the private sector is, at the same time, crucial and limited. It is crucial because entrepreneurs are put under great cooptative pressure and if they allow themselves to be absorbed by the state, there will be fewer concessions over liberalization. It is limited because, in the battle to change the state, the private sector is merely one group among many and not one of the most courageous. Thus, one should not overestimate its importance in the space that will open up if this battle leads the country from stable transition to, if not liberal democracy—which is not the case at present—at least a regime that is more compatible with the pressures of revindicative masses.

7 •

Economic Policies and the Prospects for Successful Transition from Authoritarian Rule in Latin America

John Sheahan

As Brazil and the Southern Cone countries break out of the repressive regimes established in the 1960s and 1970s, their chances for consolidating political freedom may be raised or damaged by the quality of their economic policies. If they are to have any chance of success, such policies must meet two requirements which pull in contrary directions. One is that they have the consistency necessary for a viable economy, able to function without constant crises and to achieve some economic growth. That requirement implies restraints: the ability to limit claims that would seriously damage efficiency or outrun productive capacity. The other is the ability to answer enough of the expectations of the politically aware groups in society to gain and hold their acceptance. In some of these countries, perhaps especially Argentina, competing expectations may in some periods exceed any possible capacity to respond. But it is at least conceivable that more coherent economic performance, able to provide gains to all social groups rather than taking away from some to favor others, might achieve a more sustainable balance between demands and possibilities.

The constraints on economic policy when attempting to move out of an authoritarian system vary with each country's history and economic structure, with the particular alignment of forces in the society, and with the kind of change being attempted. They also vary with world economic and political conditions. In the mid-1980s the special condition of greatest immediate relevance is the burden of external debt accumulated under the authoritarian regimes. That situation has been aggravated by exceptionally high interest rates and by the resistance of northern financial institutions to extend net new credit to the debt-ridden countries. Those special conditions tighten the constraints on economic policy, but they also introduce an angle that could be helpful to new regimes: the authoritarian systems have done so much damage that domestic social groups might at least initially be more willing than historically they have been to accept the compromises and restraints necessary to restore functioning democracies.

This chapter is particularly concerned with negotiated movements away from the ultraconservative regimes which have used military force to dismantle organizations of popular expression, to restrain real wages, to promote integration into world trade and financial markets, and to hold down social reform as well as mass consumption in the interest of favoring capital accumulation and upper-class incomes. These features are intended as a brief summary of the main economic policy orientations in the authoritarian regimes of the Southern Cone countries, Brazil, and possibly also of the Franco and Salazar regimes before the mid-1970s. They are not meant as a list of uniformly negative policies which should be reversed by democratic regimes. Some aspects of these orientations are unambiguously harmful, some mixed, and some potentially positive. This discussion is concerned with two particularly sensitive issues: wage policies and international economic relationships. They are of course closely related to each other and also to the more general question of the ways in which market forces could either harm or help nonauthoritarian regimes.

Wage Policies and Employment

Conflicts over wage policies can be crucial to the chances of survival of a nonauthoritarian government. Most Latin American countries have so much underemployment, and some have so much open unemployment as well, that if market forces were left to operate freely wage-earners would be left out of rising national income far too long for any possible political acceptance.[1] Wages need to be guided by extramarket decisions, and raised gradually, if national income is increasing, but raising them too rapidly can stop growth and worsen unemployment. Decisions on wage trends need some conception of norms consistent with the sustained growth of employment and income.

A democratic government must give much higher priority to creation of employment opportunities and reduction of poverty than the Southern Cone military regimes have done if it is to have any hope of wide public acceptance.[2] Poverty is partly a matter of low wages but much more closely associated with lack of regular employment, and with low productivity occupations in the rural sector.[3] Promoting productive employment is surely likely to bring more people out of poverty, but to do so requires balancing a complex set of relationships within which wage rates play important roles. For an immediate objective of raising employment in a new postauthoritarian context, the main determinant is the level of economic activity rather than wage rates. But the degree to which aggregate demand can safely be stimulated depends on what that does to external balance and inflation. The rapid rise of wage rates in the early stages of expansion pushes up demand for imports, makes exporting more difficult, and aggravates inflation. A slower rate of wage increase allows more space for sustained expansion.

Continuing growth will generate more employment if the costs of using labor do not rise relative to the costs of capital equipment, energy, and other inputs into production. Greater wage stability favors the growth of employment in industrial production for export, use of more labor-intensive technology, and changes in the structure of production toward products with relatively higher ratios of labor to capital inputs. Some indication of the magnitudes involved have been calculated by Marcelo Selowsky for six of the semiindustrialized Latin American countries. In these countries, real wages in the industrial sector increased 3.7 percent a year from 1963 to 1972, while industrial employment increased 3.6 percent a year. Selowsky estimates that a reduction of the rate of increase of wages to a range of 2 to 3 percent would have increased the rate of growth of employment to a range between 5 and 7 percent a year.[4]

A democratic government would be more likely to aim at raising demand and income than the Argentine or Chilean military regimes, and that aim should provide scope for increasing real wages and employment simultaneously. But the rate at which wages rise for regularly employed workers can make a great deal of difference: they cannot safely be raised faster than real income per capita. An increase at the same rate as gross domestic product per capita would allow three important conditions to be satisfied at once: (1) approximately equal rates of wage increase for workers outside of regular urban employment; (2) growth of the resources available for investment at the rate that GDP and consumption increase; and (3) growth of exports at whatever rate is necessary to keep up with that of imports, without any need for a rising external deficit. Any faster rate of growth of real wages for regularly employed workers would mean that at least one of the other conditions would necessarily be violated.

The actual rate at which wages could increase with such a norm depends on factors partly outside of national control. Rising import prices or worsening export markets would keep it down, and the reverse trends would raise it. Heavy debt service requirements from past external borrowing would keep it down; debt renegotiation or lower world interest rates would allow more room. If increases in real wages in Latin America had matched the average rate of growth of GDP per capita from 1960 to 1980 they could have risen 3.2 percent a year, or 88 percent over the twenty-year period.[5] The rates of growth for individual countries and subperiods varied greatly: they were far higher than the regional average for Brazil from 1967 to 1980, and much poorer for the Southern Cone countries. The Brazilian growth record for 1967–80 would be hard for a democratic regime to beat. But the miserable economic records of the Argentine and Chilean military regimes have at least the perverse advantage that they should allow even a moderately successful democratic government to look good in comparison.

A wage norm equating the trend rate of real wages to the growth of output per capita would mean that increasing real wages could come out of increasing output and not out of either an import surplus or a reduction of profits. On that side, use of such a norm would do nothing to pull down the pretax incomes of the wealthy. On another side, if priority is given to increasing employment then the real incomes of the underemployed and unemployed would rise faster than national income: first by gaining regular employment at going wage rates and then by rising wages along with everyone else. The degree of inequality would be reduced from the lower end, by reducing extreme poverty, rather than by pulling down the highest incomes. But that approach introduces a complication of macroeconomic imbalance: the newly employed workers would be raising their consumption faster than national product while other income receivers are trying to keep up with national product. In the absence of offsetting corrections, either investment would be squeezed or external deficits would widen. A possible answer could be to offset increasing consumption of the lower-income groups with increasing taxes on property or on the consumer goods most important to higher-income groups. Such measures could maintain overall balance, protect the availability of productive resources for investment, and still allow for reduced inequality in real terms.

Appeals for social agreements on wage norms have been tried in Latin America, and have consistently failed to work for any length of time. Albert Hirschman suggests an important reason for the failures: they cannot serve as a substitute for real changes in economic and social structures which would provide support for new behavior.[6] Why should a society be expected to act differently if basic market and power relationships remain much the same? That question points to the need to consider structural changes as components of any social agreements providing for ceilings on wage increases. For example, a change in taxation, placing more of the tax burden on property, or on consumption of the consumer durable goods of greater importance to upper-income groups, possibly accompanied by increased social welfare programs directed to lower-income groups, might help to achieve worker cooperation with wage norms. More equitable tax structures and constraints on the consumption of upper-income groups could make wage guidelines more nearly feasible, and greater consistency between output and consumption would in turn help to make it possible to carry out structural reforms without the macroeconomic imbalances that have so often undermined reformist regimes in the past.

The special circumstances of escape from the drastic political repression of the past might just possibly help to create a more durable consensus on the need for shared growth, as opposed to the antagonistic strategies which did so much to create explosive conditions in the past. The historical model underlying this suggestion is that of the French resistance movement under German occupation during World War II. A previously stagnant economy, weakened by bitter social conflict, was in a sense renegotiated by wartime resistance leaders. They were able to gain agreement on extensive nationalization, the creation of a planning commission to introduce more active government direction of investment backed by major public financing, changes in labor legislation to improve conditions for workers, and a new system of social security, all to be put in place as soon as foreign domination ended. It was all put in place, and the economy proved to be much more dynamic for the next twenty years than it had ever been before.[7] The new system in turn grew less flexible and eventually less successful, but that is the fate of all human institutions. Changes that make a significant positive difference for the better part of a generation are not all that common, and not to be disdained. In the French case, perhaps the main difference from shorter-lived wage policies was that the period in which conflicting groups were pulled together by the conscious need to find new solutions was used to prepare serious structural reforms rather than merely to suspend temporarily the struggle over income distribution.

International Economic Relations

Albert Fishlow's discussion at the Wilson Center conference on "Transitions from Authoritarian Rule" made a strong case for the desirability of an orientation toward exports of manufactured goods, but contrary comments ran through many aspects of the conference discussion. Some suggested that desirable internal changes have been sacrificed to establish the conditions necessary for an open economy: that authoritarianism itself and its specific economic characteristics are the result of tying Latin American countries too closely to world markets.[8]

The issues involved in these conflicting suggestions might be divided into three sets: (1) the costs and gains of an emphasis on industrial exports; (2) protection against imports; and (3) foreign investment. That division emphasizes specific economic questions rather than the general concept of integration with the world economy, in the belief that some kinds of integration may be helpful at the same time as others should be avoided or strictly limited.

The possible economic gain of an export orientation is that the industrial sector could contribute much more than in the past to growth and employment.[9] If incentives are made sufficiently favorable for the growth of industrial exports, those particular industries best able to contribute to rising national income would be differentially favored. Industrial employment could be generated by activities that add to the supply of foreign exchange instead of merely using it up. Economies of scale obtainable through exporting could increase real returns on investment and make possible a higher rate of growth of wages without disrupting macroeconomic stability. The rate of growth could be made more independent of fluctuations in primary exports and the economy could become less dependent on foreign credit.

Criticisms of such an orientation toward industrial exports include arguments that it simply cannot succeed in the face of protectionism by the industrialized countries, would force suppression of wages in order to price exports low, requires capital-intensive methods of production, concentrates income in relatively few fields and larger firms, or is in general just "more of the same" subjection of the domestic economy to world capitalism.[10] These are important issues which deserve analysis going far beyond the bounds of this chapter. The main suggestion offered here is only that the options depend greatly on the society's fundamental orientation. If the dominant preference as expressed in a nonauthoritarian process is for maximum possible increases in private consumption, with free choice among the most modern consumer goods, then the society cannot escape reliance on the growth of industrial exports. If the dominant preference is instead for a society oriented toward satisfaction of basic needs, with restricted access to modern consumer goods, fewer imports would be required and the country would not need to place so great an emphasis on exports. The only system that is clearly nonviable is to emphasize private consumption with free choice of modern durable goods, and of the specialized equipment needed to produce them, while failing to develop the industrial exports required to pay for them.

Issues of protection against imports involve a parallel mixture of questions about social preference and consistency. Prior to the authoritarian regimes, governments more responsive to public preferences went to costly extremes of protection for import substitution, fostering a kind of industrialization that aggravated inequality, failed to provide employment, and fostered dependence on foreign firms and technology.[11] The authoritarian regimes all took some steps to change this approach, in different ways and degrees. In Brazil, protection was reduced moderately for some fields but kept or even increased on a selective basis when considered to be helpful in stimulating particular new industries, especially in production of capital goods.[12] In Uruguay to a greater degree, and in Chile most of all, the authoritarian governments cut down greatly on protection in all directions. Chile gained in one respect, by getting rid of some high-cost activities with little constructive future. But at the same time, the sweeping reduction of protection on imports of modern consumer goods changed the composition of imports and the distribution of real income in favor of upper-income groups.

A democratic government, concerned with popular support, is bound to come under pressure from the business sector to restore high protection. What should it do? Economic analysis suggests only a partial answer: a return to indiscriminately high protection, determined mainly by the demands of individual producers, would be seriously damaging to future possibilities of growth. The criticism of earlier protection for import substitution was mostly right. But then an additional question arises: what kind of consumption pattern is desired by the society? If it is to be as modern and free as possible, as much like consumption patterns in the industrialized North as possible, then protection should probably be kept low on everything. But if the preferred consumption pattern is instead one emphasizing provision of basic needs, that would argue for keeping mass consumption goods at relatively low prices and upper-income consumer goods at high prices. That course would be favored by keeping high tariffs on imported consumer durables, provided that the tariffs are accompanied by high taxes on any domestic production aimed at replacing such imports. Instead of protection to stimulate domestic production of goods for the upper-income minority, selective protection plus internal taxes would help make the distribution of real income more equal and release resources for more adequate provision of basic needs.

Liberalization of imports for production is in general desirable for efficiency and for export potential, provided that the cost of foreign exchange is kept high relative to domestic prices, but liberalization for modern consumer goods encourages a pattern of consumption open only to a small minority at present income levels. It works against the acceptance of negotiated restraints on wages and against the possibility of any social program that tries to restrain private consumption. Given the extreme inequality of income distribution in Latin America, it does not seem easily compatible with preservation of the social consensus needed in a free society.

The third aspect of international economic policy which could be of great importance for a transition from authoritarianism is the set of national policies toward foreign firms and external credit. The scope for *any* national choice may be drastically curtailed for some years to come by the debt crisis and falloff in foreign investment in the 1980s: the outside world may no longer be trying to get in. But this impasse is not likely to last forever. Foreign firms and lenders will soon regain interest in any economy in which growth can be restored. What should a newly democratic government try to do: encourage renewed foreign investment and borrowing, or discourage them?

If one considers the question of direct foreign investment first, it would seem an unnecessary self-denial to block out foreign firms entirely, but a major risk to go to any great lengths to encourage them. On the favorable side, they can create new employment, new opportunities for learning skills, and sometimes new potential for earnings of foreign exchange. Particular firms that can offer such advantages may help national economic performance and fortify a democratic regime. On the unfavorable side, foreign firms that try to buy out existing domestic producers, or demand protection for sales in the domestic market, or need special tax advantages and administrative favors not available to domestic producers, can set back domestic entrepreneurship and weaken the growth of national capacities for development. Foreign investment is not something to be maximized. A democratic regime is likely to be safer in terms of domestic political strains, and to have better growth possibilities, if foreign investment is accepted only for well-defined particular purposes. Even apart from the special cases of firms that deliberately interfere in domestic political struggles, too much subservience to the wishes of potential foreign investors can weaken popular support for a nonauthoritarian government, and pull it away from social programs basic to its effectiveness.[13]

External credit may be restricted for some time to come for all of these countries, as both they and foreign lenders try to cope with almost unmanageable levels of debt service. In the period 1960–80 growth was speeded up by the unusual availability of external credit at low real rates of interest; in the decade ahead it may be correspondingly slowed down by the burden of service on past debt, and by the reluctance of many lenders to extend new credit. But that constraint may have advantages. The burden of debt service may pull the countries toward more active promotion of industrial exports, and thereby keep up higher rates of growth of production. Such exports may also help to achieve greater economies of scale than were possible in previously constricted Latin American industries. Similarly, pressure to keep up the value of foreign exchange will act to restrain imports of capital goods, and could stimulate more appropriate domestic technology, less dependent on foreign companies. The future may be more difficult than the past in terms of availability of external credit, but it is possible that this new constraint—like the even more drastic contraction of the 1930s—may turn out to be positively stimulating for those countries which respond in more self-determining directions.[14]

Market Forces and the Survival of Nonauthoritarian Regimes

The authoritarian regimes in Argentina, Brazil, Chile, and Uruguay were all explicitly oriented toward the use of market forces to guide production and investment. They partly contradicted this orientation by using wage controls, and Brazil also used considerable protection and subsidization, but they were clearly more inclined to rely on private markets than the preauthoritarian regimes in these countries.[15] Would a newly nonauthoritarian regime have a better chance of survival if it repudiated this basic orientation? Or would its chances be better if it followed the approach of the civilian government in Peru since 1980 and adopted, without the authoritarian repression of Chile, economic policies similar to those attempted by the authoritarian regimes? Or are both such paths likely to be mistakes?

To be wholehearted about whatever one does, including the nature of the economic regime, is enormously appealing. But sometimes the costs are too high. When the questions involve the effort to get people out of extreme poverty and the danger of renewed extremes of repression, not just degrees of efficiency in the allocation of resources, compromises are superior to purity. Neither complete repudiation of the promarket orientation of the authoritarian regimes nor attempts to stay with its more extreme forms would seem to be ideal.

The distinctive economic policies of the authoritarian regimes included potentially separable components: (1) greatly reduced control of prices, lower protection, reorientation of the practices of public firms toward accumulation of a surplus for investment, and attempts to keep interest rates positive in real terms; (2) serious efforts to limit budget deficits and the growth of the money supply, more effective taxation, and changes in patterns of public expenditures toward more support for the military and for investors at the cost of reduced social programs; (3) wage controls and strict limits on independent action by unions; (4) highly favorable conditions for foreign investors and reassurance to property owners against political action adverse to them.

The first of these categories comes closest to what economists usually mean by "reliance on market forces," or at least reduction in degrees of attempted management of markets. They are options related to efficiency and not particularly toward growth. It would be possible to follow them and get no economic growth at all, as Chile did for several years, if accompanying monetary and fiscal restraints are excessive. They could have favorable effects for exports and for employment, and would in general make it easier to achieve relatively rapid growth, if accompanied by exchange rates favorable for industrial exports and by sufficient stimulus to investment. But they would probably act to make the distribution of income less equal, given the present concentration of access to capital and education in Latin America and the existence of underemployment, unless this effect is moderated by selective protection and high taxes on consumer durable goods, by support for gradual wage increases, and by social welfare programs which are designed to avoid blocking the operation of markets. All of these are controversial issues which require concern for the implications of market forces while partly acting against them, but which would not seem likely to produce violent conflict destructive of nonauthoritarian government.

The second of these categories involves issues of macroeconomic balance. They are choices on which most governments swing back and forth all the time, according to current degrees of concern for inflation, employment, social welfare, and military strength. A nonauthoritarian coalition might well reverse the emphasis between military and social expenditures. Such a reversal could greatly change the structures of demand and production, and reduce poverty, without creating any conflict with the price mechanism or macroeconomic stability. A nonauthoritarian government seeking political acceptability could easily be pulled toward more spending and monetary growth than is consistent with stability: that outcome occurs all the time, not only in Latin America. And it may sometimes be politically expedient to give in to group pressures for increased spending, when the alternative would be a head-on confrontation likely to raise social conflict to dangerous levels.[16] The problem is that increasing inflation can be just as bad, or worse. Given the conflict, there is no abstract principle that says what to do. But repetition of the worst prior cases of extreme inflation and external deficits might be less likely if it is remembered that they have their political dangers too: whether or not they seriously damage the operation of the economy, they certainly move the middle class toward bitterness against the political system that permits them.

The third of the above categories, control of wages and suppression of unions, has involved increased state control rather than reliance on markets. It is not difficult to see why the nominally "free market" authoritarian systems so often go this way: it protects profits and suppresses a particularly likely channel of opposition. Should a nonauthoritarian government simply reject all such restraints on labor? It should surely allow independent union organization and the right to strike, or it would not be nonauthoritarian. But the questions raised in the first part of this chapter are critical. Under conditions of excess labor, determination of wages by market forces is most unlikely to be acceptable politically. Sharply differential wage trends, or rapidly increasing real wages for regularly employed workers acting to reduce employment opportunities for everyone else, can be costly too. The first part of this discussion concentrates on these questions because they are among the most sensitive for any nonauthoritarian coalition, and because the case for negotiated rather than market solutions is exceptionally strong.

The fourth category, complete acceptance of foreign investors and political reassurance to property owners, may be the one most closely linked to the authoritarian system. The discussion above argues for a shift toward greater restraint on foreign investment, rather than either the Chilean open door or the contrary of total rejection. Restriction of foreign investment to the particular kinds most useful for the society could mean slower rates of economic growth, though it need not: some kinds of foreign investment can be harmful even in purely economic terms. But even if tight selectivity does slow down growth to some degree, it should still be worthwhile for any nonauthoritarian government concerned with the goals of distribution and employment.

For domestic investors, if the society wants them to operate it will be necessary to give them some assurance against political action that takes their property without compensation. Such assurance need not exclude nationalization by purchase, as in England or France or any other country in which open political systems allow nationalization when the party that advocates it wins elections. It may be that this issue is the ultimate stumbling block for nonauthoritarian systems in Latin America: if open elections seriously threaten complete loss of private property, capitalists will all become authoritarians unless they are stepped on by anticapitalists who become authoritarian themselves.

It is easy to become pessimistic about the chances of survival for nonauthoritarian government in Latin America, whether for the particular reasons considered here or for more general reasons associated with the tensions of increased political awareness in supremely inegalitarian societies.[17] The strains are matters of objective economic and social pressures which could in principle be moderated by more constructive economic policies. To dismiss them as results of an inescapable Latin impatience with restraint is to obscure the real underlying reasons.

There are systematic forces working against the survival of open societies in these countries: such forces may become increasingly powerful if new ways are not found to counteract them. The main disasters so far have come from the extreme Right. They may make things worse for the future, both by persuading conservatives that their interests can best be served by such regimes and by convincing otherwise nonviolent reformers that force and repression are the only ways to survive. But it may also be true that the very brutality of some of these regimes has turned others, including some of their original supporters, toward increased willingness to negotiate and compromise for the sake of a more humane society. If that is so, the chances of success are real. To keep those chances alive, all sides need to recognize economic constraints. The constraints do not cease to exist if the society turns away entirely from the use of market forces, or from international trade, or from private ownership: they are imposed fundamentally by the boundaries of the productive capacity of the economy. They place upper limits on the rate of gain possible for all social groups. Probably the fundamental test for any nonauthoritarian government is its ability to keep any one group from setting the rest of society back by trying to raise its gains at the cost of others, to keep all groups participating in the gains collectively possible through the use of coherent economic policies.

Notes

Chapter 1 International Aspects of Democratization

1. In Robert Dahl's list of the twenty-six so-called polyarchies (by which he meant practical approximations to the theoretical ideal of democracy) that existed in 1969, four were the direct product of external imposition by the U.S.A. (Federal Germany, Italy, Japan, and the Philippines); at least seven more were shaped or recreated in substantial measure under U.S. military influence; and several others may be regarded as economic clients or political satellites whose choice of internal regime must have been significantly affected by their international alignments. In contrast, only seven out of the twenty-six were historical fixtures, in the sense that no undemocratic regime had been known in the present century. Robert A. Dahl, *Polyarchy: Participation and Opposition* (New Haven: Yale University Press, 1971), pp. 248–49.

2. Salazar as quoted in Albano Nogueira, "The Making of the Alliance, A Portuguese Perspective," *NATO Review*, no. 5, 1980, p. 9. Nogueira describes Salazar's "selective reading" of NATO principles as "an act of high statesmanship" (p. 10), and this official NATO journal offered no demur even in 1980. The same issue records the Turkish military coup of September 1980 as if it were a success for NATO principles.

3. Phyllis Parker, *Brazil and the Quiet Intervention, 1964* (Austin: University of Texas Press, 1979), p. 63.

4. See Edward S. Herman and Frank Broadhead, *Demonstration Elections: U.S.-Staged Elections in the Dominican Republic, Vietnam, and El Salvador* (Boston: South End Press, 1984), and Laurence Whitehead, "International Aspects of Democratisation in Central America" (Paper delivered to the Annual Meeting of the American Political Science Association, Washington D.C., 1 September 1984).

5. Christian Deubner, "The Southern Enlargement of the European Community," *Journal of Common Market Studies*, March 1980, p. 231.

6. William Minter, *Portuguese Africa and the West* (Harmondsworth: Penguin, 1972), p. 43.

7. At its tenth congress in Caracas in December 1983 the ODCA adopted a manifesto that stated that "the number one problem in Latin America is called 'dictatorship' and its solution 'democracy.' " According to ODCA's president, Ricardo Arias Calderón, "the content of democracy is identified in terms of three principles: the respect for human rights; the affirmation that free, regular elections, while not the 'whole' of democratic participation, are fundamental to it; and the public character of all governmental activity, as well as the responsibility of all governmental agents. It is also identified with the validity of certain institutions and organizations: the revaluation of parties as organs of political mediation; the independence of the legislative and judiciary; freedom of the media, as well as free access to them by representative sectors of the community; and freedom of labor unions and of other intermediary associations and groups."

8. The Final Resolution of the October 1984 Bureau meeting reaffirmed that "in order to establish democracy firmly in Latin America and the Caribbean it must find expression at every level of society. This must be achieved in economic and social terms. Only economic and social democracy can provide the guarantee for a durable political democracy." It should be noted that the New Jewel Movement, which ruled

Grenada prior to the U.S. invasion of October 1983, was a full member of the SI. Since that invasion the U.S. State Department has published numerous captured documents, many of which concern the NJM's support for revolutionary, as opposed to social democratic, positions within the SI.

9. One of the first acts of the reconstituted SI, in July 1951, was to send a telegram to Secretary of State Dean Acheson: "We express the concern of 43 million Socialists at the present resolution to associate Franco Spain with the community of democratic peoples. Democracy cannot be defended by measures which would reinforce the position of dictatorship in any part of the world."

10. The quotation is from a "Statement on Argentina and Chile" issued by the International Department of the British Labour party in 1977, which said that "the Labour party fully agrees with Mitterrand's statement." It does not follow that ministers in the then Labour government necessarily agreed, but it is the party, not the ministers, that sends delegates to the Socialist International.

11. Robert A. Packenham, *Liberal America and the Third World* (Princeton: Princeton University Press, 1973) provides a useful insight into American "Cold War Liberalism" written from the standpoint of a reluctant and far from ruthless critic. His analysis of the Kennedy administration's perspective on Latin America is especially relevant here. See pp. 53–56, 69–81, 163–73.

12. Perón had risen to power following a coup in 1943 by nationalist, and in some cases pro-Axis officers in Argentina, but in fairly honest elections in 1946 Perón won in the face of State Department censure. "Many Latins charged that the U.S. opposition to Perón was inconsistent with its toleration of other Latin American dictatorships. Although it is true that the kind of attack the U.S. waged on Perón was withheld from Somoza of Nicaragua and Trujillo of the Dominican Republic, consideration has to be given to the fact that these dictators had been loyal in their observance of inter-American commitments." J. Lloyd Meecham, *The U.S. and Inter-American Security, 1889–1960* (Austin: University of Texas Press, 1961), p. 290.

13. Quotations are from document PPS-26, dated 22 March 1948, classified secret, as printed in Department of State, *Foreign Relations of the United States: 1948*, vol 9 (Washington D.C.: U.S. Government Printing Office, 1972), pp. 194–201. (Henceforth referred to as *FRUSA*.)

14. It is not unusual for democratic regimes that are fragile, internally, to engage in activist foreign policies designed to promote democracy in their region and to combat adjacent authoritarian regimes. Thus, for example, the insecure Betancourt regime in Venezuela (1945–48) broke relations with Franco, Trujillo, and Somoza. In 1946 Betancourt advocated a "prophylactic cordon" around the antidemocratic governments of Latin America, adding that as long as there was a single government in the Americas not practicing Roosevelt's "Four Freedoms," the liberty of all the others was threatened. Arévalo's Guatemala took an even more vigorous antidictatorial line at the same time, and for the same reasons.

15. In 1974 the OAS General Secretariat published a document entitled "The Marxist-Leninist Process in Chile," which concluded: "Morally Mr. Allende disqualified himself as the President of the Nation when he said 'I am first a Marxist and then President' " (p. 353).

16. The quotation is from the speech by Mr. Birkelbach, presenting his report on behalf of the political commission, 23 January 1962. *Debates* of the European Assembly.

17. Stanley Henig, *External Relations of the European Community* (London: PEP [Political & Economic Planning], 1971), p. 91. The brackets are mine. The Athens Agreement was not actually frozen, but restricted to "current administration" so that tariff barriers were gradually dismantled on both sides, while the dictatorship subsisted.

18. The subtleties of the interplay between EC pressures and domestic realignments within Greece are nicely captured in Panos Tsakaloyannis and Susannah Verney,

"Linkage Politics: The Role of the European Community in Greek Politics in 1973," forthcoming in *Byzantine and Modern Greek Studies*.

19. S. M. Lipset, *Political Man* (London: Heinemann, 1963; Expanded edition, Baltimore: Johns Hopkins University Press, 1981), p. 79.

20. *The Report of the President's National Bipartisan Commission on Central America* (New York: Macmillan, 1984), p. 75. Although the report can be read as favoring multilateralism, and depoliticization of the aid program, it also expresses Washington's great reluctance to allow any dilution of its discretionary control in the region.

21. See my conclusion to G. di Palma and L. Whitehead, eds. *The Central American Impasse* (Beckenham: Croom Helm, 1986).

22. Federico G. Gil, Enrique A. Baloyra, and Lars Schoultz provide a valuable description of the activities of these organizations during the 1970s, in "U.S. Interest Groups and Democracy in Latin America," an annex to their draft report to the State Department, "Democracy in Latin America: Prospects and Implications" (Washington D.C., December 1980).

23. Robert Alexander, "Socialism in Latin America," *Socialist World* 1, no. 3 (December 1947–February 1948): 24.

24. James Petras claims that the West German SPD contributed 60 percent of the SI's total budget and that "the proposition that German Social Democracy is oriented toward creating a political base for German capital in Latin America is generally accepted in European circles." *Class, State, and Power in the Third World* (London: Zed Press, 1981), p. 143. This is a mechanistic viewpoint, however. The Latin countries most affected by SI activism are those of least interest from a commercial standpoint. In any case, German and Swedish supremacy in the SI was a temporary phase, with France and Spain taking the lead thereafter. One of the first acts of the new (probusiness) German government that took power in November 1982 was to cancel the SPD's policy of sending aid to Nicaragua.

25. President Reagan's speech to both Houses of Parliament, 9 June 1982.

26. N. Gordon Levin, Jr., *Woodrow Wilson and World Politics: America's Response to War and Revolution* (New York: Oxford University Press, 1968), p. 43.

27. Ibid., p. 156.

28. R. A. Humphreys, *Latin America and the Second World War*, vol. 2, pp. 42–45 (London: Athlone, 1982), includes sketches of how various Latin American republics responded to the imminence of an Allied victory by adopting at least superficially more "democratic" forms of government.

29. See Packenham, *Liberal America*, pp. 27–32. He considers that, between the end of the Greek Civil War and the outbreak of the Korean War, the Truman administration repeatedly strove to "bring about a more genuine democracy in Greece," before admitting failure (p. 30). But he also states that "American officials underplayed the repressive and corrupt features of the Greek regime in 1947; they did the same thing after the coup in 1967" (p. 170). For a thoughtful survey of recent scholarship on the Greek Civil War see R. V. Burks, "Hellenic Time of Troubles," *Problems of Communism* 33 (November–December 1984).

30. *FRUSA: 1948*, vol. 9 (Washington D.C., 1972), p. 116.

31. Romulo Betancourt, *Venezuela: Oil and Politics* (Boston: Houghton Mifflin, 1979), pp. 237–42. In a footnote, he judiciously accepts Truman's assertion that no malice was intended. The Truman letter is printed in *FRUSA: 1949*, vol. 2 (Washington D.C., 1975), pp. 797–99.

32. *FRUSA: 1949*, p. 751.

33. Extracted from a long secret appraisal of U.S.-Guatemalan relations, dated 2 May 1951, in *FRUSA: 1951*, vol. 2 (Washington D.C., 1979), pp. 1416, 1417.

34. *FRUSA: 1949*, p. 445.

35. Ibid., p. 665.

36. Ibid., p. 800.

37. Jerome Slater, *The OAS and U.S. Foreign Policy* (Columbus: Ohio State University Press, 1967), p. 240. See, in particular, his account of OAS policy toward the Dominican Republic during the failed democratic experiments of 1960–63, and of the lack of U.S. diplomatic backing for Venezuela and Costa Rica in their condemnations of the military coups in other Latin countries in 1962–63 (pp. 245–50); also his conclusions (pp. 282–88).

38. Packenham, *Liberal America*, p. 69.

39. According to Mrs. Jeane Kirkpatrick, who became an ambassador in the Reagan administration, dictatorships of the Left are "totalitarian" and therefore more oppressive toward civil society than the "authoritarian" dictatorships of the Right. Also, the former never evolve into democracies, whereas the latter do. This sweeping system of classification enables her to argue that true democrats must support "authoritarian" regimes whenever they confront a "totalitarian" threat. Since authoritarian regimes always claim the existence of such a threat, and indeed frequently try to force their domestic critics into the arms of the revolutionary opposition, this schema means in practice that Washington can find *any* kind of right-wing authoritarianism compatible with America's democratic conscience. There is *some* empirical basis for this convenient dichotomy, but as this chapter may have illustrated, the real world is more complex and troubling to the American conscience. Was Guatemala 1944–54 more oppressive to civil society than Guatemala 1954–82? Which was more capable of evolving into a democracy? More generally, this dichotomy demands democratization in countries under Soviet military control, where America has no influence, and where, indeed, its exhortations may well be counterproductive. It simultaneously excuses Washington from antagonizing undemocratic allies who may be more susceptible to influence, and it grants respectability to almost any cosmetic moves the entrenched authoritarians may make to legitimize and extend their prerogatives.

40. *The Rockefeller Report on the Americas* (Chicago: Quadrangle, 1969) gave a semiofficial imprimatur to some of these arguments. "Democracy is a very subtle and difficult problem for most of the other countries in the hemisphere. . . . The authoritarian tradition . . . of most of these societies does not lend itself to the particular kind of popular government we are used to. . . . For many of these societies, therefore, the question is less one of democracy or lack of it than it is simply of orderly ways of getting along" (p. 58).

Chapter 2 Some Problems in the Study of the Transition to Democracy

Editors' Note: When the idea of convoking a working group on "Transitions from Authoritarian Rule: Prospects for Democracy" first surfaced in the Latin American Program of the Wilson Center, we were confronted with a paucity of theoretical material to guide such a venture. The volume edited by Juan Linz and Alfred Stepan on *The Breakdown of Democratic Regimes*, published by Johns Hopkins University Press, 1978, served as a model for our efforts, but dealt with the "other end," so to speak, of the change process. Most contemporary theorizing about democracy was oriented exclusively toward explaining how such regimes functioned, *not* how they came into being. Our response was to commission three "think pieces" to help get the project started. This one by Adam Przeworski is the only one to be included in this, the Working Group's final product. The other two have been published and circulated, but we chose to omit them in part because some of their better ideas and concepts have been picked up in subsequent chapters by project participants, and in part because these have been developed in the fourth volume of this collection in which two of us reflect on "Tentative Conclusions about Uncertain Transitions." For those readers who are curious enough to wish to see these initial efforts at dealing with the topic, they are: Guillermo O'Donnell, "Notas para el estudio del processo de democratización política a partir del estado burocrático autoritario," *Desarrollo Económico* 22, no. 86 (July–September 1982): 231–48; and Philippe C. Schmitter, "Speculations about the Prospective Demise of Authoritarian Regimes and Its Possible Consequences" (Working Paper no. 80, Latin American Program, Wilson Center, Washington, D.C., 1980, subsequently revised and reprinted as Working Paper of the European University Institute, Florence, Italy, 1984).

1. Barrington Moore, *Social Origins of Dictatorship and Democracy* (Boston: Beacon, 1965).

2. Karl Marx, *The Class Struggles in France, 1848–1850* (Moscow: Progress, 1952) and *The Eighteenth Brumaire of Louis Bonaparte* (Moscow: Progress, 1934).

3. Juan Linz, *Crisis, Breakdown, and Reequilibration* (Baltimore: Johns Hopkins University Press, 1978).

4. Etienne Balibar, "The Basic Concepts of Historical Materialism," in *Reading Capital*, ed. Louis Althusser and Etienne Balibar (New York: Pantheon, 1970).

5. Jon Elster, *Logic and Society: Contradictions and Possible Worlds* (New York: Wiley, 1978), p. 190, notation slightly changed.

6. Giandomenico Majone, "On the Notion of Political Feasibility," *European Journal of Political Research* 3 (1975): 261.

7. Guillermo O'Donnell and Philippe Schmitter, "Prospects for Democracy: Transitions from Authoritarian Rule—A Proposal for a Series of Discussions at the Wilson Center" (Washington, D.C.: Latin American Program—Woodrow Wilson International Center for Scholars, 1979).

8. Max Weber, *Economy and Society*, vol. 1 (New York: Bedminster, 1968), p. 213.

9. Ibid., vol. 3, p. 953.

10. Ibid., vol. 1, p. 214.

11. Ibid., emphasis added.

12. Bolivar Lamounier, "O discurso e o processo" (Paper presented at workshop on "Prospects for Democracy: Transitions from Authoritarian Rule in Latin America and Latin Europe" sponsored by the Latin American Program of the Woodrow Wilson International Center for Scholars, Washington, D.C., 25–26 September 1979).

13. Arthur Stinchcombe, *Constructing Social Theories* (New York: Harcourt, 1968), p. 162.

14. On this issue, see Jürgen Habermas, *Legitimation Crisis* (Boston: Beacon, 1975), pp. 97–102.

15. Adam Przeworski, "Material Bases of Consent: Politics and Economics in a Hegemonic System," *Political Power and Social Theory* 1 (1980): 23–68.

16. Thomas C. Schelling, *Micromotives and Macrobehavior* (New York: Norton, 1978), chap. 7.

17. Nicos Poulantzas, *Political Power and Social Classes* (London: New Left Books, 1973), pp. 99–109.

18. *El Mercurio*, 5 September 1970, author's translation.

19. The quotation is cited in Pablo Lucas Verou, *Crítica Jurídico-Política de la Reforma Suarez* (Madrid: Editorial Tecnos, 1976.)

20. The quotation is cited in Dankwart A. Rustow, *The Politics of Compromise: A Study of Parties and Cabinet Government in Sweden* (Princeton: Princeton University Press, 1955), p. 59.

21. Douglas Verney, *Parliamentary Reform in Sweden, 1866–1921* (Oxford: Oxford University Press, 1957), p. 168.

22. Roque Sáenz Peña, *La Reforma Electoral* (Buenos Aires: Editorial Raigal, 1952), p. 124.

23. *Le Monde*, 6 July 1979.

24. See Przeworski, "Material Bases of Consent: Politics and Economics in a Hegemonic System" for details.

25. Antonio Gramsci, *Selections from the Prison Notebooks* (New York: International, 1971), pp. 160, 181.

26. Adam Przeworski, "Social Democracy as a Historical Phenomenon," *New Left Review* 122 (July–August 1980).

27. Santiago Carrillo, *Demain L'Espagne* (Paris: Seuil, 1974), p. 187; author's translation.

28. A correlation of +0.41 in a sample of 3,000 was reported by Peter McDonough, Samuel H. Barnes, and Antonio López Piña in "The Spanish Public and the Transition to Democracy," (Paper presented at the 1979 meeting of the American Political Science Association, Washington, D.C.).

Chapter 3 Paths toward Redemocratization: Theoretical and Comparative Considerations

1. See Sverre Kjelstadli, "The Resistance Movement in Norway and the Allies, 1940–1945," and L. de Jong, "The Dutch Resistance Movement and the Allies, 1940–1945," both in *European Resistance Movements, 1939–1945: Proceedings of the Second International Conference on the History of the Resistance Movements Held at Milan, 26–29 March 1961* (New York: Macmillan, 1964). See also Henri Michel, *The Shadow War: European Resistance, 1939–1945* (New York: Harper & Row, 1972), esp. pp. 301–2, 336–38.

2. In Holland, however, the restoration was accompanied by some criticisms to the effect that the prewar political parties had been responsible for the parlous state the armed forces found themselves in on the eve of hostilities. There was also a perceptible shift toward greater secularism in Dutch politics and a nonconfessional Labor party emerged.

3. Per Nutrup, *An Outline of the German Occupation of Denmark, 1940–1945* (Copenhagen: Danish National Museum, 1968) and Henning Poulsen and Marlene Djursaa, "Social Basis of Nazism in Denmark: The DNSAP," in *Who Were the Fascists?: Social Roots of European Fascism*, Ed. Stein Ugelvik Larsen, Bernt Hagtvet, and Jan Petter Myklebust (Bergen: Universitetsforlaget, 1980).

4. Michel, *The Shadow War*, pp. 302, 337–38; Val R. Lorwin, "Belgium: Religion, Class, and Language in National Politics," in *Political Oppositions in Western Democracies*, ed. Robert A. Dahl (New Haven: Yale University Press, 1966), pp. 168–69, 177; Jacques Pirenne, *Dossier du Roi Leopold III* (Luxembourg: L'Imprimerie St. Paul, n.d.), and Brian Bond, *France and Belgium, 1939–1940* (London: Davis-Poynter, 1975), pp. 143–57.

5. Robert Owen Paxton, *Vichy France: Old Guard and New Order, 1940–1944* (New York: Knopf, 1972), p. 20; see also Robert Aron, *Histoire des Années 40* (Paris: Librairie Jules Tallander, 1976), vol. 1, pp. 61–226.

6. John F. Sweets, *The Politics of Resistance in France, 1940–1944: A History of the Mouvements Unis de la Résistance* (De Kalb: Northern Illinois University Press, 1976), pp. 33–70, 115–48.

7. Paxton, *Vichy France*, pp. 291–98.

8. Aron, *Histoire des Années 40*, vol. 10, pp. 406–19.

9. Ibid., vol. 9, pp. 16–31.

10. The PCF had two members in de Gaulle's CFLN (National Liberation Committee) as early as 1944, and Communist ministers were also in the Provisional government. See Sweets, *The Politics of Resistance in France*, pp. 115–49.

11. Thomas T. Mackie and Richard Rose, *The International Almanac of Electoral History*, 2d ed. (New York: Facts on File, 1982).

12. For Greece consult Richard Clogg, *A Short History of Modern Greece* (Cambridge: Cambridge University Press, 1979), pp. 133–226; P. Nikiforos Diamandouros, "Regime Change and the Prospects for Democracy in Greece: 1974–83," in Volume I of this series; George Th. Mavrogordatos, "From Ballots to Bullets: The 1946 Election and Plebiscite as Prelude to Civil War" (Paper presented at the Symposium of the Modern

Greek Studies Association on "Greece in the 1940s," 9-12 November 1978, American University, Washington, D.C.); Nicos Mouzelis, "Regime Instability and the State in Peripheral Capitalism: A General Theory and a Case Study of Greece," (Working Paper no. 79, Latin American Program, Wilson Center, Washington, D.C., 1980); and Nicos C. Alivizatos, "The Greek Army in the Late Forties: Towards an Institutional Autonomy," *Journal of the Hellenic Diaspora* 3 (Fall 1978): 37-45.

13. See the excellent chapter by Gianfranco Pasquino, "The Demise of the First Fascist Regime and Italy's Transition to Democracy: 1943-1948," in Volume I of this series.

14. F. W. Deakin, *The Brutal Friendship: Mussolini, Hitler, and the Fall of Italian Fascism* (New York: Harper & Row, 1962), pp. 419-85.

15. Pasquino, "Demise of the First Fascist Regime," chap. 3 in Volume 1.

16. Armed anti-Fascist parties and organized resistance only began to show their presence to any appreciable extent after September 1943. See Charles F. Delzell, *Mussolini's Enemies: The Italian Anti-Fascist Resistance* (Princeton: Princeton University Press, 1961), pp. 261-314 and Michel, *The Shadow War*, pp. 302-4.

17. See Norman Kogan, *Italy and the Allies* (Cambridge, Mass.: Harvard University Press, 1956) and his *A Political History of Post-War Italy* (London: Pall Mall Press, 1966).

18. Pasquino, "Demise of the First Fascist Regime," chap. 3 in Volume 1.

19. Ibid.

20. Kogan argues that in 1943 the Allies demanded "the provisional abandonment of all goals of social reform for the duration of hostilities. . . . The preservation of the social structure for its own sake was not the only motive behind Allied demands. . . . Reform and change would mean political conflict and headaches for Allied administrators. So for immediate, practical reasons the Allies threw their weight behind the status quo." See Kogan, *Italy and the Allies*, pp. 60-61.

21. Pasquino, "Demise of the First Fascist Regime." See also the articles by M. De Cecco, "Economic Policy in the Reconstruction Period, 1945-1951," and B. Salvati, "The Rebirth of Italian Trade Unionism, 1943-1954," in *The Rebirth of Italy, 1943-1950*, ed. S. J. Woolf (New York: Humanities Press, 1972), pp. 156-80, 181-211.

22. Juan Linz in a commentary on an earlier version of my chapter notes that in Germany "the Allied high command in the western sectors implemented a controlled process of redemocratization defining the rules of the game, the timing of the process, excluding some potential political forces by limiting the number of parties, the *Lizenparteien*, and giving them a series of advantages which would assure the future strengths of some of them, at the same time that they exercised considerable influence on the constitutional framework, imposing their version of federalism and supporting a particular model of social economic organization." See his "The Transition from Authoritarian Regimes to Democratic Political Systems and the Problems of Consolidation of Political Democracy" (Paper prepared for the International Political Science Association, Tokyo Round Table, 29 March–1 April 1982), p. 25.

23. For one of the few comparative analyses of all four cases see Linz, "Transition from Authoritarian Regimes," pp. 23-28. For a standard history of monitored installation in Germany see Hans W. Gatzke, *Germany and the United States: A Special Relationship* (Cambridge, Mass.: Harvard University Press, 1980), pp. 154-78, and Edward N. Peterson, *The American Occupation of Germany: Retreat to Victory* (Detroit: Wayne State University Press, 1977). For a revisionist account, see Bruce Kuklick, *American Policy and the Division of Germany: The Clash with Russia over Reparations* (Ithaca: Cornell University Press, 1972). For Japan see Edwin O. Reischauer, *The United States and Japan* (Cambridge, Mass.: Harvard University Press, 1965), and for a revisionist version see John Dower, *Empire and Aftermath: Yoshida Sigero and the Japanese Experience, 1878 1954* (Cambridge, Mass.: Harvard University Press, 1979).

24. Robert A. Dahl, *Polyarchy: Participation and Opposition* (New Haven: Yale University Press, 1971), p. 15.

25. For the argument that "it is *within the nature of democracy that no one's interests can be guaranteed*" and that "democratic compromise cannot be a substantive compromise; it can only be a contingent institutional compromise," see Adam Przeworski, "Some Problems in the Study of the Transition to Democracy" in this volume. (Emphasis added.)

26. Some examples of authoritarian regimes in which the civilian or civilianized military is dominant over the military-as-institution are Spain after the death of Franco, the first Vargas regime in Brazil (1930–45), the Mexican government since the late 1930s, and Turkey in the 1940s.

27. For example, in terms of these three factors, the conditions in Egypt and Cuba after Nasser and Castro came to power were such that factor 3 was supportive of a choice for democratization (both Nasser and Castro would have won), but factor 2 pressure was absent in both countries, and in neither country was there significant pressure for democratization from below (factor 1).

28. Linz, "Transition from Authoritarian Regimes," p. 28. In the first version of this chapter I overemphasized the role of the leadership of the authoritarian regime and Linz in the cited manuscript urged a greater attention to the role of the opposition in Spain. I gratefully acknowledge my debt to Linz for this observation.

29. Ibid.

30. Ibid. For the Spanish transition see also José María Maravall and Julián Santamaría, "Political Change in Spain, and the Prospects for Democracy," in Volume 1 of this series; Juan Linz, "Spain and Portugal Critical Choices," in *Western Europe: The Trials of Partnership*, ed. David S. Landes (Lexington, Mass.: Heath, 1977), pp. 237–96, and John F. Coverdale, *The Political Transformation of Spain After Franco* (New York: Praeger, 1979).

31. For an analysis of the aborted movement toward greater democratization in Mexico in the 1970s, see the chapter by Kevin J. Middlebrook, "Political Liberalization in an Authoritarian Regime: The Case of Mexico," in Volume 2 of this series.

32. For a comparative analysis of political institution building that demilitarized the Turkish and Mexican revolutions see Samuel P. Huntington, *Political Order in Changing Societies* (New Haven: Yale University Press, 1968), pp. 255–58. For Atatürk's conscious depoliticization of the army see Dankwart A. Rustow, "The Army and the Founding of the Turkish Republic," *World Politics* 11 (July 1959): 543–52. There is much to learn from Turkey in the 1930s, and 1940s, but it has not been included here because it was a case of first-time democratization, not redemocratization.

33. A borderline case is Turkey in 1961. See Walter F. Weiker, *The Turkish Revolution 1960–1961: Aspects of Military Politics* (Washington, D.C.: Brookings Institution, 1963) and Ergun Ozbudun, *The Role of the Military in Recent Turkish Politics* (Cambridge, Mass.: Harvard University, Center for International Affairs, Occasional Papers in International Affairs, No. 14, November 1966). It falls short of being a pure example because the weightiest element of the "military-as-institution" also urged the extrication from office. Another virtual borderline case of a military-as-government-led redemocratization would be that of Argentine General Aramburu's decision to initiate the process that eventually resulted in the election of Frondizi in 1958. As in Turkey it is not quite a pure case because much of the support also came from the military-as-institution. For a discussion of the Argentine military during this period see Robert A. Potash, *The Army and Politics in Argentina, 1945–1962* (Stanford: Stanford University Press, 1980), pp. 214–71.

34. See my "O Que Estão Pensando os Militares," *Novos Estudos CEBRAP* 2, no. 2 (July 1983): 2–7 and my "State Power and the Strength of Civil Society in the Southern Cone of Latin America," in *Bringing the State Back In*, ed. Peter Evans, Dietrich Rueschemeyer, and Theda Skocpol (New York: Cambridge University Press, 1985).

35. There are, of course, a variety of cases. For example, there can be a moderate threat when the military-as-institution withdraws its support from a civilian authoritarian regime (Vargas in 1945) or a greater threat when the military-as-institution, with some civilian support, moves against a civilianized populist military figure who is mobilizing autonomous forces (Perón in 1955).

36. For Greece see Diamandouros, "Regime Change and the Prospects for Democracy in Greece: 1974–83," Clogg, *A Short History of Modern Greece,* and Mouzelis, "Regime Instability and the State in Peripheral Capitalism."

37. For Portugal see Kenneth Maxwell, "Regime Overthrow and the Prospects for Democratic Transition in Portugal" in Volume 1 of this series. See also Antonio Rangel Bandeira, "The Portuguese Armed Forces Movement: Historical Antecedents, Professional Demands, and Class Conflicts," *Politics and Society* 6, no. 1 (1976): 1–56.

38. See Alfred Stepan, *The State and Society: Peru in Comparative Perspective* (Princeton: Princeton University Press, 1978), pp. 298–301. See also the chapter by Julio Cotler, "Military Intervention and Transfer of Power to Civilians in Peru," in Volume 2 of this series. I was in Argentina in July 1982 after the surrender in Malvinas. In interviews with a number of military officers a strong argument repeatedly articulated was that the internal political mission of the military-as-government had made the military incompetent and divided in regard to its central military mission and that the corporate survival of the military-as-institution necessitated that it withdraw from power as soon as possible. As in Greece in 1975, the military's perception of the urgency of the need to extricate from power decreased its will and capacity to resist posttransition reprisals against central members of the military-as-government.

39. Two cases of society-led regime transition were Iran during the movement against the shah and the French Revolution before Napoleon. Korea during the revolt against General Park was an attempted case but it reverted to a military regime.

40. Arend Lijphart, *Democracy in Plural Societies: A Comparative Perspective* (New Haven: Yale University Press, 1977).

41. For the role of party pacts with consociational elements in Colombia see Alexander Wilde, "Conversations among Gentlemen: Oligarchical Democracy in Colombia" in *The Breakdown of Democratic Regimes: Latin America,* ed. Juan J. Linz and Alfred Stepan (Baltimore: Johns Hopkins University Press, 1978), pp. 28–81 and Robert H. Dix, "Consociational Democracy: The Case of Colombia," *Comparative Politics* 12 (April 1980): 303–21. For party pacts in Venezuela see Daniel H. Levine, *Conflict and Political Change in Venezuela* (Princeton: Princeton University Press, 1973) and his "Venezuela since 1958: The Consolidation of Democratic Politics," in *The Breakdown of Democratic Regimes,* ed. Linz and Stepan, pp. 82–109.

42. This statement is the central argument of Terry Karl, "Petroleum and Political Pacts: The Transition to Democracy in Venezuela" in Volume 2 of this series. Jonathan Hartlyn discusses consociational exclusion in his "Consociational Politics in Colombia: Confrontation and Accommodation in Comparative Perspective" (Ph.D. diss., Department of Political Science, Yale University, 1981).

43. See Linz, "The Transition from Authoritarian Regimes to Democratic Political Systems," p. 66.

44. This statement was the reluctant conclusion of a number of senior Christian Democratic leaders, including Eduardo Frei, in interviews with the author in Santiago after the plebiscite.

45. I analyze the Uruguayan and Chilean comparison with greater detail and documentation in my "State Power and the Strength of Civil Society in the Southern Cone of Latin America," in *Bringing the State Back In,* ed. Evans, Rueschemeyer, and Skocpol.

46. The Costa Rican case is not a simple case of redemocratization, however. There are numerous ambiguities. For example, despite the government's attempt to annul the presidential election results in 1948 an argument could be made that up to that time Costa Rica did not have a full-blown authoritarian regime, but rather one in which the

standards of open electoral contestation had been deteriorating for about eight years. Also the goals of José Figueres, who led the victorious forces in the Civil War, were not simple *restoration* but *reformulation*. In fact he had long urged the need to create a "Second Republic" and had been organizing an armed uprising *before* the presidential electoral fraud. Finally, despite the social reforms that were carried out, Figueres *narrowed* the range of political and legal participation in Costa Rica by outlawing the Communist party and by using a variety of methods virtually to destroy one of Latin America's best organized and most powerful Communist trade union movements, a movement that had originally helped put on the books many of the reforms that Figueres and his followers eventually implemented and claimed for their own. For a book that discusses the broad outlines of the 1948 Civil War and analyzes the ambiguities see John Patrick Bell, *Crisis in Costa Rica: The 1948 Revolution* (Austin: University of Texas Press, 1971). For a more hagiographic account see Burt H. English, *Liberación Nacional in Costa Rica: The Development of a Political Party in a Transitional Society* (Gainesville: University of Florida Press, 1971).

47. The most complete account of this sad cycle is James M. Malloy, *Bolivia: The Uncompleted Revolution* (Pittsburgh: University of Pittsburgh Press, 1970).

48. See Karl, "Petroleum and Political Pacts."

49. See Alex Pravda, "Elections in Communist Party States," and Juan J. Linz, "Non-Competitive Elections in Europe," both in *Elections without Choice*, ed. Guy Hermet, Richard Rose, and Alain Rouquié (New York: Wiley, 1978), pp. 169–212, 36–65.

50. See Richard Weinert, "The Nicaraguan Debt Re-Negotiation," *Cambridge Journal of Economics* 5, no. 2 (1981): 187–94.

51. For the important role of the domestic bourgeoisie in the struggle against Somoza see Harold Jung, "Behind the Nicaraguan Revolution," *New Left Review* 117 (September–October 1979): 69–90. All the Nicaraguan bishops signed the important statement in support of the then still unresolved revolutionary struggle. See Conferencia Episcopal de Nicaragua, *Mensaje al Pueblo Nicaragüense: Momento Insurreccional, 2 de Junio 1979*. Even more significant was a pastoral letter, again signed by every Nicaraguan bishop, almost four months after the revolution was successful, explicitly acknowledging, if a few key safeguards were maintained, a role for the Sandinistas in carrying out the postrevolutionary government. See Carta Pastoral del Episcopado Nicaragüense, *Compromiso Cristiano para Una Nicaragua Nueva* (Managua, 17 November 1979).

52. For a thoughtful discussion of the dilemmas of the Nicaraguan Revolution by an important thinker and participant see Xabier Gorostiaga, "Dilemmas of the Nicaraguan Revolution," in *The Future of Central America: Policy Choices for the U.S. and Mexico*, ed. Richard R. Fagen and Olga Pellicer (Stanford: Stanford University Press, 1983), pp. 47–66. See also Richard R. Fagen, "The Nicaraguan Revolution," (Working Paper no. 78, Wilson Center, Latin American Program, (Washington, D.C., October 1980).

Chapter 4 Liberalization and Democratization in South America: Perspectives from the 1970s

Editors' Note: This chapter is a revised and shortened version of a paper originally prepared in 1980, comparing Argentina, Brazil, Chile, and Uruguay in the 1970s. For obvious reasons we advised the author not to incorporate new material referring to developments since 1980. These are discussed separately in the respective country studies in Volume 2. The debt crisis and the South Atlantic conflict, together with other factors, would require extended treatment giving rise to a new and different comparative paper. The experiences of the 1970s deserve comparison in their own right without the distortions produced by hindsight.

1. Fernando Henrique Cardoso and Enzo Faletto, *Dependency and Development in Latin America* (Berkeley and Los Angeles: University of California Press, 1978); Guillermo O'Donnell, *Modernization and Bureaucratic-Authoritarianism: Studies in South American Politics* (Berkeley: Institute of International Studies, University of California, 1973); "Reflections on the Patterns of Change in the Bureaucratic-Authoritarian State," *Latin American Research Review* 12, no. 1 (Winter 1978): 3–38 and "Tensions in the Bureaucratic-Authoritarian State and the Question of Democracy," in *The New Authoritarianism in Latin America*, ed. David Collier (Princeton: Princeton University Press, 1979), pp. 285–319.

2. See the critical discussions of these issues in Collier, ed., *The New Authoritarianism*.

3. I have elaborated some of these points more fully in Robert R. Kaufman, "Industrial Change and Authoritarian Rule in Latin America: A Concrete Review of the Bureaucratic-Authoritarian Model," in *The New Authoritarianism*, ed. Collier, pp. 165–255.

4. See Cardoso and Faletto, *Dependency and Development*, pp. 142–79.

5. See ibid., pp. 149–216.

6. Thomas E. Skidmore, "The Politics of Economic Stabilization in Postwar Latin America," in *Authoritarianism and Corporatism in Latin America*, ed. James M. Malloy (Pittsburgh: University of Pittsburgh Press, 1977), p. 181.

7. See Hollis Chenery et al., *Redistribution with Growth* (London: Oxford University Press, 1974).

8. For a more extended version of this crossnational proposition, see Kaufman, "Industrial Change and Authoritarian Rule," pp. 217–44; and "Mexico and Latin American Authoritarianism," *Authoritarianism in Mexico*, ed. José Luis Reyna and Richard S. Weinert (Philadelphia: Institute for the Study of Human Issues, 1977), pp. 193–233. Venezuela, arguably the single "deviant" case, will be dealt with in more detail.

9. For an exceptionally persuasive argument about the avoidability of at least one bureaucratic-authoritarian crisis, see Arturo Valenzuela, *The Breakdown of Democratic Regimes, Chile* (Baltimore: Johns Hopkins University Press, 1978).

10. Cardoso and Faletto argue that although "dependent development" may be possible under "restricted democracies" as well as authoritarian rule, such development is not "structurally compatible" with "substantive forms of mass democracy . . . since in these regimes the requisite policies leading to the expansion of industrial dependent capitalism become difficult to implement, because of the masses' interest in economic redistribution and political participation" (*Dependency and Development*, p. 211).

11. I have deliberately substituted references to exclusionary *processes* and bureaucratic-authoritarian *governments* for the more customary references to bureaucratic-authoritarian "states" or "regimes." The terms "state" and "regime" imply a degree of sociopolitical equilibrium and "institutionality" that, in my judgment, has not been established in the cases discussed in this chapter.

12. See O'Donnell, "Reflections" and "Tensions in the Bureaucratic-Authoritarian State."

13. See Adam Przeworski, "Some Problems in the Study of the Transition to Democracy," in this volume, for a more general discussion of the "bandwagon" effect.

14. O'Donnell, "Tensions in the Bureaucratic-Authoritarian State."

15. O'Donnell, "Reflections."

16. Robert A. Dahl, *Polyarchy: Participation and Opposition* (New Haven: Yale University Press, 1971).

17. The example of Leonel Brizola is illustrative. A man who during the early 1960s was publicly calling for direct action and the formation of guerrilla forces has now returned to Brazil as a moderate "social democrat."

18. Daniel H. Levine, *Conflict and Political Change in Venezuela* (Princeton: Princeton University Press, 1973).

19. James C. Scott, "Corruption, Machine Politics, and Political Change," *American Political Science Review* 63 (December 1969): 1142–59.

20. Franklin Tugwell, *The Politics of Oil in Venezuela* (Stanford: Stanford University Press, 1975).

21. Richard Scase, *Social Democracy in Capitalist Society: Working-Class Politics in Britain and Sweden* (London: Croom Helm; Totowa, N.J.: Rowman & Littlefield, 1977).

22. Fernando Henrique Cardoso and José Luis Reyna, "Industrialization, Occupational Structure, and Social Stratification in Latin America," in *Constructive Change in Latin America*, ed. Cole Blasier (Pittsburgh: Pittsburgh University Press, 1968).

23. See Juan J. Linz, "Crisis, Breakdown, and Reequilibration," in *The Breakdown of Democratic Regimes*, ed. Juan J. Linz and Alfred Stepan (Baltimore: Johns Hopkins University Press, 1978).

24. Dankwart Rustow, "Transitions to Democracy," *Comparative Politics* 2, no. 3 (1970): 330–67.

Chapter 5 Demilitarization and the Institutionalization of Military-dominated Polities in Latin America

Editors' Note: Analyses of regime transitions can follow many different research strategies, as the chapters in this volume clearly illustrate. The two that particularly appealed to us were contextually rich examinations of the multitude of actors conflicting and coalescing in a historically specific place and period (these case studies have been collected in Volumes 1 and 2) and more conceptually bounded comparisons which focussed on the motives and behavior of a specific, hopefully analogous, set of actors coping with the choices generated by liberalization and, eventually, democratization in different national settings.

At the beginning we ambitiously thought of commissioning analyses focusing on a large number of actor-types which we thought to be particularly crucial—classes such as capitalists, workers, and petty bourgeois; institutions such as the military, civil service, church, trade unions, and party organizations. We quickly discovered how difficult it is both to delimit such groups across countries, and, most important, to identify scholars with such a wide range of knowledge and interest.

We were fortunate to find as a collaborator a distinguished French scholar, Alain Rouquié, who was not only working on the one institution most obviously circumscribable in structure and most crucial in its impact on the transition—that is, the armed forces—but who also had the expertise to cover the great variety of experiences in militarization and demilitarization in contemporary Latin America. Although developments in this institutional realm have been happening at an accelerated pace in recent years, Rouquié has helpfuly updated his original contribution.

1. The reference is to General Odría, who left power in July 1956 and organized free elections in which his candidate was defeated. For the waves of militarism, see Edwin Lieuwen, *Generals versus Presidents, Neo militarism in Latin America* (New York: Praeger, 1964).

2. See Adam Przeworski, "Some Problems in the Study of the Transition to Democracy," chap. 2 in this volume.

3. The idea of a "permanent military government" seems as transitory and dated as that of the irresistible rise of democracy. Cf. Mario Esteban Carranza, *Fuerzas armadas y estado de excepción en América Latina* (Mexico: Siglo XXI, 1978), chap. 5.

4. See Alain Rouquié, *Pouvoir militaire et société politique en République argentine* (Paris: Presses de la Fondation Nationale des Sciences Politiques 1978), passim.

5. Cf. Alain Rouquié, "L'Uruguay, de l'Etat providence à l'Etat garnison," *Etudes* (Paris), June 1979, p. 750.

6. Speech by General Pinochet on 11 September 1973, cited by Cristina Hurtado Beca, "Le processus d'institutionnalisation au Chili," *Problèmes d'Amérique Latine* (Paris) 58 (December 1980): 78.

7. See *El Mercurio*, 26 and 28 September 1975.

8. Jorge de Esteban and Luis López Guerra, *La crisis del estado franquista* (Madrid: Editorial Labor, Colección Politeia, 1977), pp. 28–29.

9. Cf. Carlos Semprun Maura, *Franco est mort dans son lit* (Paris: Hachette, 1980).

10. Cf. Yves Le Bot, "Bolivie: Les militaires, l'Etat, la dépendance: Une décennie de pillage," *Amérique Latine* (Paris), July–September 1980, p. 8.

11. According to Edelberto Torres Rivas, "Vie et mort au Guatemala, réflexions sur la crise et la violence politique," *Amérique Latine*, April–June 1980, p. 5.

12. See "El Salvador: The Process of Political Development and Modernization," in *Party Systems and Election in Latin America*, ed. Ronald McDonald (Chicago: Markham, 1971), pp. 260–63.

13. In this the PCN was not alone; in *El Salvador, Election Factbook, 1967* (Washington D.C.: Institute for the Comparative Study of Political Systems, 1967) one reads: "Ninety percent of the dozen political parties which have functioned since 1944 have been in reality military cliques or factions in disguise."

14. Cf. "Mixed Blessings for Government in Panamanian Poll Result," *Latin American Weekly Report*, 3 October 1980.

15. "La visite à Paris du président Royo," *Le Monde*, 3 May 1979.

16. Victor Meza, "Honduras; crisis del reformismo militar y coyuntura política," *Boletín del Instituto de Investigaciones Económicas y Sociales*, Universidad Autónoma Nacional de Honduras (Tegucigalpa), no. 98, September 1980; author's translation.

17. Ibid., and *Latin American Weekly Report* (22 August 1980).

18. Cf. Salvador Sánchez Estrada, "La represión des indiens dans la frange transversale nord du Guatemala," *Amérique Latine*, April–June 1980, pp. 73–77.

19. The anti-Communist Right consists of six parties. In 1979 the legal opposition included the Christian Democrat party, the Social Democratic party, and the United Front of the Revolution. These legal opposition parties have lost numerous cadres assassinated by paramilitary forces.

20. Cf. Susanne Jonas and David Tobis, *Guatemala, una historia inmediata* (Mexico: Siglo XXI, 1974), p. 318.

21. The "plebiscitary deadlock" was according to the formulation of José Alvaro Moises, "Crise política e democracia a transicao dificil," *Revista de Cultura e Política* (São Paulo), no. 2, August 1980, p. 13.

22. Cf. Luciano Martins, "La réorganisation des partis politiques et la crise économique au Brésil" *Problèmes d'Amérique Latine* 55 (March 1980): 23.

23. See Alain Rouquié, "Le modèle brésilien a l'épreuve," *Etudes*, May 1977, pp. 628–32.

24. F. H. Cardoso, "Les impasses du régime autoritaire: Le cas brésilien," *Problèmes d'Amérique Latine* 54 (December 1979): 104; quotation translated by author.

25. The plans for electoral reform designed to give an advantage to those in power and to conservative parties would thus be associated with sophisticated forms of "gerrymandering," assuring a comfortable majority to the "system." But even in the heart of the PDS there is no agreement on the use of such strategies. Cf. "Golbery Plots on Strategy for the Rest of the Year," *Latin American Regional Report (Brazil).* (London) October 1980.

26. Cf. *Le Monde*, 29 November 1980, and *La Prensa* (Buenos Aires), 3 December 1980.

27. Cf. Luis Rico Ortiz, "Uruguay, un análisis del plebiscito" (Paris, 1981), mimeo, p. 37.

28. Cf. Alain Rouquié, "Le retour du général Perón au pouvoir," "Les élections générales du 11 Mars 1973 et l'élection présidentielle du 23 septembre," *Problèmes d'Amérique Latine* 33 (September 1974): 20.

29. Ibid., p. 31.

30. *Le Monde*, 14 July 1978.

31. See my article, "Argentine: Les fausses sorties de l'armée et l'institutionnalisation du pouvoir militaire," *Problèmes d'Amérique Latine* 54 (December 1979): 109–29.

32. General Pavia, in 1874, at the head of an infantry battalion, dissolved the Cortes and put an end to the ephemeral Republic before delivering power to Serrano, who governed dictatorially. Cf. F. G. Bruguera, *Histoire contemporaine d'Espagne, 1789–1950* (Paris: Editions Ophrys, 1953), p. 286, and Manuel Tuñon de Lara, *La Espagna del siglo XIX, 1808–1914* (Paris: Club del Libro Espagñola, 1961), p. 194.

33. Wanderley Guilherme dos Santos, "A ciência política na América Latina (notas preliminares de autocritica)," *Dados* (Rio de Janeiro) 23, no. 1 (1980): 24; quotation translated by author.

34. Cf. Sergio Spoerer, *América Latina, los desafíos del tiempo fecundo* (Mexico: Siglo XXI, 1980).

35. Thus, retirement will henceforth be established on a system of individual "capitalization," and not as a function of the principle of national solidarity; cf. "Reforma provisional. Compare su futuro," *Ercilla* (Santiago) (26 November 1980).

36. On this subject, the reader should see my article, "Révolutions militaires et indépendance nationale en Amérique Latine (1968–1971), *Revue Française de Science Politique* 21, nos. 5–6 (October and December 1971).

37. Cf. "Declaración del Pacto Andino contra el golpe militar," *El País* (Madrid), 14 November 1979.

38. J. Schumpeter, *Capitalisme, socialisme et démocratie* (Paris, 1965), p. 368; published in English as *Capitalism, Socialism, and Democracy* (New York: Harper, 1942).

39. Mariano Grondona, *Visión* (Mexico), 1 May 1976. See the discussion of this point of view by Daniel Waksman Schinca in *El Día* (Mexico), 11 May 1976.

40. According to Lucía Pinochet, the president's daughter, *Hoy*, no. 151, 11 June 1980, quoted by C. Hurtado Beco, "Le Processus d'institutionnalisation . . . ," p. 89.

41. Cf. Alain Rouquié, "La Hipótesis bonapartista y el surgimento de sistemas políticos semi-competitivos," *Revista Mexicana de Sociología*, no. E, 1978; pp. 164–65.

42. Cf. on this point Elizer Rizzo de Oliveira, "Conflits militaires et décisions sous la présidence du général Geisel," in *Les partis militaires au Brésil*, ed. Alain Rouquié et al., (Paris: Presses de la FNSP, 1980), pp. 134–39.

43. Oliveira, ibid., and *As forças armadas: Politica e ideologia no Brasil (1964–1969)* (Petropolis, Brazil: Editora Vozes, 1976), pp. 10–11.

44. Goes Monteiro, Dutra, Teixeira Lott, or Albuquerque Lima all had been such leaders in their time.

45. The comment on the military establishment is what General Morales Bermúdez stated in an interview in April 1979, "Un entretien avec le président du Pérou," *Le Monde*, 13 April 1979.

46. The observer is Hugo Neira, "Au Pérou le retour de l'oligarchie," *Etudes* (Paris), October 1980, p. 304.

47. "Posición oficial ante la Comisión fue expuesta anoche al país por Harguindeguy," *La Nación*, 24 September 1979.

48. *Movimento*, 23 February 1981.

49. The formulation is by Ricardo Balbin, leader of the Argentine Radical party, who would accept the imposition of this "law."

50. The relations with the narcotics mafia and the self-interested protection given by the present leaders of the country to the drug traffickers (see *Newsweek*, 2 February

and 9 March 1981, and *Le Matin-Magazine* (Paris) 18 October in fact cover over structural, permanent phenomena that one might characterize as "privatization of the state" or "patrimonialization of the bureaucracy" and that Laurence Whitehead has analyzed as an "absence of relations of legitimate authority" and of "group domination" in his article "El estado y los intereses seccionales: el caso boliviano," *Estudios Andinos*, no. 10, 1974–75.

51. See the conclusion of my book *Pouvoir militaire et société politique.*

52. Gerard Fenoy, "L'armée en Colombie," *Cahiers du monde hispanique et luso-brésilien* (Toulouse), no. 26, 1976, pp. 86–7. Only supporters of the conservative Laureano Gómcz were opposed to the military solution to the crisis.

53. See Constantino Urcuyo Fournier, "Les forces de securité publiques et la politique au Costa Rica, 1960–78" (Thesis, Paris, September 1978), chap. 1.

54. Régis Debray, "Nicaragua, une modération radicale," *Le Monde Diplomatique*, September 1979, p. 8.

55. This is the military program of the Sandinista government; see "Organización de un nuevo ejército nacional," in Programa de la Junta de Gobierno de Reconstrucción Nacional de Nicaragua, published in *Bohemia* (Cuba), 3 August 1979.

56. Samuel Huntington, *Political Order in Changing Societies* (New Haven: Yale University Press, 1968).

57. Jorge I. Domínguez, "The Civic Soldier in Cuba," in Catherine Mardle Kelleher, ed. *Political-Military Systems, Comparative Perspectives* (Beverly Hills: Sage, 1974), pp. 209–37.

58. See Alfonso Camacho, "Bolivia: militares en la política," *Aportes*, October 1971, pp. 73–6.

59. This is the position defended by the leadership of the Spanish Socialist Worker's party (PSOE) against its left wing. This position was reinforced by the failed putsch of 23 February 1981. See the interview of Felipe González, general secretary of the PSOE, in *L'Unité*, 7 March 1981.

60. One has been able to witness joint action at the time of the great demonstration for democracy which followed the antiparliamentary putsch, by former high officials of the Franco regime like Fraga Iribarne and the Communist, Socialist, and syndicated leaders of the opposition.

61. Post-Kemalist Turkey offers this type of scenario in the framework of an elected regime set up by the postmilitary state. But one can scarcely offer it as an example of demilitarization of the political system, with a coup d'état every ten years since 1960.

Chapter 6 Entrepreneurs and the Transition Process: The Brazilian Case

1. See F. H. Cardoso, *Empresário industrial e desenvolvimento econômico no Brasil* (São Paulo: Difel, 1964), last chapter; and also note 3 below.

2. L. Martins, *Industrialização, burguesia nacional e desenvolvimento* (Rio de Janeiro: Saga, 1968).

3. F. H. Cardoso "Hégémonie bourgeoise et indépendance économique: Racines structurales de la crise politique brésilienne," *Les Temps Modernes* 257 (October 1967): 680.

4. For an excellent summary, see H. Trindade, "La bourgeoisie brésilienne en question," *Amérique Latine* (CETRAL) (1981): 35–46.

5. I am, of course, referring to P. Schmitter, *Interest Conflict and Political Change* (Stanford: Stanford University Press, 1971).

6. Cf. F. H. Cardoso, "Hégémonie bourgeoise.,"

7. In the academic sphere there was one writer who continued to pay extraordinary attention to the "bourgeois revolution" and thus to the formation of entrepreneurial groups: Florestan Fernandes. See his *A revolução burguesa no Brasil*, 3d ed. (Rio de Janeiro: Zahar, 1976).

8. I will not make any further reference to this point or to the attempts to make a dialectical analysis of authoritarian regimes. I refer the reader to D. Collier, *The New Authoritarianism* (Princeton: Princeton University Press, 1979).

9. See, for instance, E. Diniz, *Empresariado, estado e capitalismo no Brasil (1930–1945)* (Rio de Janeiro: Paz e Terra, 1978).

10. I do not linger on the subject of technobureaucrats which has been the object of wide-ranging debate, especially between Luís Carlos Bresser Pereira and Carlos Estevam Martins.

11. See V. Figueiredo, *Desenvolvimento dependente brasileiro* (Rio de Janeiro: Zahar, 1978).

12. See E. Diniz Cerqueira and R. R. Boschi, "Elite industrial e estado," in *Estado e capitalismo no Brasil*, ed. C. E. Martins, (São Paulo: HUCITEC/CEBRAP, 1977).

13. See F. H. Cardoso, *Autoritarismo e democratização* (Rio de Janeiro: Paz e Terra, 1975).

14. C. Lessa, "A descoberta do estado totalitário," *Gazeta Mercantil* (São Paulo), 29 April 1980, pp. 32–34. Lessa's earlier study, "A estratégia do desenvolvimento, 1974–1976: sonho e fracasso," (Rio de Janeiro: 1978, unpublished) contains a more thorough analysis of enterpreneurial action and economic policy in this period.

15. Another analyst considers that "the II PND expresses the spirit of nationalism and the desire for autonomy which characterize the technocratic-military coalition controlling the bureaucratic apparatus. This is an unequivocal demonstration of state autonomy." P. Faucher, "The Paradise that Never Was: the Breakdown of the Brazilian Authoritarian order," in *Authoritarian Capitalism: Brazil's Contemporary Economic and Political Development*, ed. T. C. Bruneau and P. Faucher, (Boulder, Colo.: Westview Press, 1981).

16. C. Lessa, "A descoberta do estado totalitário," p. 32.

17. Public declaration in *Veja*, 19 May 1976.

18. Since 1977 the São Paulo newspaper *Gazeta Mercantil* (which is the chief financial newspaper in Brazil) has annually consulted thousands of businessmen to elect the ten most influential leaders in the business community. Those elected then meet for a debate (the Forum) and issue a signed document about the political, social, and economic state of the nation.

19. Declarations made during the elections to the Forum in 1977. *Gazeta Mercantil* (São Paulo) 13 September 1977.

20. Declarations made to *Gazeta Mercantil*, 13 September 1977. One should note that at this point, when asked by reporters if the ideas he was putting forward were those of "opposition," Gomes replied cautiously, without making a break with Geisel.

21. To be exact, the two studies by Carlos Lessa referred to above present different interpretations. In the book on development strategy, the relationship between economic interest and political stance is clearly defined. In the article on the discovery of the authoritarian state, the democratic motivation of the business community seems to appear of its own accord.

22. The Geisel government did limit itself to declarations in support of the capital goods sector. The ninth resolution, on 13 March 1977, of the Economic Development Council, directed the BNDE to give priority to financing programs in the national sector of the economy. The links between Brazilian and foreign capital concerns should have forced the latter to make a real transfer of technology; investment studies and engineering projects should have growing local participation, and the CDI (Industrial Development Council) should prevent competition with local investments.

The CDI contributed 5 percent and 18 percent respectively in 1973 and 1977 of the total investments in the basic sectors, and as little as 5.5 percent and 2.6 percent in the consumer goods sector. The participation of Brazilian industry in the supply of equipment for investment projects approved by the CDI was more than 35 percent and 68 percent. The BNDE created three subsidiaries (EMBRAMEC, FIBASE, and IBRASA) to provide national enterprises with fixed capital, and another of the BNDE's subsidiaries, FINAME, guaranteed finance with fixed interest rates well below inflation, to capital goods industries. Cf. P. Faucher, "The Paradise that Never Was," p. 21.

23. Industrialist's declaration quoted by Carlos Lessa in the *Gazeta Mercantil* article referred to note 14.

24. See C. Lessa, "A estratégia," and P. Faucher, "The Paradise that Never Was." See also L. Martins, "La Joint-venture état-firme transnationale-entrepreneurs locaux au Brésil," *Sociologie et Société* (Paris) 11, no. 2 (August 1979): 169–90. The unfulfilled promises of state sector investments led to overcapacity in the capital goods manufacturing sector: from 1975 orders declined, from index number 135 (1972 = 100) to 97 in 1978.

25. In the particular case of the Geisel government one should add that the Economic Development Council was personally chaired by the president of the Republic, who made his opinions on economic matters abundantly plain and took responsibility for the council's decisions.

26. It is as well to remember that many industrialists directly supported the system of repression and torture.

27. Severo Gomes, then minister of industry and commerce, took up the criticism as did conservative industrialists, like the president of the Federation of Commerce of the State of São Paulo. The major business associations (ANFAVEA, ABDIB, ABINEE) and even FIESP (Federation of Industries of the State of São Paulo) endorsed liberal-leaning positions.

28. "Primeiro Documento dos Empresários," Forum da *Gazeta Mercantil*, July 1978.

29. The entrepreneurs who signed the document were, in order of election: Cláudio Bardella, Severo Gomes, José Mindlin, Antônio Ermínio de Morais, Paulo Villares, Paulo Velhinho, Laerte Setúbal, and Jorge Gerdau.

30. Forum of *Gazeta Mercantil*: "Íntegra do documento." *Gazeta Mercantil* 2 October 1980. Those elected were: A. E. Morais, C. Bardella, L. E. Bueno Vidigal Filho, Olavo Setúbal, Abílio Diniz, José E. Morais Filho, Laerte Setúbal, Mário Garnero, Jorge Gerdau, José Mindlin. From previous Forums, the following also signed the document: Manoel Costa Santos, Paulo Villares, Paulo Velhinho. The general tone of criticism and the search for "elevated solutions," above immediate interests, even affected more conservative entities. See, for instance, the document of Brazilian Confederation of Commercial Associations: "A empresa e a economia." *Digesto Econômico* 271 (January 1981).

31. Because of this paragraph, Severo Gomes, who was already an active member of the opposition party, did not sign the document.

32. Declarations made by the president on receiving a group of entrepreneurs who presented him with the 1980 Forum document. *Gazeta Mercantil*, 23 October 1980.

33. Antônio Ermínio de Morais, *Gazeta Mercantil*, 23 October 1980. A. E. Morais continued to step up his criticism of economic policies and to defend the necessity for democratization throughout 1981.

34. Questions were extracted from the results of an opinion poll carried out by *Gazeta Mercantil* published on 29 April 1980. Thirteen thousand questionnaires were distributed and 1,353 replied by post from all over Brazil. It is difficult to reach objective conclusions about the replies because the questions, in some cases, do not provide contrary options. In any case, as there was no obligation to answer, one must assume that the entrepreneurs endorsed some of the proposed opinions.

35. In a recent round table on the role of industrialists, Cláudio Bardella, who was one of the more outspoken participants, drew attention to this point. *Gazeta Mercantil*, 29 April 1980. This aspect of the political liberalization process in Brazil is interesting:

civilian society was "reinvented" as a political force mostly by the mass media. The creation of the *Gazeta Mercantil*'s Forum is an excellent example. Independent of parties and the government, leaderships were becoming institutionalized and assumed.

36. Moreover, just as the "liberal bourgeoisie" was being brought into the political arena, its more reactionary sector—which had predominated during the emergence of the authoritarian regime—also made its views known. On 2 June 1978 *Gazeta Mercantil* published a document signed by 100 businessmen which protested simultaneously about state intervention in the economy and about the apparent reigning liberalism which they in fact said might be a return to Communism. However, this sort of discourse was overshadowed by more liberal discourse from 1979 on.

37. In recent lectures, Alfred Stepan has drawn attention to a peculiar aspect of the return to democracy in Brazilian society: "horizontal connections." In other words, there is a permeability that allows for contact and articulation between sectors of society that exist on structural levels that are distinct, and, at critical moments, opposed. Church leaders, workers, journalists, lawyers, industrialists, teachers, representatives of base organizations, intellectuals, politicians, and so on frequently come into contact and mutually aid each other in putting pressure on the state.

38. One should not make mechanical assumptions in this case, however, as there were divisions that had nothing to do with democratization and that played an important role.

39. Recent declarations by the president of the Federation of Industries of the State of São Paulo are significant: he will not join any political party so as not to run the risk of becoming the "Lula of my class—which would not necessarily make me the leader of my colleagues." *O Estado de São Paulo*, 3 May 1981.

40. After a decade analyzing Latin American authoritarianism, political scientists have turned their attention to the breakdown of authoritarian regimes. See, especially, the essay by G. O'Donnell, "Tensions in the Bureaucratic Authoritarian State and the Question of Democracy," in *The New Authoritarianism*, ed. D. Collier, (Princeton: Princeton University Press, 1979); see also F. H. Cardoso, "A Bias for Democracy" (Paper presented to the Wilson Center in 1978).

41. One should not put too much emphasis on the parallel, though; the pressure applied by Spanish workers was and is much greater than in the Brazilian case. On the other hand, the regional issue does not exist and what terrorism there is, is right wing and limited.

Chapter 7 Economic Policies and the Prospects for Successful Transition from Authoritarian Rule in Latin America

Editors' Note: In the third conference of the Wilson Center's "Transitions" project, held in June 1981, Albert Fishlow presented a paper entitled "Are Economic Constraints an Empty Intellectual Box?" which considered in summary form the degrees of freedom on economic policy issues that might be available to newly emergent democracies. Clearly there are definite limits to the extent that economic policies can be varied in response to the new demands that inevitably accompany democratization. If the new regime is to achieve medium-term viability, it must practice skill and restraint in the design of its economic policies. But equally, for the fledgling democracy to consolidate its social appeal at least some of the more unattractive features of the authoritarian regime's economic policies will require modification. Indeed, in the absence of an authoritarian regime, some major elements of previous economic strategy become literally unsustainable. How much scope is there for creative innovation in the choice of economic strategies, drawing on the additional sources of strength that social participation and consultation could offer to democratic policy-makers? Clearly the answers will depend for the most part on the particular trajectory taken by the transition process and on the general economic context in which it occurs. Nevertheless, some generalizations can be formulated that are of rather widespread applicability. John Sheahan has expanded his response to Fishlow's presentation into this full-scale contribution.

Author's Note: I would like to thank Laurence Whitehead for his helpful suggestions and the Social Science Research Council for their research grant to work on these issues.

1. Prior to their authoritarian regimes, the Southern Cone countries were not characterized by excess labor to anything like the degrees in Brazil and the rest of Latin America. But continuing higher levels of unemployment became more common under the authoritarian regimes, especially in Chile, even before the severe economic contractions of 1982–83. See Victor E. Tokman, "Dinámica de los mercados de trabajo y distribución del ingreso en América Latina," *Colección estudios cieplan* 3 (June 1980): 121–50; Oscar Muñoz, "Crecimiento y desequilibrios en Chile," *Colección estudios cieplan* 8 (July 1982): 19–41; and Patricio Meller, René Cortazar, and Jorge Marshall, "Employment Stagnation in Chile, 1974–78," *Latin American Research Review* 16, no. 2 (1981): 144–55.

2. Oscar Muñoz, "La economía mixta como camino al pleno empleo. Lecciones de un cuarto de siglo," *Colección estudios cieplan* 9 (December 1982): 107–38; "Hacia una neuva industrialización: elementos de una estrategia de desarrollo para la democracia," *Apuntes cieplan* 33 (May 1982).

3. Tokman "Dinámica de los mercados," table 4, p. 126; O. Altimir, *La dimensión de la pobreza en América Latina* (Santiago: CEPAL, 1978).

4. Marcelo Selowsky, "Income Distribution, Basic Needs and Trade-offs with Growth: The Case of Semi-industrialized Latin American Countries," *World Development* 9 no. 1 (January 1981: 73–92. See also Patricio Meller, "Enfoques sobre demanda de trabajo: relevancia para América Latina," *Estudios cieplan*, no. 24, (June 1978).

5. Interamerican Development Bank, *Economic and Social Progress in Latin America, 1983 Report* (Washington, D.C.: IDB, 1983), table 3, p. 345.

6. Albert Hirschman, "The Social and Political Matrix of Inflation: Elaboration of Latin American Experience," in *Essays in Trespassing: Economics to Politics and Beyond*, ed. A. Hirschman (New York: Cambridge University Press, 1981), pp. 177–207.

7. John Sheahan, *Promotion and Control of Industry in Postwar France* (Cambridge, Mass.: Harvard University Press, 1963). Colombia's Frente Nacional is another example of an agreement negotiated by previously warring groups which proved effective, within its own objective of political stabilization, for the next sixteen years. "During this period, repressive extremism did not prevail in this remaining South American democracy. The Front was a welcome departure from the violence and crude authoritarianism of the immediate past": *Politics of Compromise: Coalition Government in Colombia*, ed. R. Albert Berry, Ronald G. Hellman, and Mauricio Soláun (New Brunswick, N.J.: Transaction Books, 1980), p. 457.

8. Albert Fishlow, "Are Economic Constraints an Empty Intellectual Box?" (Paper presented at the Wilson Center conference, June 1981). No individual conference paper developed an argument against active participation in external trade; its undesirability for national welfare seemed rather to be taken for granted. Robert Kaufman's paper, now revised as Chapter 5 in the present volume, came closest to an explicit discussion, suggesting that participation in the international economy is a burden which may have to be accepted as a political compromise.

9. In addition to the discussion by Fishlow see Bela Balassa, "Export Incentives and Export Performance in Developing Countries: A Comparative Analysis," *Welwirtschaftliches Archiv* 114 (1978): 24–61.

10. Cf. Laura Guasti, "The Peruvian Military Government and the International Corporations," in *The Peruvian Experiment Reconsidered*, ed. Cynthia McClintock and Abraham Lowenthal (Princeton: Princeton University Press, 1983), pp. 181–205; Javier Iguíñiz Echeverría, "Reflexiones polémicas sobre dos alternativas a la situación

económica actual," Fundación Frederick Ebert, ILDIS, Serie Materiales de Trabajo no. 15, Lima, April 1978; and Martin Landsberg, "Export Led Industrialization in the Third World, Manufacturing Imperialism," *Review of Radical Political Economy* (Winter 1979): 50–63.

11. Of the many discussions of the ways in which protection for import substitution damaged developing countries, one of the clearest remains that of Ian Little, Tibor Scitovsky, and Maurice Scott, *Industry and Trade in Some Developing Countries* (Oxford: Oxford University Press for the Organization for Economic Cooperation and Development [OECD], 1970).

12. Gary Gereffi and Peter Evans, "Transnational Corporations, Dependent Development, and State Policy in the Periphery: A Comparison of Brazil and Mexico," *Latin American Research Review* 16, no. 3 (1981): 31–64.

13. Peter Evans, *Dependent Development: The Alliance of Multinational, State, and Local Capital in Brazil* (Princeton: Princeton University Press, 1978).

14. Carlos Díaz Alejandro, "Latin America in the 1930s" (Yale University Discussion Paper, mimeo, April 1982).

15. John Sheahan, "Market-oriented Economic Policies and Political Repression in Latin America," *Economic Development and Cultural Change* 28, no. 2 (January 1980): 267–91.

16. Albert Hirschman, "The Turn to Authoritarianism in Latin America and the Search for Its Economic Determinants," and "The Social and Political Matrix of Inflation: Elaborations on Latin American Experience," in *Essays in Trespassing, Economics to Politics and Beyond*, ed. A. Hirschman. Cf. John Sheahan, "The Elusive Balance Between Stimulation and Constraint in Analysis of Development" (Paper presented at the Conference on Economic Development and Democracy, at the University of Notre Dame, April 1984; revised as Williams College Research Memorandum 89, July 1984).

17. Guillermo O'Donnell, *Modernization and Bureaucratic-Authoritarianism* (Berkeley and Los Angeles: University of California Press, 1973).

Index